D1568315

NARRATING SCOTLAND

An Accurate Map of Scotland. Drawn from all the Particular Surveys hitherto Published, by James Dorret (London: R. Sayer, 1761). Courtesy of the National Library of Scotland, Edinburgh.

NARRATING SCOTLAND

The Imagination of
Robert Louis Stevenson

BARRY MENIKOFF

University of South Carolina Press

© 2005 Barry Menikoff

Published in Columbia, South Carolina, by the
University of South Carolina Press

Manufactured in the United States of America

09 08 07 06 05   5 4 3 2 1

Library of Congress Cataloging-in-Publication Data

Menikoff, Barry.
Narrating Scotland : the imagination of Robert Louis Stevenson / Barry Menikoff.
    p. cm.
  Includes bibliographical references and index.
  ISBN 1-57003-568-7 (cloth : alk. paper)
  1. Stevenson, Robert Louis, 1850–1894—Knowledge—Scotland. 2. Stevenson,
Robert Louis, 1850–1894—Knowledge—History. 3. Historical fiction, Scottish—
History and criticism. 4. Scotland—Intellectual life—19th century. 5. Literature and
history—Scotland. 6. Scotland—In literature. I. Title.
PR5497.M46 2005
828'.809—dc22
                                                                    2004020593

For my mother
Blanche Goldman Menikoff
1906–52

Sleep softly while I sing my song

CONTENTS

ILLUSTRATIONS

PREFACE

Stevenson was quite attached to his thick copy of Alexander Findlay's ocean *Directory,* else how would he have known where he was going when he sailed those island chains in the Pacific? Yet the *Directory* could not always tell him with certainty where he was, and on occasion it even misled him. So it is with the making of books. Some follow a plumb line as smoothly as a seasoned sailor and are composed with punctilious rectitude. Others are written in a kind of white heat, possibly with the end point in view, but no sure sign of how to get there. Still others, like this one, absent a plumb line and carried on too long to sustain a white heat, follow a more elusive path. *Narrating Scotland* was prompted by one of those familiar facts that lose their resonance because they are so well known, in this case that *Kidnapped* was inspired by an old incident in Scottish history that had been recorded in a printed trial. The book slowly evolved from a circuitous process of reading and research, a process that at times seemed to mirror the story it set out to relate. But that was only a seeming. Tracing the books that Stevenson read did not entail balancing on choppy seas or coursing through high roads, as David and Alan did, and which might at least have given the enterprise some panache. But, as these things are done, it was managed in the dim stacks and sedate reading rooms of privileged libraries, places whose mission is to collect and conserve the unending artifacts of what Stevenson wryly called the ruins of the Roman Empire.

The story of that tracing appeared on the face of it simple enough: what were the books that went into the making of *Kidnapped?* Finding them might prove a challenge, reading them a chore, yet in the end—such was the hope—something substantive would surely emerge, some clue, or set of clues, that would unlock the compositional secret of a brilliant text. But as each found book led to another, documents uncovering documents, much like those Russian dolls that disclose themselves anew as you open them, it became clear that finding the books alone was not the answer, that the true source of the work, however polished or rough-hewn, was both obvious and impenetrable at the same time. It was nothing less than the creative imagination. And fathoming that mystery is ultimately beyond the reach of the critic, and possibly of the writer himself. Henry James called it the sacred fount. Stevenson would have balked at the sacral imagery, but he would have agreed with the idea. On a contrary note, Roland Barthes declared with great élan that the author was dead, and some years later Robert Altman literally killed him, giving a cinematic reality to a rather dry academic thought. But Barthes was wrong, as readers who are continually bewitched by books keep reminding us. When new people insist on discovering Austen's Hampshire, Hemingway's Paris, or Stevenson's South Seas, knowing nothing of the truth or falsity of those made up places, they become sharers in the imagination of those authors and witnesses to the magic of their invention. Thus the books live, and they work their way into the lives of generations, long after the noise of the writers' lives and the critics' carpings have passed into oblivion. In the making of a book, to loosely paraphrase the Master, we do what we can, we work in the dark, and the rest is the madness, and the doubtful pleasure, of art.

If David Balfour's wanderings were often arduous, at least he had good company in that voluble bantam, Alan Breck Stewart. For me, many people have lightened the carriage along the way. In the early 1990s I met Paul Karlstrom at lunch in The Huntington. At the time Paul was the regional director of the Archives of American Art, and as stylish in his life as the art and artists he wrote about. Those were heady days, in our open-air Algonquin, when the conversation was ever keen, the skies knew only the color blue, and the women were always gorgeous. After the publication of the Huntington Library Press edition of *Kidnapped* in 1999, and the inaugural Stevenson conference in Scotland a year later, I met many who contributed to my work and my pleasure. Bill Jones, by profession a lawyer, in practice a smart writer on popular culture and a shrewd literary critic, was a gracious host and witty guide to Little Rock, the city that spawned a president. Eric Massie fashioned that seminal conference in Stirling through indomitable energy and hearty good spirits, and in the process made friends of strangers, and made strangers friends. Richard Dury, of English birth and Italian spirit, whose close attention to language and art bears the elegance of his literary mentor, and whose work for the Garda conference will live long in the memories of all who were there. And Richard Ambrosini, Roman, a man whose intellectual passions run as deep as his private ones, and who contrived a tour of his beloved city that was at least the equal of that celluloid holiday immortalized long ago by William Wyler. Returning to California, there was Cathy Turney, whose noir scripts for Joan Crawford, Betty Davis, and Ida Lupino gave no hint of her regal splendor. Cathy was a reigning presence at The Huntington when I met her thirty years ago, with her great, rich hair piled high on her head, as if crowning her statuesque body. She knew the great and the less-than-great, and treated them all with the same natural courtesy and tart humor that was her own easy manner. Cathy left before she could read these words on an author dear to her, but I can still make out her smile, and hear her own indulgent words of approval. Finally, three who have witnessed this wandering longer and more steadfastly than all others: Carrie, Alec, and Aaron Menikoff. To them, and to a new generation that will soon read their names here, and perhaps smile, Max, Rachel, and Jonah Menikoff, these pages are inscribed.

NARRATING SCOTLAND

PROLOGUE

Robert Louis Stevenson is an anomalous figure in literary and cultural studies. There is not a single writer in the United Kingdom and America whose name is more universally recognized and who is, at the same time, so little understood. Stevenson survives in the popular imagination for his romantic life story (to fall in love in France, to marry in California, to live and die in the South Seas). He survives in popular culture for his authorship of *Dr. Jekyll and Mr. Hyde,* a shilling thriller that has given an eponymous phrase to the English language. And he survives more broadly in the countless illustrated editions of *A Child's Garden of Verses* and *Treasure Island.* But this picture of Stevenson obscures the serious artist who was considered, at the time of his death in 1894, the most brilliant and original writer of his generation. That was the judgment of those, like Henry James and Oscar Wilde, who read him as contemporaries. It was the judgment of younger writers, like Rudyard Kipling and John Galsworthy, who studied him in order to learn how to write. And it was the conviction of those that came much later, like Jorge Luis Borges and Robertson Davies, who saw in him not just an inventive and versatile writer but a profoundly modern theorist of fiction. Yet even Stevenson's most attentive readers would be astonished to discover how original were his theories of fiction—and how modern was his practice. Stevenson himself is largely to blame for this. When he dedicated *Kidnapped* to his good friend Charles Baxter he made a point of apologizing for the minor historical errors and topographical inaccuracies in the text, mistakes that no one but a captious antiquarian would even have noticed. But then he defended himself in a manner that was as misleading as it was self-deprecating, suggesting that the book was "no furniture for the scholar's library" but simply an escape from reality with no higher purpose than to serve as a soporific at the end of a long day.

For anyone who knew Stevenson, the falsity of such a remark would have been immediately obvious. A member of the Scottish bar, Stevenson was a profound student of law and history. These twin interests reflected two salient features of Edinburgh life that he knew from firsthand experience and from deep study: that the law was the traditional means of advancement for intellectually ambitious Scots, and that history constituted a major component of the law. Stevenson's first writings focused heavily on historical subjects, alternating between eighteenth-century Scotland and medieval France, and he occasionally exploited his material for dual purposes. For example, in his first published short story, "A Lodging for the Night" (1877), Stevenson took as his subject the French medieval poet, François Villon. He had written a review of a recent biography of Villon, and his invented story used the known facts of the poet's life as they were reported in the biography. The story incorporated themes from the poetry and concluded with Villon the character walking away into the Parisian night just as the real Villon disappeared from the historical record. On a small scale, Stevenson constructed a fiction that operates as a stand-in for history. Villon—as a medieval French poet, original, imaginative, and rebellious—was a natural for him. "A Lodging for the Night" was one of Stevenson's most admired short stories, yet critics had no idea of its historical exactitude.

A voracious reader of everything from current popular literature to abstruse German philosophy, Stevenson's early career as an essayist was prompted by his habit of studying books as opposed to merely reading them. Thus the image of the "scholar's library" was not an accidental one. It was the deliberate choice of a writer whose preparation for his own texts always involved the indefatigable reading of those of others. But Stevenson was not writing for an academic audience; he was writing fiction, or what passed for fiction, and his scholarship had to be concealed, submerged beneath the rapid succession of engaging incidents and surprising climaxes. Why inform anyone that *Treasure Island,* already the work of an accomplished researcher, depended for its chilling detail on Daniel Defoe's pseudonymous history of pirates?[1] What benefit would readers derive from seeing the scaffolding erected for the plot's construction? It was a point of pride with Stevenson never to intrude the smallest detail into his text if it was in any way extraneous. The writer, he once told a reporter, should be prepared to spend five hours in order to save the reader five minutes, and nowhere is he obliged to let the reader know how he does it, or even that he has done it. Stevenson's compact with his audience was, on the surface, a simple one: readers need to be compelled by the story and made to turn the page, with a passionate and even unthinking fervor. That, in short, was success in fiction.

But that was not at all what Stevenson's fiction was about. Or that was not all that it was about. *Kidnapped* (1886) and its sequel *David Balfour* (1893) were among the most serious works of Stevenson's career. In these two novels he placed his extensive historical and legal training in the service of his country's past. Stevenson had long planned to write a traditional history of Scotland, and he had even applied in 1881 for a professorship in law and history at Edinburgh University, an episode that has been misconstrued by all his biographers. But the purchase in Inverness of *The Trial of James Stewart for the Murder of Colin Campbell* (1753), an account of one of Scotland's most celebrated political trials, along with the rejection of his application for the professorship, changed all that. Stevenson immediately saw the *Trial* as a documentary symbol of the profound divisions in Scottish national life, a "tragedy . . . highly typical of the place and time." And from its exhaustive recounting of the assassination of a king's agent, a man collecting rents from a Jacobite chief's forfeited estate, he conceived the plan for dramatizing the nature and dissolution of the Highland clan system. Reading the printed trial, as he later said in an unpublished note to *Kidnapped,* he determined to found upon it a "narrative of fact" that would faithfully reflect the realities of Highland life after the rebels' defeat at Culloden in 1746. Stevenson's experiment in fiction was successful beyond his own imaginings, and in its form and originality it anticipated by nearly a hundred years Truman Capote's self-declared invention of a new genre, the nonfiction novel.

The genesis and composition of *Kidnapped* and *David Balfour* reveal not only Stevenson's deep immersion in Scottish history and culture, but the creative process by which he reconstructed that culture in fiction. For the two novels constitute an epic account of eighteenth-century Scottish life woven together from contemporary trials, memoirs, letters, and histories. Why did Stevenson not name these texts? The short answer is political. While *Kidnapped* and *David Balfour* have always been read together, as a single story of comradeship, courage, and adventure, behind the written texts stand a political allegory of colonial dominance, of the subjugation of a native people by an alien and aggrandizing foreign culture. Stevenson was writing for a predominantly English audience, and he was inevitably constrained in his discourse (just as the Scots idiom in both books was flattened when it was not converted outright into English). Rather than disturb his readers with a disquisition on their country's violent suppression of a hereditary Scottish culture, he offered a narrative that appeared to reinforce the conventional English wisdom that the defeat of the Highland clans prepared the way for the development of modern Scotland. This was a view propounded by Walter Scott in the Waverley novels. But Stevenson, admiring as he was of Scott, never subscribed to his countryman's roseate progressivism. He concentrated, instead, on the loss suffered by the indigenous culture, focusing on how the law of the state was utilized for ends that had nothing to do with justice and everything to do with the preservation of power.

How did Stevenson subvert the English view of Scottish history and inscribe his own historical culture upon a common novel of adventure? For one thing, the texts that provided the material and intellectual resources for *Kidnapped* and *David Balfour* were reconstituted as hidden texts within the novel. In essence, the novel as story was a shadow of the documents that dominated Stevenson's imagination and that he never stopped reading. And the *Trial* was only the most obvious of these, the one he cited in the dedication to Charles Baxter. But that very naming was a feint, for it deflected readers from contemplating the existence of other texts, such as Edmund Burt's *Letters from a Gentleman in the North of Scotland,* or David Stewart's *Sketches of the Highlanders,* or the compelling *Trials of Three Sons of Rob Roy.* These are just a few of the extraordinary accounts of Highland life that make up the tapestry of Stevenson's great epic. For the novelist was engaged in a dialogue with his ancestors, a panoply of Scottish authors—advocates and legal historians, missionaries and travel writers, church pietists with their eyes on the next world, and careful folklorists with their ears pitched to the odd stories of this one. In short, Stevenson silently coopted all the neglected and forgotten scholars who labored in obscurity to record both the blood and the glory of their people's lives. If he failed to credit them in print, he immortalized them in art, for in their preservation of Scottish history and culture they are, among all else, the inspiration for the great character portraits of Alan Breck Stewart, James Macgregor, and the Lord Advocate Prestongrange.

Chapter 1

A SCOTS HISTORIAN

I have a fierce combat with my wife & try to prove
that you are quite as great a historian as Carlyle.
—Walter Grindlay Simpson

Few modern authors were more attentive to their dedication pages than Robert
Louis Stevenson. For a man who cherished his friendships almost as much as he
cherished life itself, each new book was an opportunity for a public toast to auld
lang syne as well as a timeless gift to those who shared the privacy of his days and
nights. Stevenson was often deliberate and even sly in matching the book with
the person. *An Inland Journey* was inscribed to his riverway companion, Sir Walter
Simpson, and to Simpson's canoe. *Kidnapped* (and later *David Balfour*) was addressed to Charles Baxter, his closest friend from university days and the one he
most deeply identified with Edinburgh and Scotland. The dominant impulse in all
his previous inscriptions had been one of friendship, but the dedication to Baxter
was more than this. For the first time, the dedication served as a preface to the
text itself—even as it was so veiled and deprecating as to pass unnoticed. "If you
ever read this tale," Stevenson began, as if it were a matter of real doubt, "you will
likely ask yourself more questions than I should care to answer: as for instance
how the Appin murder has come to fall in the year 1751, how the Torran rocks
have crept so near to Earraid, or why the printed trial is silent as to all that
touches David Balfour." Given Baxter's background in the law and his intimacy
with the writer, these questions have a veneer of reasonableness about them. Yet
no reader—Baxter included—would ever have conceived them. Apart from those
Highlanders who passed along their clan's history, the murder of a rural land agent
in 1752 was hardly a topic of conversation in London or Edinburgh in 1886. Nor
was the exact placement of a group of rocks near a tiny islet in western Scotland
of interest to any but the most addicted readers of esoteric gazetteers. As for the
printed trial, barring a few antiquarians and a handful of legal historians, none
would even have heard of the document. Stevenson, of course, knew this. The
questions he posed for Baxter were openly directed at the reader. They establish
his forthrightness as a serious writer drawing on historical and topographical

materials, with the appealing touch that he admits his own failure to explain these discrepancies of fact—"These are nuts beyond my ability to crack."

All this is quite disarming. Stevenson introduces a series of questions that would have occurred to no one, and he apologizes for not answering them. Then he turns around and justifies a major departure on his part from the printed trial. In the matter of Alan Breck Stewart's culpability in the murder of Colin Campbell, the king's factor on the estates of Appin and Lismore, he declares the man innocent. Thus, in the space of a single paragraph, Stevenson professes his inability to explain the minor historical mistakes in his own text, and then he soberly asserts that the important findings of earlier texts may themselves be wrong. His book might, therefore, serve as a useful corrective to the historical record. At this point, a prospective reader of the novel, unfamiliar with the arcana of Scottish history, might well find himself spinning. But Stevenson dismisses these near contradictions out of hand. Untroubled by questions of accuracy, he concludes his opening paragraph with a striking passage that has effectively framed the reception of the novel for more than a century.

> This is no furniture for the scholar's library, but a book for the winter evening school-room when the tasks are over and the hour for bed draws near; and honest Alan, who was a grim old fire-eater in his day, has in this avatar no more desperate purpose than to steal some young gentleman's attention from his Ovid, carry him awhile into the Highlands and the last century, and pack him to bed with some engaging images to mingle with his dreams.

It would be hard to overstate the hold this one sentence, less than a hundred words long, has had on the popular and critical understanding of *Kidnapped*. It sets up an opposition between serious work and play; it identifies the book's audience; and it insinuates an idea as to the nature or genre of the text itself. The problem is that these assertions may not be true—or they may be, at best, only half-true. For example, setting the book in the Scottish Highlands just after the Jacobite rebellion, with its implicit promise of adventure, might beguile a tired reader at the end of the day's work. But why would a young man trade the libidinous pleasures of Ovid—a writer more likely to be read under the sheets than in the classroom—for the plain and even grim episodes of deceit, death, and loneliness that follow Stevenson's preface? Stevenson here plays upon the disparity between the two texts—the one work, the other pleasure—inverting our instinctive assumptions and making us believe that Ovid's easy Latin is the work while his own unfamiliar and often unpronounceable Scots is the pleasure.

Stevenson is engaged in both a sly deception and a revealing truth, for his novel sits as easily on a scholar's bookshelf as it does on an end table by a comfortable chair. The image of the scholar was not an accidental one. It was the deliberate choice of a writer whose prodigious preparation for the construction of his text was, in fact, a scholar's work. But Stevenson was not writing for a scholarly audience; he was writing fiction, or what passed for fiction, and the scholarship had to be veiled. So *Kidnapped* was presented as a book for "young gentlemen," however indeterminate that audience description. None need mistake it for serious work. Hence his dismissal of the historical discrepancies as insignificant, of no concern to the reader. Yet despite his denial—indeed, the denial may be the proof— Stevenson was intensely committed to accuracy, both as a principle in itself and as homage to the past. The first of his two-part preface refers to the history in the text, while the second reflects on his and Baxter's personal histories. Addressing his friend, Stevenson recalls their early days in Edinburgh and takes pleasure in remembering things past. And just as the lines to Baxter bring back days long gone, alive now only in memory, so does the reconstitution of an earlier Highlands bring back days and lives either long forgotten or misremembered. Veracity and error may lie both in actual history and in its reconstruction as printed text, but the past must still be recovered, if only because it is all we have to explain our present. To give it life for the armchair reader is not to rob it of its substance for the scholar but simply to make it accessible to everyone.

Stevenson was a voracious reader with an extraordinary range of interests. Proficient in English literature, he was equally at home in French medieval history and popular fiction, German political memoirs and correspondence, and American experimental poetry and prose. As for Scotland, he read everything from border ballads to Robert Burns, from church history and martyrology to folklore, philosophy, and criminal jurisprudence. Coming from a professional family who always had books in the home, he early on developed the habit of buying books for work and for pleasure. While he never bought as a collector, he nonetheless had a keen sense of how attached a person could become to his books, as he indicated to John Hill Burton when he learned that the famous historian of Scotland was disbursing his library (*L,* 3:99).[1] After he settled in Samoa he arranged for the shipment from England of his own library, which now included his father's books, and he added heavily to this collection during those last years in the Pacific. The breadth of the collection is quite remarkable. Yale University, the largest repository, catalogues only those books that have Stevenson's markings; their actual holdings are far more extensive. And Yale by no means has all his books. Dispersed in stages after his death, they can be found in the pages of the numerous auction catalogues that periodically record the sales of Stevensoniana.

But the books in an author's library are not necessarily an indication of what that author has read. Where Stevenson's books can be identified, however, there are characteristic markings—a vertical pencil line in the margin of the printed text—that indicate how closely he read. He was critical, even skeptical, and did not take what he read on faith. Just where, or how, he developed this habit is not easy to say. It may have been a vestige of the Scottish philosophical tradition that alternately emphasized the limits of our knowledge (David Hume) and the necessity of our knowing (Thomas Reid, Dugald Stewart); it was surely a part of his home life, given the omnipresence of a family of engineers; and it was certainly reinforced by his intense preparation for the law. There is no question that Stevenson's deep reading was, at its core, a profound matter of temperament. His very sharp and precise critical writing—*all* his writing had a critical component to it —was the product of an acute and a broad literary culture. When he was not reading for pleasure, which he largely dispensed with after he became a professional writer, he read to a purpose. That is, his reading served to found and buttress his writing.

Stevenson's reading began to inform his composing as early as 1866, when the sixteen-year-old author published *The Pentland Rising.* Stevenson here transports material wholesale from James Kirkton's and Robert Wodrow's histories of the Covenanters' early battles. In the manner of a college history essay, he recounts an old Scottish story replete with character, incident, and drama. He supplies a range of footnotes for his authorities, and in a manner consistent with all his subsequent work, they are impeccable in their accuracy. If Thomas Stevenson privately printed this exercise merely out of pride in his son's accomplishment, he was certainly unaware that it might prove the source of an incurable "lead poisoning" like that which Dr. Oliver Wendell Holmes warned could strike a writer the first time he saw his name in print. What is notable about *The Pentland Rising* is its example of a working practice that Stevenson was to adapt and refine throughout his writing career. Eleven years later, this was shown to advantage in "A Lodging for the Night: A Story of Francis Villon." Although the colloquy between the cold and vagrant poet and the staid and comfortable ex-soldier was invented, other incidents (like the murderer Montigny and the magnificent gallows) were taken directly from a French biography that Stevenson had reviewed for the *Cornhill Magazine.* Unlike *The Pentland Rising,* however, there are no footnotes and no references in "A Lodging for the Night." This is fiction that calls attention to its history, but the lines between the fact and fiction are blurred, and Stevenson does nothing to clarify them for the reader.

Ten years later, Stevenson was an accomplished, international author. He had just left England for the United States when he wrote to Charles Scribner, his American publisher, from Saranac Lake in upstate New York, asking Scribner to send him books for his work-in-progress, *The Master of Ballantrae.*

I telegraphed you today for the "Memoirs of the Chevalier Johnstone," *on which I depend;* I cannot go on without it. I have to ask you now for works that will enable me to touch on colonial life here about 1760. I want any travellers book of early days; the best you can recommend. I want Dr. Eggleston's book if that be out; and how about somebody called McMasters. A journey in the woods at that date (1760–70) I have to make; can anything be produced? A missionary of that time; a military report of an expedition; what not? Likewise I have to deal (Save us and bless us, how like me!) with Buccaneers on the coast of the U.S. (1764– and around) and if you can help me, why so much the better. Cooper's Waterwitch, I believe, is somewhere about my date. I might look at that. But that is quite apart; what I want is *originals* (B, 3248; *L,* 6:80).[2]

For Stevenson, originals are key to his project. If the novel is historical then every detail of its representation must be accurate. Therefore he requires first-person accounts by people who were there. This does not mean that he assumes those accounts are invariably reliable. But he clearly distinguishes between firsthand reports and secondhand narratives, and his preference is always to work with primary materials. Hence his discomfort with using a nineteenth-century text like *Waterwitch,* since that would force him to depend upon James Fenimore Cooper for his data and, in effect, get his history from a novel.

While still composing *Ballantrae,* Stevenson wrote to E. L. Burlingame, the editor who was going to serialize the novel in *Scribner's Magazine.*

Don't trouble about any more French books, I am on another scent, you see, just now. Only the French in Hindustan I await with impatience as that is for Ballantrae: the scene of that romance is Scotland—the States—Scotland—India—Scotland—and the States again; so it jumps like a flea. I have enough about the States now, and very much obliged I am; yet if Drakes Tragedies of the Wilderness is (as I gather) a collection of originals, I should like to purchase it. If it is a picturesque vulgarization, I do not wish to look it in the face. Purchase, I say; for I think it would be well to have some such collection by me with a view to fresh woods ([January 6, 1888], P; *L,* 6:100).

Again we see Stevenson's determination to have original accounts that will enable him to site his fiction accurately. His derision of secondary sources—"picturesque vulgarization"—is that of the historian who is dismissive of all but the real thing, the document itself. Stevenson had a high regard for authors who worked with original documents and for editors who made them available, and he always had an eye for good design and printing as well as for good scholarship. But the main point is that he insisted upon authentic documents when constructing his fiction. In fact, the work could not proceed if there were no documents. If this is barely recognized with respect to his major fiction, it is virtually unknown with regard to the less familiar work. During his composition of *St. Ives,* he wrote to Burlingame from Honolulu on October 16, 1893:

> Will you please send me something as definite as you can find as to the American privateers of 1812–14? Of course I have Adams; but what I want is some log of a voyage, or some popular book containing actual facts and faces, or any historic and detailed publications. I am willing to go (if necessary) fifty dollars on this. . . . The above request is for my (not very good) novel of St. Ives.

And then on October 24: "Here is a book I shall require *quam primum:* Memoires d'un conscrit de 1808 par L. F. Gille. Paris: Havard. See and let me have it, and register the packet."[3] In all these letters there is the repeated request for logs, journals, memoirs, or reports. He is interested in the plain prose of the period, unadorned, and unselfconscious—the very antithesis of belletristic writing, with its concern for posterity and audience.

Clearly Stevenson used other books extensively in the composition of his own. As an essayist (and his early fame rested largely on his essays) he regularly drew upon essential sources for the exposition of his subject. Stevenson composed two entries for the Ninth edition of the *Brittanica,* one on the French popular poet and songwriter, Pierre Jean de Béranger, and another on Robert Burns. The latter of these utilized the most current editions of Burns's poetry, which he borrowed from the Advocates' Library. If the Burns entry was rejected, it was not rejected for its scholarly defects but for its sounding of a less than laudatory note in its review (and judgment) of Burns's career. Yet even when he wrote about his own experience, as in *Travels with a Donkey,* he drew heavily on books about the Cévennes, histories that shored up the authenticity of his own narrative. In short, it did not matter what Stevenson was writing—if a work merely touched on historical matters he felt obligated to ensure its accuracy and augment its historical density and texture through reference to authorities both common and obscure. Essentially, Stevenson had a scholar's attitude toward history. The habit of historical research, begun early, was especially fortunate as he moved toward a subject that enabled him to reinforce it through practice. In other words, as he began working with more complex historical material, his ability to utilize fundamental sources became more pronounced and far more sophisticated. Stevenson's work was always grounded in actuality—in names, places, and characters drawn from life and etched on plate, words scrambled and rearranged from the most common to the most esoteric, from Latin tags to archaic proverbs to dialectal phrases, from the jargon of the sea to the language of the law. Printed sources were as much a part of that actuality as personal observation. As such, they became a part of his own writing. The process was imaginative as well as technical. On one side, they provided the inspiration for the architecture of the text; on the other, they were the struts that supported its construction.

Starting in the early 1880s, in a succession of short stories and novels, Stevenson embarked on a major project to recreate an important era in his country's history. But he did this quietly, without calling attention to the historicity of his texts, and one consequence has been a tendency to understate or overlook entirely their historical significance. One of the paradoxes of Stevenson's historical novels is that they appear to be contemporary—that although they are set in the past, their rapidity of movement reads as if they took place in the present. This may be dismissed as sleight of hand, a trick of Stevenson's narrative and stylistic brilliance, but the effect is to mute the reader's awareness of and interest in the text's historicity. And Stevenson—unlike Sir Walter Scott, who effectively embedded the historical nature of his Waverley novels in the reader's mind before and during the course of the narrative—did not provide introductions and explanatory notes. It is curious that no one doubts the historical basis of *Waverley,* set sixty years after the Jacobite rebellion, while few readers consciously think of *Kidnapped* as historical, although it is placed just five years after Culloden. At one time, in a letter to E. L. Burlingame, Stevenson mused on the tantalizing prospect of preparing editions of his novels in the manner of Scott, an enterprise suddenly made commercially attractive by the imminent passage of the copyright bill: "If *that bill* ever passes, I shall revise the text of all my books, and add an introduction and (where it may be) notes after the manner of Sir Walter; and that should do something for your edition. Treasure Island, Kidnapped, some of the Merry Men, and the Master of Ballantrae would all support a considerable and amusing gallery of notes; and these, and Dr. Jekyll, and the Dynamiter, and perhaps Prince Otto would take good introductions. How does the idea like you?"[4]

It would be a mistake to think that Stevenson's historical intentions were restricted to subjects in the distant past. Even when writing about his own early days in Paris in *The Wrecker,* he is conscious of using the past as historical material. Burlingame, who was reading the novel for serial publication in *Scribner's,* questioned Stevenson on his use of possible anachronisms. Stevenson replied with complete assurance and in the process delivered a discourse on historical fiction.

> As to anachronism, I must explain. There are two anachronisms, which I cannot help; but oddly enough niether is situate in San Francisco. The S.F. is that of 79–80, as I lived in it, and almost all that Dodd saw, I saw;—only

perhaps the telephone had scarce gone the length of the ships in the harbour; though even that I do not know. So the middle is right enough. But the beginning is a little too early—for the Latin quarter is that [of] '73—and the sequel is a trifle too late, for the directories are those of '87. So far I plead guilty, and I don't think the charge is serious. A little stretching of dates might even bring Dodd back as far as 75, which is near enough; and for the directories, who ever reads them but myself, and Clark Russel[l], and sundry old particular and pickled skippers, who are little likely, even if they read the book at all, to verify the date of Hoyt's directory or the Admiralty book on the Islands Vol III? Most people will suppose the passage fanciful altogether; and in that case none would have thought of blame. In a historical novel, who looks so close? Were the conditions so anywhere over fifty years? That is all we ask. May I not claim my license of say 12 years instead of five or six?[5]

What is important is not that Stevenson erred about his dates—he noted a similar discrepancy in the dedication to *Kidnapped*—but that he is completely confident about the fundamental nature of his method. For all intents, or rather for all readers, *The Wrecker* was a contemporary novel. But insofar as it was set in the past, even though not more than ten to fifteen years earlier, Stevenson was extremely conscious of his details. Navigational directories were among his reliable tools. He clearly did not expect his readers to have any idea where he got his material or of what sources were available to him. Except for W. Clark Russell, the foremost sea writer of the day, the people who would know about ocean directories—old "pickled" skippers—were not likely to be reading novels. As for dates, as long as the fictional ones came close enough to the historical reality an author has "license" for minor alterations. And by saying "fifty years" Stevenson gives himself a wide latitude, although he personally maintained a close rein on the events and dates in his own fictional frames. Thus the slight inexactitude of a few years in Loudon Dodds's Latin Quarter will hardly affect the broader picture of Bohemia in Paris. Although set in the very recent past, Stevenson knows that *The Wrecker,* in time, will be a part of history, that it will itself become a historical fiction.

From the beginning, Stevenson was comfortable with documents and skilled in adapting them to fiction.[6] But he was never under any illusions about their meaning. For one thing, he did not automatically accept them as true in any representational sense. In the case of the memoir, for example, he was invariably skeptical as to how much should be taken at face value. A logbook or nautical directory had a higher truth-value, but even they were problematic since sea directories were often limited in their reliability (as Stevenson discovered during his voyage through the Pacific with Alexander Findlay's *Directory* as his guide). But the significant thing about a document for Stevenson was its status as an artifact, as a linguistic relic of a past time. Its importance resided in its archeological value, its capacity to reveal a past culture in the smallest ways—by its dress, its turns of speech, its crimes and punishments. Documents were an archeology of social history, an unmediated gaze into the past, provided that the person sifting them had a knowledge broader than that of the individual items and the sharpness to see their significance. One of the reasons Stevenson was so drawn to criminal trials was his recognition, as Hugo Arnot earlier observed, that they are the truest and most intimate register of a culture's history. Stevenson's intellectual understanding of the nature and function of documentary materials was crucial to his pursuit of historical research. It is an aspect of his career that has often been misunderstood. If we can see how sources were, in a sense, the lifeblood of his fiction—living printed forms that revealed past lives—then we will begin to understand some fundamental issues in Stevenson's art.

Stevenson's extraordinary dependence upon documents had its origins in his singular intellectual history and its convergence with his country's culture. Although biographers have customarily dismissed Stevenson as a desultory student, his admission to the Scottish bar in 1875 was no small accomplishment. The course of study for the bachelor of law was rigorous. The faculty required, first, a degree in arts from any Scottish or English university. Since Stevenson did not have this, he was first given a general examination that he completed successfully. Then, to become an advocate, he had to "pass examinations in Civil Law, Scots Law, Scots Conveyancing, Constitutional Law and Constitutional History, and Medical Jurisprudence."[7] This was not a simple task. The calendar of classes for Edinburgh University lists these courses and the nature of the material covered. For the civil law course:

> The subject-matter . . . is the external and internal history and general and special doctrines of the Law of Rome, as developed in the Institutes of Gaius and Justinian. . . . The law of possession, property and real rights, and (2) the law of obligations. . . . (1) The law of the family relationships, and (2) the law of succession.[8]

The Scots Law course also covered a wide range of subjects including: the history and literature of Scots law, its sources, and the interpretation of statutes; personal relations, marriage and the methods for proving it; rights of husband and wife, and the dissolution of marriage; the origin of property, its acquisition and possession, heritable and movable; contracts and obligations; and the law of evidence, procedure, succession, and criminal law (*EUC*, 87–88). Conveyancing covered the whole area of deeds, which was central to Scottish law. The course Law and History included the history of Scotland, "with special reference to the origin and history of the Constitution of Scotland, and the progress of Civilisation" (*EUC,* 92). John Hill Burton's *History of Scotland*—a text Stevenson retained in his private library—was one of the recommended books for this course. Stevenson compressed a suggested two-year course of study into a brief period where he prepared himself for the examinations. That he succeeded is a testament both to his powers of concentration and to his ability to absorb an enormous amount of technical as well as historical information.

What was the nature of the legal studies in which Stevenson had immersed himself? To answer this we might consider how the term "law" was defined. A prominent dictionary defined the term as "the different systems of rules by which the subjects in this country are associated; by which they conduct themselves in their intercourse with other nations; or by which the conduct of individuals is regulated, or their rights and interests in property ascertained." Constitutional law was the law of the state "by which the reciprocal obligations of the governors and governed to each other are regulated." And civil law was "that branch which includes the rules by which property is preserved or vindicated, and the rights and interests of individuals ascertained."[9] Rules and regulations are repeatedly used to define the law in Bell's *Dictionary.* System and order, rule and principle— these are the characteristics of the law as it was understood and taught in Scotland. There was an exceptionally strong emphasis on relations in the law, on what we could call social relations, including contractual relations. Even in the area of medical jurisprudence, the focus was on the social aspects of illness, and on social labeling, since the way in which individuals were defined was important to their personal status (their enfranchisement, their legitimacy). An individual's health was also viewed in the context of public health, and the treatment of illness was directed toward the larger end of a healthier social body.

The areas of Scots law that were voluminous had to do with conveyancing and criminal law. As for the former, the key to the conveyance is the "deed," which the *Dictionary* defines as follows:

> a formal written instrument executed and authenticated according to certain technical forms, setting forth the terms of an agreement, contract, or obligation, whether in relation to persons or things, and comprehending every description of formal writing required for the voluntary constitution, transmission, or discharge of rights or obligations . . . relating either to heritable or moveable property, with all the modifications, qualifications, and combinations of which such documents are susceptible, in order to fit them for the various and complicated transactions to which they may be applied (*DLS,* 383).

The definition of deed runs to three pages and is cross-referenced under nine other titles. Yet there are two essentials: every deed "requires a party or parties capable of contracting obligation," and every deed "contains a definite and distinct obligation or agreement, capable of explication" (*DLS,* 383). Scots law is characterized by a profusion of contracts and rules that are largely written down. Scotland is remarkable for the number of writers who prepared texts on the principles and practice of the various branches of the law. Viscount Stair's *Institutions of the Law of Scotland* is only the most famous. There are Sir George Mackenzie's *Institutions* and Lord Bankton's *Institute.* (The latter models itself explicitly on Stair's great achievement.) Stair and Mackenzie both "were scholars and humanists, as well as practicing lawyers . . . [and] both brought to their exposition of the law all the apparatus of scholarship and literature."[10] In addition, other major treatises were less theoretical and more practical in their objectives. John Erskine—"the lawyer of common sense," as Aeneas Mackay called him—aimed his *Institutes* at the working lawyer, while George Bell, author of the prestigious *Commentaries* on Scottish law, prepared a popular textbook for students, *Principles of the Law of Scotland.* Both Erskine's *Institutes* and Bell's *Principles* were being sold and recommended when Stevenson was studying. The Scots have always been determined to codify, on the Roman model, the principles of their law.[11]

The emphasis on order and system in the law was buttressed by a solid focus on the document and its crucial role in the legal process. Scotland's institutional writers divided the law of their country into "written and unwritten"—the former being the rules prescribed in the acts of parliament and sederunt, the latter consisting of everything that derived from custom or was adopted from Roman, canon, or feudal law (*DLS,* 173).[12] The Scots were famous, perhaps even notorious, for their record keeping: "In no country is property better secured, or protected with more legislative wisdom, than in Scotland. Our system of records gives a degree of security to the transmission of property which is peculiar to Scotland" (*DLS,* 173–74). Bell's conviction that the genius of Scottish property rights is rooted in hard copy is visible at the opening of *Kidnapped,* when David Balfour is given his father's testamentary letter, a piece of writing that establishes David's legal claim to the estate of Shaws. But nowhere is the Scottish concern for documents more revealing than in the view of evidence that emerges in Scots law. We will remember how David, after his captivity on the Bass Rock, attempts to deliver his evidence for the defendant at the trial of James Stewart. In William Bell's *A Dictionary and Digest of the Law of Scotland* the definition of "evidence" runs to fourteen closely printed pages.[13] Simply put, "evidence is the proof, either written or parole, which the parties in a civil or criminal cause, may legally adduce in support of facts and circumstances on which their respective pleas or defences depend" (366). But the salient point is that "the evidence afforded by writing is accounted the highest description of legal proof." This type of evidence by writ includes "formal deeds," "notarial instruments," "acts of court, extracts from judicial records," and "public instruments and documents not by officers of the law" (366–68). Documents were instruments for getting at the legal issues in cases, and written documents were preferred to oral testimony. Scottish law, with its roots in Roman law and its focus on private and social relations, supported and legitimated documentary evidence above all others. This may be why we see in Stevenson's writing so much questioning of his own sources' "authority." He wants to examine original documents, but as a good lawyer he is aware of the potentially tainted nature of their testimony. The Scottish preoccupation with documents and written materials was even recognized by people beyond the country's borders. "An English counsel observed some years ago, 'That the Scotch lawyers write all they speak, and print all they write.'"[14] This is not the place to bring in the legion of religious writers, who were at least as industrious as the lawyers in compiling records for posterity, but it may be enough to say that the Scots were habituated to print, perhaps even fixated on it. Stevenson, in this respect, was a consummate Scotsman. He was trained to revere the document as the source of hard evidence. To pass the bar he absorbed quantities of printed information that predicated the rules governing people's behavior. But in the very act of honoring the printed word lies the doubt as to its reliability. For the document is merely a record, and the human being who made that record may have erred or lied. Yet without the document there is no source at all. There is merely fancy. Stevenson himself may ultimately have questioned the foundation of our knowledge—of our ability to penetrate the meaning of our experience—but his characters never completely relinquish their need for the tangible evidences of their existence, their documentary validation.

At this point we can reconstruct, in a small measure, Stevenson's association with the Faculty of Advocates. He first had to be admitted to candidacy for the law, and the records in the Advocates' Library reveal the following:

Edinburgh, 2nd Nov. 1872

Mr. Alexander Moody Stuart, second surviving son of the rev. Alexander Moody Stuart, Minister of Free St. Luke's Church, Edinburgh, and Mr Robert Louis Stevenson, only son of Thomas Stevenson Esq., C.E. Edinburgh, appeared before the examinators and having been examined, the former in Latin, Greek, Logic and Ethical and Metaphysical philosophy and the latter in Latin, Ethical and Metaphysical Philosophy, Mathematics, French and German were found sufficiently qualified.

T. Hill Jamieson Cl.Int.[15]

Sir Walter Grindlay Simpson, Stevenson's friend and companion on the inland voyage, had been admitted on July 16 of that year on the basis of having received a B.A. from Cambridge University.[16] Stevenson is next listed in the Faculty of Advocates' *Register of the Private Examinators (Law),* a volume covering the years

1857 through 1908. On July 14, 1875, "Mr Robert Louis Stevenson, only son of Thomas Stevenson, Esq., C.E. Edinburgh," along with two other men, "appeared before the Examinators, were examined, found qualified and recommended. T Hill Jamieson Cl Int."[17] As Lord Guthrie said in his memoir, "Fellow-students for the Scotch Bar, we became advocates the same year, 1875" (LG, 2). According to Guthrie, passing the bar involved the "*payment of about* £350, *in fees, stamp-duty, etc. Of this sum a large part goes to the support of the Advocates' Library, with the valuable privilege of borrowing twenty books at a time*" (LG, 36). The treasurer's account book lists Stevenson as having paid £10 as a fee for the examination in law (between December 1874 and December 1875) and £6 6[s.] during that same period as payment for use of the Library.[18] Guthrie even went so far as to discover some of Stevenson's borrowings from the Library: "The lists show that Stevenson borrowed in 1878 a large number of books relating to the Cevennes, in connection with his *Travels with a Donkey in the Cevennes,* published in 1879." (LG, 36, 38).

Although Guthrie is off by a year—the books on the Cévennes were borrowed in 1879—what is most interesting is his judgment on Stevenson and the law. He claims he "knew him intimately" during his period "as a student of law qualifying for the Scottish Bar" (LG, 30). Then he proceeds to comment:

> He had no natural taste for law. . . . Not even the love for the curiosities of legal history and legal lore which fascinated Sir Walter Scott. Nor had he the comprehensive insight into human nature, the balance of mind and sobriety of judgment, which, with his industry and his predilection for law, might have made Sir Walter a great judge, if not a great advocate (LG, 40–41).

This is altogether baffling. Stevenson had a powerful attachment to legal history and the ability to transform it into narrative fiction of the first order. That someone who knew him well as a student, and considered him one of only two figures of that generation of Speculative Society students to have achieved enduring fame, could so misread both his aptitude and his work, should give all readers pause for reflection.

Over the course of a decade, between 1875 and 1885, Stevenson borrowed books regularly from the Advocates' Library. The years are as follows: 1875, 1876, 1878, 1879, 1880, 1882, and 1885. The years of heaviest borrowing are 1879, when he checked out just over two dozen texts, many of them multiple volumes, and 1882, when he checked out twelve. Roger Swearingen, drawing on Guthrie's earlier declaration about Stevenson's use of the library for *Travels with a Donkey,* first identified the books Stevenson used.[19] If we examine the faculty records, he borrowed the English language *A Complete History of the Cevennes* (London, 1703) on March 24, 1879, and twice checked out *Histoire des troubles des Cevennes* (1760) in 1879 (January 8 and March 27) and once in 1880 (September 23). But clearly his favorite book was Cavalier's *Memoirs* (2nd ed., London, 1726). Stevenson borrowed it in 1879 (January 8 and March 24) and again in 1880 on September 23.[20] Stevenson marked this edition in the margins, undoubtedly for an essay on Cavalier of which a draft paragraph remains, and which Swearingen, in *The ProseWritings of Robert Louis Stevenson,* dates June 1881 (59). Before his work on the Cévennes, Stevenson borrowed a number of books for his essay on Charles of Orleans that was published in the *Cornhill* in December 1876. *Histoire de Charles VI* was checked out on December 14, 1875; Comines' *Memoires fur les principaux faits & gestes de Loys XI. & Charles VII* (1747) was checked out on March 19, 1876; J. J. des Ursins' *Histoire de Charles VI* (1614) and another two volume study, possibly by J. le Laboureur (1663), were checked out on June 5, 1876.[21]

The recovery of Stevenson's borrowings from the Advocates' Library is a small side story. My working assumption was that the library would keep written records of anyone who borrowed books, and since we know that Stevenson used the library it was just a matter of locating those records. But that was not as simple as it sounded. When the National Library of Scotland was formed in 1925 it acquired the bulk of the Advocates' Library holdings, with the exception of its records and the law books that could still be used by working attorneys. In effect, the National Library and the Advocates' Library, although joined physically, became two separate entities, the one open to the general public and the other restricted to attorneys. Since there was no reliable catalogue listing the Advocates' manuscript holdings, I could only guess at the existence of a record indicating Stevenson's use of the original collections. When I did indeed discover that record, in the form of a large ledger book devoted solely to members' borrowings, it had "Robert Louis Stevenson" written at the top of one of the pages, with the dates and titles of his borrowings scratched in a late nineteenth century cursive script. But as one might expect, since the book titles were often long, and the scribe's patience short, abbreviated titles were often used. Fortunately, a seven volume printed catalogue of the Advocates' Library had been published in the 1860s and 1870s, and by simple trial and error most of the titles on the Stevenson pages could be identified by their complete forms in the catalogue. I then attempted to match the printed titles with those in the National Library's own catalogue, and given the disparities between the two systems, the task was a bit mazelike. The test for success was simple: I called up a book, leafed through it, and looked for Stevenson's characteristic markings—a single vertical line drawn along the margin of the page, occasionally double or triple lines when a passage was given special notice. Stevenson could never read seriously without a pencil in his hand, and books that were important for his work had to be marked. The fact that they were the library's property made no difference. But those texts that went to building *Travels with a Donkey* and the essays on Burns and Charles of Orleans are still there for public use—at least Stevenson returned them.

Stevenson's imagination was rooted in historical detail, and it soon came to focus on Scotland. After his return home from the United States in 1880, having married in San Francisco and camped out in Calistoga, he and his wife traveled with his parents to the Scottish Highlands. He had been turning over in his mind a book on Scotland, and this trip energized that idea, as he later wrote in a letter to Principal Tulloch of the University of St. Andrews: "While studying for the book of which I spoke to you at Strathpeffer, I fell in love with the Highlands; and have it in my heart to write of them from the '15 to the present day: a very strange story, but so little opened up that it may be long before I can find my way from the one end to the other" (*L,* 3:196). But his real enthusiasm for the project can be gleaned from an earlier, more intimate letter to his cousin Bob, which he wrote in Strathpeffer:

> I am in a great scheme now of a history book; you will recoil from it as it relates to Scotland; but it will be very interesting, when done, to any class of mind; and in the meantime what I particularly desire, supply me with business while I am still so little able for serious work. It is to be called Scotland and the Union. And it is to be an attempt to posit Scotland as she was at that epoch, socially, economically, religiously; hill clergymen, hill robbers, highland chiefs dealing at St Germains, Darien scheme, Cameronians, Ferguson the Plotter, Carstares, Simon Fraser, &c &c—You have no idea what interesting material I can see to get together for it.[22]

This is not the rambling of an amateur but the elliptical shorthand of an adept. Stevenson knew what he was about. At Strathpeffer he also wrote to the eminent historian John Hill Burton and asked him three questions. First, he wanted to know where he was "likely to find material relative to the career of . . . John Cavalier, the ex-Camisard," whom Stevenson had been interested in for some time as we know from his reading in the Advocates' Library. "And, by the way, do you believe in his memoirs? I fear they are to be taken with a very large allowance." Second, he asked for material about Robert Fergusson, "outside of two meagre memoirs prefixed to two editions of his poems." Third, he inquired as to the worthiness of the endeavor he was about to undertake:

> 3rd An old idea, first started while I was reading your history of Scotland. . . . That is to write a circumstantial history of the Union. This takes one among so many curious characters that I think the book ought to be interesting. . . . I suppose I should find no want of material, and I should

be obliged if you would tell me briefly whether or not I am deceived in this expectation.

After receiving a reply Stevenson wrote back: "I shall soon be in Edinburgh. And then I shall be very glad to tell you my idea, if you will allow me, and get any advice you can spare. I believe there is a book to be written, as I see the subject; but I feel already what a huge task it would be without some of that guidance you could give me" (L, 3:98–99). That Stevenson refers to his project as an "old" idea, first generated when he read Burton's *History of Scotland,* suggests how early and deep was his passion for national history. Whatever a reader today makes of *The Pentland Rising,* it stands as an emblem for the writer's abiding conviction that his country's history contained all that narrative and drama could allow. On a personal level, approaching Burton without any timidity—for he was not just a distinguished historian but an important biographer and legal commentator as well—reflected a high degree of confidence, notwithstanding the self-effacing humility. Finally, the letter to Burton reveals a pattern that emerges in Stevenson's correspondence, a constant demanding of books or information needed for his work. These requests varied from cajolery to peremptoriness. It is understandable that Stevenson, a pampered only child, should carry through life the habit of expecting people to accommodate him. For the most part they did, which was hardly surprising given his personality and charm. He may even have been unconscious of just how demanding he was, since people so readily acceded to his wishes, as well as his needs.[23]

In the fall of 1880 Stevenson was at Davos, in Switzerland, and the project was still at the front of his mind. Indeed, the concept had undergone considerable development. A well-known letter to his father outlined the book's subjects. There were five proposed sections covering all the major episodes in Scottish history from 1715 through the end of the eighteenth century. Stevenson realized that he was carried away by a grand plan: "All this of course will greatly change in form scope and order; this is just a bird's eye glance. Thank you for Burt which came and for your union notes. I have read one half (about 900 pages) of Wodrow's correspondence, with some improvement but great fatigue."[24] Graham Balfour, Stevenson's relation and his chosen biographer, was the first to review this episode of the writer's life: "An outline of the Highland history may be found in the *Letters,* but the book itself remained unwritten, and is never likely now to become what Stevenson would have made of it. But he spent some time in preparatory reading, and even began to learn Gaelic for the purpose, though he never got beyond the rudiments of the language."[25] Balfour's summary comment exhibits the attitude toward this project that shows up regularly in the biographies and criticism—that it was an understandable, perhaps even admirable enthusiasm, but it could hardly be taken seriously.

That was not Stevenson's attitude. "You have no idea what interesting material I can see to get together for it," he writes his cousin. And he knew how to get that material. His father purchased books for him, to be sure, in keeping with his need for research materials, but Stevenson read them. Apart from ecclesiastical historians, and social historians, it is hard to imagine too many readers for Robert Wodrow. But when Stevenson says he read half the *Correspondence* he meant just that. What must be appreciated is that although he read this for a purpose, he found a genuine interest in it. He wrote to his father again in December: "Briefly all that has to do with the (1) hereditary jurisdictions (2) the forfeited estates (3) the evictions (4) the men, the church & the disruption in the Highlands. . . . I breathe after this Highland business; feeling a real, fresh, lively & modern subject, full of romance & scientific interest in front of me. It is likely it will turn into a long essay. The Highlands in the 18th–19th century" (B, 3459; *L,* 3:129). During his stay at Davos, and especially during the month of December, Stevenson's mind was filled with his book. On December 21 he wrote to his father:

> Thanks for your notes; that fishery question will come in, as you notice, in the Highland Book, as well as under the Union; it is very important. I hear no word of Hugh Miller's *Evictions;* I count on that. What you say about the *Old and New Statistical* is odd. It seems to me very much as if I were gingerly embarking on a *History of Modern Scotland.* Probably Tulloch will never carry it out. And, you see, once I have studied and written these two vols., *The Transformation of the Scottish Highlands* and *Scotland and the Union,* I shall have a good ground to go upon (*L,* 3:145).

And to Sidney Colvin, also in December:

> It is a most interesting and sad story, and from the '45 it is all to be written for the first time. This of course will cause me a far greater difficulty about authorities; but I have already learned much, and where to look for more. One pleasant feature is the vast number of delightful writers I shall have to deal with: Burt, Johnson, Boswell, Mrs Grant of Laggan, Scott. There will be interesting sections on the Ossianic controversy and the growth of the taste for Highland scenery. I have to touch upon Rob Roy, Flora Macdonald, the strange story of Lady Grange, the beautiful story of the tenants on the Forfeited Estates, and the odd, inhuman problem of the great evictions. The religious conditions are wild, unknown, very surprising. And three out of my five parts remain hitherto entirely unwritten (*L,* 3:149).

Reading Stevenson's correspondence from the summer through the fall of 1880 we see him filled with energy and enthusiasm for this story, commenting repeatedly on its "interest" and "beauty" and "romance," or on its "strangeness" and "sadness."

With legends like Rob Roy and Flora Macdonald, enigmas like Lady Grange, and tragedies like the evictions, the "romance" and the "sadness" are clear to see. But it would be a mistake not to recognize another plane of Stevenson's perception, that the story possessed an intellectual fascination for a modern writer, or put another way, that a modern story lived inside it. Stevenson's passion for his subject—for the people of the Highlands and their history—coexists with his cooler, more dispassionate and scientific view. On one side we see a romantic artist drawn to the eighteenth century and the Scottish Highlands, to a world of lawless adventurers and political rebels and religious martyrs.[26] On another we see a gifted scholar determined to trace Scotland's history from the time of the Union, an act which abolished Scotland as a separate nation and created in its place a poor province of a larger and more powerful country. To be sure, it was a history that contained limitless opportunities for romance and poetry. Sir Walter Scott, after all, was never at a loss for heroic legends—if he did not himself create the history he did a good job of transforming it. But Stevenson was another matter. He was capable of greater detachment than Scott, and he was not driven by a historical idea that was to be revealed in his writing. And he was a far more deliberate writer. He could be viscerally attracted to his material and at the same time view it as a technical challenge. Stevenson sensed the epic scale of Scotland as a subject, but he was unsure of just what to do with it. His uncertainty, and in a way his miscalculation, is reflected in one line of the letter to his father: "It is likely it will turn into a long essay."

Stevenson's intense interest in Scottish history leads into one of the more curious episodes of his career. In 1881 his name was submitted as a candidate for the chair in constitutional law and history at the University of Edinburgh that was being vacated by Professor Aeneas Mackay. According to Lord Guthrie, Thomas Stevenson was responsible for the application, having asked Guthrie "to nominate Louis" to the Faculty, and Guthrie came to believe the father was the primary force behind the scheme to secure a professorship.[27] But Stevenson needed no prompting, as he himself had written to Mackay before the chair was even cold:

> What is this I hear? that you are retiring from your chair. It is not, I hope, from ill-health?
>
> But if you are retiring, may I ask if you have promised your support to any successor? I have a great mind to try. The summer session would suit me; the chair would suit me—if only I would suit it; I certainly should work it hard: that I can promise. I only wish it were a few years from now, when I hope to have something more substantial to show for myself. Up to the present time, all that I have published, even bordering on history, has been in an occasional form, and I fear this is much against me.[28]

If this all seems strange—Stevenson supplicating for a university post for which he has no academic qualifications—it was, in fact, not as ill-conceived as we might think. To begin with, the chair carried few duties. Essentially it required the holder to spend the summer in Edinburgh delivering a series of lectures for which he was paid £250. Stevenson clearly needed the money—"it is perhaps the only hope I may have of a permanent income"[29]—and the prospect of working just three months and having the other nine to himself was hard to turn away from. Of course, he knew that his writing was not academic; and he even worried that his actual publications might be held against him and that he was simply too popular for serious consideration: "My works are unfortunately so light and trifling they may interfere."[30] Setting aside the deprecating note, Stevenson's experience in pursuit of a professorship reflects a pattern in academic life as invariable as the laws of nature.

Stevenson proceeded to solicit letters of recommendation for the electors, and a bound pamphlet of fourteen testimonials was printed.[31] Stevenson's biographers viewed the entire project as "quixotic" (Guthrie), "bound to fail" (Steuart) and "markedly unreal" (Furnas). Yet what made it seem so odd? The unlikelihood that he would succeed? His inappropriateness for the post? His lack of qualifications? The suggestion that runs through the biographical commentaries is that it was audacious, if not presumptuous, of Stevenson to submit an application. Even Rosaline Masson, who was attracted to just about everything connected with Stevenson, writes in a note of amazement that he "actually offered himself as candidate."[32] But the testimonial writers did not consider it at all astonishing. Despite the inclination to dismiss their letters as nothing more than friendship's offerings, the referees were considerable figures. J. M. D. Meiklejohn, professor of education, the University of St. Andrews:

> He possesses in a quite rare degree the most needful qualification for a historian—a keen and true insight into the life of man, and a strong sympathy with all shapes and forms of it . . . and I am quite sure he, more than any man I know or know of in Scotland, would make the past of our Scottish history live again. . . . He is one of the most subtle and acute debaters I ever heard; and he possesses a power of explanation and illustration—qualities required in a lecturer or professor—which in him rise to the level of genius (6).

Louis Campbell, professor of Greek, the University of St. Andrews: "His knowledge of the history of some periods, especially of Scottish History, is intimate and minute" (7). And John Tulloch, vice-chancellor of St. Andrews: "Stevenson has a genuine interest in historical research, and possesses capacities fitted . . . to advance the study of History in our Universities" (17). There are also (as we would expect) general testimonials from Edmund Gosse, Sidney Colvin, and Leslie Stephen. And what do the biographers say of these letters? Balfour blankets them all as "a tribute to the ingenuity of the human intellect."[33] Masson quotes the phrase, as does Furnas (although all three saw the printed pamphlet, none noticed that there were fourteen testimonials, not thirteen). In effect, Balfour claimed that the letters did not mean what they said, that they were simply puffs by friends and acquaintances and were not to be taken seriously, that they were, in his words, "wholly disregarded by the Electors." But all the letters, whether general or substantive, make a single, conclusive point: Stevenson was a serious student of Scottish history.[34]

Of course, the letters do not address the question of constitutional law, which was the chair's other responsibility. But the important consideration in this case is to determine the nature of the position itself. For a long time, university chairs were not much more than sinecures, some entailing no responsibilities at all. The chair that Stevenson was after (which was jointly held by the Faculty of Law and the Faculty of Arts) had a better history. For years it was held by Cosmo Innes (1846–74), "perhaps the greatest record scholar of nineteenth century Scotland."[35] Aeneas Mackay succeeded Innes and occupied the position with distinction. None of the candidates vying for the chair in the election of 1881 were in Mackay's league, let alone Innes's. The successful applicant, John Kirkpatrick, had updated an earlier edition of Lord Mackenzie's *Studies in Roman Law* (1876). A year later he edited and revised J. M. Bell's *Treatise on the Law of Arbitration*. Kirkpatrick apparently did not shine as a legal scholar, for Guthrie remarks that his talents were in modern languages: "[He] knew German, Dutch, and Italian, as well as French, and was a good classical scholar" (LG, 48). Although these hardly seem like desiderata for a professor of constitutional law and history, if we look at George Seton, who came in second with fifty-one votes, according to Guthrie, we find a candidate whose qualifications appear even more problematic (LG, 47). Seton's major interest was genealogy and heraldry. At the time of the election he had published *The Law and Practice of Heraldry in Scotland* (1863). Seton was a superintendent of civil service examinations and a secretary to the register-general in Scotland. He delivered lectures on odd topics like "Cakes, Leeks, Puddings, and Potatoes," a lecture on the nationalities of the United Kingdom, 1864, and "The Causes of Illegitimacy particularly in Scotland," 1860. He also wrote ephemera like "Gossip about Letters and Letter-Writers" (1870) and "St. Kilda past and present" (1878).

If we consider closely the résumés of Kirkpatrick and Seton we discover there were few, if any, special requirements for the professorship. Kirkpatrick had studied in Heidelberg, where Mackay had been, and that might have given him an advantage. But the only common denominator was admission to the bar—Stevenson,

Kirkpatrick, and Seton were all advocates. As for expertise, none had any particular knowledge of constitutional law, and judging solely from the printed record, Stevenson clearly knew more history than Kirkpatrick. There is no question he outclassed Seton, who was essentially an antiquarian with neither the breadth of interest nor depth of knowledge of a Cosmo Innes. Guthrie states that Sir John Skelton, the historian, had declined Thomas Stevenson's request that he propose Stevenson for the post. But Skelton had previously declined to propose Seton, and he told Guthrie that if he attended the election, which was doubtful, he would vote for Stevenson. But the applicant was not in Edinburgh at the time of the election. He was "on the Continent," unavailable to "personally meet with the Electors," as the note below the title of the pamphlet of testimonials declared. Clearly he was not politicking, or even going out of his way to make himself known. Yet it is not as if he had spent six years in anonymity from the time he passed the bar to the moment he applied for the chair. And writing for literary reviews and publishing books outside the specialized area of constitutional law and history, it is worth remembering, was not an automatic disqualification for the post. Sir John Skelton was a prolific writer for the magazines. And John Hill Burton was himself connected with magazine writing for virtually his entire career. What the people who supported Stevenson were saying was quite simple: he had both a detailed knowledge of Scottish history and an interest in exploring the forces that constituted that history. Thomas Baynes of St. Andrews, a professor of logic and English literature who had also received an honorary doctor of laws degree from Edinburgh seven years earlier, put it this way: "He seems able not only to realise the very form and pressure of a great national crisis, but to detect the more obscure personal and social causes which, while helping to develop the national character, gradually change the direction of its activities, and give a new complexion to its polity and public life" (13).

Walter Grindlay Simpson attended the election and sent Stevenson a description on November 5, 1881:

> I went down & gave your father a note of the voting today, which I suppose he will send you. He seemed a little disappointed but I suppose that was paternal. I was not—did not expect you would do as well. Why did they take the patronage from the town council. Shopkeepers can at least appreciate learning as a worshipful thing; but these lawyers get it into their head that a knowledge of law is learning. So help me they do. Is it because they call each other "my learned brother"? And yet it is no more learning than a knowledge of piece goods. I got this a dozen times. "No doubt S. is the best qualified—awfully able writer but—scarcely one of us . . . & then Kirkpatrick is such a plodding fellow &c &c"

One fellow said ought to elect K. "for the best lawyer" which was neither an argument nor a fact. Another card said you were not serious in going in—a mere youth. The idea seemed to be that a professor without side whiskers and a plug hat was inconceivable.

Into the first lobby the only known persons who went with me were Shaw & Macgill. (Mac & I concluded yesterday we would be alone. The others were youths unknown to me, either smarting from dull lectures or as yet unnarrowed by law. Your contemporaries? . . .

Shaw seconded you because Guthrie was suddenly called away, & because I suppose he liked his name brot forward.

Numbers voted for K because he was hard up. The history chair is a more purely administered charity than the Heriot Trust. And he will certainly uphold the traditions of the chair which are 3 sleeping students.

It is a curious fact that town councils & governments seem the least corrupt electioneering bodies for universities.

Do you know I was nevertheless astonished how unanimous people were in admitting your true position in literature. I was astonished to find I could class a living author with classical writers of past generations & not be laughed at by learned lawyers. (B, 5506)

Simpson's letter is engaging for its sly look at academic politics and for its remarkable revelation of just how widely admired was this thirty-year-old advocate by his "learned" colleagues. Simpson is forced to admit that the lawyers do indeed recognize Stevenson's gifts and his superiority to the other applicants, but the professorship was not about those things. For us, it is important to understand that if Stevenson's application was impulsive, it was not capricious. It is hard to imagine how he would have managed to spend summers in Edinburgh, preparing and delivering lectures year after year. But it is equally true that within the context of that small, closed world of Parliament House, Stevenson's candidacy was not only conceivable but plausible.

He has for some years been occupied with studies of the religious, social, and political history of Scotland and of the Highlands. If appointed Professor, he would no doubt enrich literature with works on these themes; and it seems certain that he would succeed in engaging the interest and securing the affections of any class of young men with whom he might be thrown (11).

Even Andrew Lang, who had the highest regard for Stevenson's talents, could not have foreseen how prophetic these words of his would become.

Chapter 2

COUNTRY OF THE POOR

The Highlands

But, good God! you could not conceive there was
such misery in this Island.

—Edmund Burt

During Stevenson's early enthusiasm for composing a history of the Highlands he
referred regularly to authors who could provide him with ready and usable material, as we saw in his letter to Sidney Colvin in late December 1880. A year later,
during the episode of the law professorship, Stevenson still had his primary
sources in mind: "This winter I mean to write an article on Burt, Boswell, Mrs.
Grant and Scott" (*L,* 3:243). Graham Balfour viewed this statement as a retreat
from the grand project envisioned the year before: "The Scottish history had fallen
into abeyance, or had come down to an article on 'Burt, Boswell, Mrs. Grant, and
Scott,' and a paper on the Glenure murder, afterwards the central incident in *Kidnapped,* but neither of these was even begun."[1] Despite Balfour's dismissive note,
Stevenson's remark reflected the persistent attraction that Scottish history exercised over his imagination, for these writers were among the most important
observers and interpreters of that history. And this attraction of his intersected
with the law professorship, for although technically separate, the two interests
converged. The one was made to do service for the other. Stevenson's knowledge
of history was the rationale for his application, and the application would in turn
further his research. None of this was to be. The book went the way of the chair.
But looked at another way, as Stevenson saw it, he did come to write his history,
only in a form as original as it was unexpected. He selected the historical novel
for his design, but he gave it a deliberate twist. He chose to reproduce and conceal history, to invent a fiction that would paradoxically reveal and veil historical
truth. Stevenson used his knowledge of documents and his understanding of
men's behavior to fashion a text that would serve jointly as the illumination and
the preservation of Scottish history.

How did Stevenson go about reconstructing the past? It goes without saying that
the Highland history, which he was so possessed by, was not going to be discarded.

Stevenson has a reputation, not altogether undeserved, for having started more projects than he was capable of finishing. Usually the judgement implies a moral criticism of his habits; rarely does it acknowledge the astonishing fertility of his imagination. But he was determined not to let this major project get away from him. It is not by chance that his greatest work drew on his most passionate intellectual and personal commitments—to Scottish history, to the law, and to his native country. *Kidnapped* and *David Balfour* are two parts of an epic novel, impelled by a studied reading of the past and an inventive manipulation of narrative art. That Stevenson managed for more than a century to deceive readers as to the origin and purpose of this work is a testament to his artistry. It is also, paradoxically, a reflection of his peculiar ambivalence toward the work of an artist and the products of his own imagination. That said, Stevenson never truly wavered from his bedrock conviction that first *Kidnapped,* and then *David Balfour,* were the best things he had done in fiction.

Stevenson kept a working notebook during his projected history of the Highlands. This manuscript volume, now in the Huntington Library (HM, 35317), contains thirty-four pages of notes drawn from two major sources: Edmund Burt's *Letters from a Gentleman in the North of Scotland to His Friend in London* and Colonel David Stewart's massive *Sketches of the Character, Manners, and Present State of the Highlands of Scotland.* We have already seen Stevenson refer repeatedly to Burt in his letters, and he could even be quite specific about the particular text: "Wade's report is appended to an edition of Burt; this edition would be the one to send me now, if the other vol II be truly lost" (B, 3459; *L,* 3:131). Originally published in two volumes in 1754, Burt's *Letters* were instantly recognized as an important source of information about the Highlands.[2] As for the two-volume Stewart text, that was sent to Stevenson by his father.[3] It was definitely a find: "Stewart's Sketches have filled me with hope and interest. . . . It is simply one of the most interesting fields of inquiry in the world, and there is a noble book to be written on the Highlands from then to now, social, religious and military."[4]

Stevenson's autograph notebook records material from both texts, copied verbatim, with occasional ellipses or paraphrase, and with little or no commentary on the passages copied.[5] The first five pages of the notebook are devoted to Burt, and the remaining twenty-eight are devoted to Stewart. This is not unreasonable, given the size of Stewart's study and its importance as a source of both oral and documentary history. What is interesting about the writer's notebook, apart from what he copied, is its illustration of how closely Stevenson studied such sources. It was not uncommon for him to splice passages from widely separated sections of Stewart's tome in order to build up a single telling excerpt. He was working as a scholar, using his source for the acquisition of information (the revelatory anecdote) and for a sophisticated (albeit partisan) interpretation of events.

Burt's *Letters*, although published in 1754, were apparently written twenty to thirty years earlier, during his stay in the Highlands as an army officer in charge of the construction of roads, a project undertaken by the English after the Jacobite rebellion of 1715 in order to secure the region and prevent another uprising. The letters are a firsthand account of the Highlands, notable for their raw and graphic picture of life in a remote and essentially unknown area of northern Scotland. The description of the countryside, the commentary on the food and accommodations, the almost indescribable poverty and destitution of the people, the dirt and the stench, the cold and the hunger—all are presented, as *Gentlemen's Magazine* noted, in a "colloquial" style "without affectation," and, in the words of the *Monthly Review,* with an "air of honesty" through the whole work.[6] The absence of "order or method" was not a discouragement to Burt's contemporary readers since the material itself was of primary interest (*MR,* 349). His subject was the "common people," and he was "at no small pains to inform himself very particularly concerning their customs and manners" (*MR,* 343, 356). What must be kept in mind is that for English readers in the 1750s (and even later) the customs and manners of the Highlanders were, to use a recurrent analogy from the magazine literature of the time, as alien and exotic as "those of the wild barbarians in the heart of *Africa*" (*GM,* 342). And even if Burt's letters were written twenty years prior to their publication, the conditions he described were in no way affected by that difference. For all intents and purposes, Burt was a wonderful source for Stevenson, providing him with an authentic eyewitness account of life in the Highlands at a particular historical moment: "Nothing will be set down but what I have personally known, or received from such whose Infirmation I had no Reason to suspect, and all without Prejudice or Partiality."[7] Although Stevenson was always vigilant, or perhaps always conscious of the potential for error or distortion in a firsthand account, that vigilance was balanced by the riches those accounts provided. They gave him the material unfiltered. That is, they gave him the language, the dress, and the habits as they were, without the intervening commentary and interpretation of later writers and ages. Thus Stevenson could use a nineteenth-century edition of the *Letters,* utilizing the editor's notes while incorporating in his own work the matter from the original texts. Burt, and others like him, provided Stevenson with the documentary evidence that gave his fiction life and reality. If Stevenson was serious about making his work an accurate representation of a historical period, then he had no choice but to rely upon the keen and pungent details he found in writers like Burt.

Stewart's *Sketches* presented a more complex problem. For one thing, his book —some one thousand pages, with extensive notes—was first published in 1822, so it was not contemporary with the period of Stevenson's novel. And its ostensible purpose was to record the history of the Highland regiments. Yet the book

was, in fact, a history of the Highlands of approximately fifty to sixty years earlier
—the period of the 1760s. At the outset Stewart justified the procedure of his
long narrative by defending his sources: "My statements . . . are grounded on
authentic documents; on communications from people in whose intelligence and
correctness I place implicit confidence; on my own personal knowledge and
observation; and on the mass of general information, of great credibility and con-
sistency, preserved among the Highlanders of the last century."[8] Although much
of Stewart's material depended upon oral information from old officers—and
even from some of the officers' wives—that went back as far as the mid 1700s,
virtually all reviewers agreed that he had amassed a body of information that was
unsurpassed in its scope and authenticity. Indeed, they repeatedly noted his enormous accumulation of facts and original information, the truth and reality of his
general descriptions, and his historical details and recreation of the past. From
its first appearance in print, *Blackwood's Magazine* said the *Sketches* would take its
"place in the English library."[9]

But Stewart's text was also more complicated than Burt's *Letters*. Burt was primarily interested in the depiction of customs and manners. Stewart, on the other
hand, was concerned with historical process. He had a more pronounced point
of view and was decidedly more political. Stewart was writing about a period in
the Highlands that had already passed into history and about a people whose economic lives had changed so utterly that neither they nor their culture were any
longer the same. His book is at one and the same time a paean to the Highland
soldier and a lament for the passing of the Highland way of life. It is Jacobite in its
leanings (just as Jamieson, Burt's editor, was partial to the Stewarts) and antago-
nistic, even bitter, regarding the development of Highland history after the collapse of the Jacobite army in 1746. Thus Colonel David Stewart, the author, not
only bears the name of the royal line whose cause was defeated, but his work is
suffused with an attitude that can only be called elegiac. The political bias was
strong enough to elicit a sixty-six page book that was a direct challenge to those
sympathies, even though the author began by praising Stewart's "minute knowledge" of the Highland clans, his use of "authentic documents," "eye-witness accounts," and his "judicious remarks on the management of Highland estates."[10] Yet
Stewart's political bias was not a stumbling block to Stevenson's use of him for his
own history. His work had been instantly received by Scots reviewers as a fount
of information, and if much of that information derived from conversations with
old people, the greater part rested in the extraordinary collection of documents
that he had incorporated in his narrative. Given the assemblage of so much material, it is surprising how often reviewers commented on the clearness of the style
and its freedom from all affectation.

The first page of Stevenson's "Highlands" notebook, with its initial reference to "Burt's letters." From Edmund Burt, *Letters from a Gentleman in the North of Scotland*. Reproduced from the original in the Henry E. Huntington Library and Art Gallery, San Marino, Calif.

In his Highlands notebook Stevenson recorded what he gleaned from Burt's *Letters* and Stewart's *Sketches*. Stevenson maintained a margin on the left side of the page, and next to the copied anecdote he provided an identifying tag or heading. For Burt, the tags are "poverty" (three times), "emigration," "education," "chiefs," "Forbes of Culloden," "patronymic," "provisions" and "fishery." The headings for Stewart are far more extensive. Chief among them is "the change," or simply "change," which is Stewart's inclusive term for the alteration in Highland life after the Jacobite defeat. The second part of his first volume is devoted to this subject: "Present State and Changes of Character, Manners, and Personal Appearance." Stevenson cited twenty-three passages under this heading. For the rest, the categories relate to the character of the Highlanders ("fidelity," "virtue," "hospitality"), the conditions of Highland life ("emigration," "poverty," "evictions," "smuggling"), important historical figures ("Cluny," "Argyle," "Lovat") and the Highland regiments ("recruiting," "loyalty of troops," "military character"). Except for "the change," Stevenson draws his passages randomly from Stewart's two massive volumes, exhibiting a predilection for some of the most commonly remarked aspects of Highland life (e.g., poverty, dress, virtue, loyalty).

If Stevenson failed to use his notebook for a conventional Highland history, he made very good use of it for a fictional counterpart. Both Burt and Stewart are in *Kidnapped* and *David Balfour*. And together with a third writer, John Buchanan, they formed the background for David Balfour's travels through the Highlands following the shipwreck of the *Covenant*.[11] Indeed, David's journey would not have been possible were it not for their texts, since his introduction to Highland life and Highlanders replicates the experiences of Burt and Buchanan. (Buchanan provided an account written from his own knowledge, just as Burt and Stewart did.) With David Balfour, Stevenson collapses into one the actual travelers and creates his own innocent abroad, whose "Journey to the Wild Highlands" draws and builds upon the observations and experiences of his historical predecessors.

Without question, the condition of Highland life that was most immediately visible to contemporary travelers was the poverty of the people. Burt commented extensively on this subject. Buchanan, whose book was widely reviewed in the press, talked about the Highlanders' "misery" and "starved" condition, as did John Knox, whose narrative Stevenson checked out from the Advocates' Library and scored in the margins.[12] So it was quite appropriate for David Balfour, after landing on Mull, to offer the following observation:

> They seemed in great poverty; which was no doubt natural, now that rapine was put down, and the chiefs kept no longer an open house; and the roads (even such a wandering, country by-track as the one I followed) were infested with beggars. And here again I marked a difference from my own part of the country. For our lowland beggars, even the gowns-men themselves who beg by patent, had a louting, flattering way with them, and if you gave them a plack and asked change, would very civilly return you a boddle. But these Highland beggars stood on their dignity, asked alms to only to buy snuff (by their account) and would give no change.[13]

> The Beggars are numerous, and exceedingly importunate for there is no Parish-Allowance to any.

I have been told, that before the Union, they never presumed to ask for more than a Bodle or the sixth Part of a Penny, but now they beg for a Baubee or Half-penny. And some of them, that they may not appear to be ordinary Beggars, tell you it is to buy Snuff. Yet still it is common for the Inhabitants, (as I have seen in Edinburgh) when they have none of the smallest Money, to stop in the Street, and giving a Half-penny, take from the Beggar a Plack, i.e. two Bodles, or the third Part of a Penny in Change (EB 1: 165–66)

Stevenson was determined to introduce the most crucial aspects of Highland life into *Kidnapped* from the moment David stepped foot on this alien ground. The defeat at Culloden and the post-Culloden laws disrupted the Highlands' traditional familial and economic structure. The people of the country, who depended upon their chiefs for support and sustenance, were thrown upon indigenous resources that were severely limited, hence John Knox's effort (the purpose behind his *Tour*) to promote a fisheries industry in the coastal areas. Buchanan compared the Highlands before the rebellion, when the tenants contentedly worked the lands for their chiefs, with the current situation where the tacksmen, "strangers who . . . obtained leases from absent proprietors . . . treat the natives as if they were a conquered, and inferior race of mortals," working them "like slaves attached to the soil."[14] Poverty was endemic and visible throughout the Highlands and islands. Stevenson makes a direct connection between the conclusion of the rebellion and its consequences: "Now that rapine was put down, and the chiefs kept no longer an open house." He thus draws attention to one of the causes of the poverty. He then appropriates an anecdote from Burt that he had recorded in his notebook.

Ere the union, beggars asked a bodle (penny/six), now asked a baubee, often with the delicious flourish that it was to buy snuff. Burt has seen in Edinburgh, people stop, give a baubee and get back a Plack (penny/three) in change I.144.[15]

Privately, Stevenson is amused at the pretense that the beggar is asking money to buy snuff, as if it were not really begging so much as requesting funds for a necessity. But in the text of his novel he alters the tone, making a sharp distinction between the Edinburgh beggars and Highland beggars—to the decided advantage of the latter. For the Lowland beggars are almost unctuous, as if their business is begging, and in making change they are merely working according to their trade. But the Highland beggars do not make change. They ask only for money to purchase snuff. Stevenson highlights the pride of the Highlanders, a characteristic remarked upon in all the sources and a motif in his own text: "But these Highland beggars stood on their dignity, asked alms only to buy snuff (by their account) and

Scottish Beggars Resting Near a Well, 1750, by Paul Sandby. From *75 Etchings of Landscape and Genre Scenes,* Yale Center for British Art, Paul Mellon Collection, New Haven, Conn.

would give no change." In his revision of Burt, Stevenson maintains the fundamental integrity of his source—the parenthesis insinuates a note of doubt that the original presents straightforwardly—while emphasizing the essential dignity of the Highlanders.

Stevenson's purpose was simply to illustrate those qualities in the Highlanders that were most attractive, even noble. Poverty, after all, was not of their own doing. And it did not prevent them from maintaining their natural courtesy and manners, as David discovers when he first lands on Mull and encounters an "old gentleman" to whom he tells his harrowing yet comical story:

A south-country man would certainly have laughed; but this old gentleman (I call him so because of his manners, for his clothes were dropping off his back) heard me all through with nothing but gravity and pity. When I had done, he took me by the hand, led me into his hut (it was no better) and presented me before his wife, as if she had been the Queen and I a Duke (*K,* 15:127).

The shabbiness of the old man's clothes—"many of those who are poor . . . appear in their tattered clothes and dirty shirts, without either stockings or brogues, quite barefooted, even in frost and snow"—does not touch his innate courtesy.[16] This was a feature of Highland character that Stevenson was immensely drawn to. Robert Jamieson, in his extensive introduction to Burt's *Letters,* remarked on this quality in all classes of Highlanders, not merely the gentry: "In 1745 the Scotish Highlanders, of all descriptions, had more of that *polish of mind and sentiment,* which constitutes *real* civilization, than in general the inhabitants of any other country we know of, not even excepting Ireland."[17] The courtesy was retained, according to Stewart, despite the profound change in their circumstances: "It is a principle among the Highlanders never to allow poor and distressed persons to apply in vain, or to pass their door without affording them some charitable assistance."[18] Thus David is taken into the old man's hut: "The good woman set oatbread before me and a cold grouse, patting my shoulder and smiling to me all the time . . . and the old gentleman (not to be behind) brewed me strong punch out of their country spirit" (*K,* 15:127).[19] Stevenson takes the most ordinary incident in Highland life and, through it, elevates the Highlanders themselves. He copied from Burt other examples of Highland poverty that he did not use, including his first notebook entry, an example that illustrates as well his ability to summarize and compress the gist of an anecdote.

And here I cannot forbear to give you an Instance of the extreme Indigence of some of the Country People, by assuring you, I have seen Women with heavy Loads, at a Distance from the Bridge, (the Water being low) wade over the large Stones, which are made slippery by the Sulphur, almost up to the Middle, at the Hazard of their Lives, being desirous to save or unable to pay, one single Bodle (EB, 1:46–47).

Burt has seen women hazard their lives to save the bodle for Inverness Bridge. I.41 (HN, 1).

There are also examples of Highland poverty in Stewart's work that Stevenson draws upon. In the same scene David seeks a lodging for the night and a guide for the morning.

I bethought me of the power of money in so poor a country, and held up one of my guineas in my finger and thumb. Thereupon, the man of the house

. . . agreed for five shillings to give me a night's lodging and guide me the next day to Torosay (*K*, 15:130).

The five shillings is a good deal more than the bodles and placks in the incident with the beggars. David here offers a guinea to the "man of the house" who holds out for five shillings. The Stewart passage that Stevenson draws his coinage from follows a tale about the "incorruptible fidelity" of the Highlanders, of the many who knew of Prince Charles's hiding places yet failed to turn him in, and of one poor man who thought the reward of £30,000 would not pay for his conscience. Stewart then provides a footnote and a long anecdote of the years 1746–47, when two ladies wishing to visit gentlemen in hiding asked a "poor half-witted creature" to show them the way. He did, thinking they were friends, until they offered him five shillings, at which point he stopped, doubting their intentions, and proceeded in a false direction.

> When questioned afterwards why he ran away from the ladies, he answered, that when they had offered him such a sum (five shillings were of some value eighty years ago, and would have purchased two sheep in the Highlands), he suspected they had no good intention, and that their fine clothes and fair words were meant to entrap him into a disclosure of the gentlemen's retreat (ST, 1:64n).

In his notebook, Stevenson reduced the story to its most telling details: "Five shillings was of some value seventy years ago and would have bought two sheep in the Highlands."[20] He introduced just the sum into his text, without comment, though its use can be understood within the context of Stewart's anecdote. The guide in Stewart's story is replicated in the novel, and the sum is kept intact. There is no way a reader would know the relative value of the money David is obliged to pay; it merely seems an extravagant figure in context, which it is. But it serves Stevenson's purpose of authenticating both the value and usage of currency. He is quite deliberate throughout *Kidnapped* and *David Balfour* in his use of specific coinages and sums. Apart from the thematic and metaphorical function that money serves, on a quite practical level it enforces the local realism and highlights the poverty of the period. In each of the novels the reader is always conscious of how much actual cash—or how little—is available to the characters. Money is a central element in the transaction of life in Stevenson's refigured Scotland. It has to do with economy and the health or impairment of the country. It forms part of the historical commentary of the travelers as they journey through the Highlands, noting the price of fish and beef and even solan geese, and it is central in recognizing the destitution of the people's lives.

Stevenson also calls attention to the poverty of the Highlanders when he has Mr. Henderland remark upon the money the tenants pay to the King's factor. "'It's

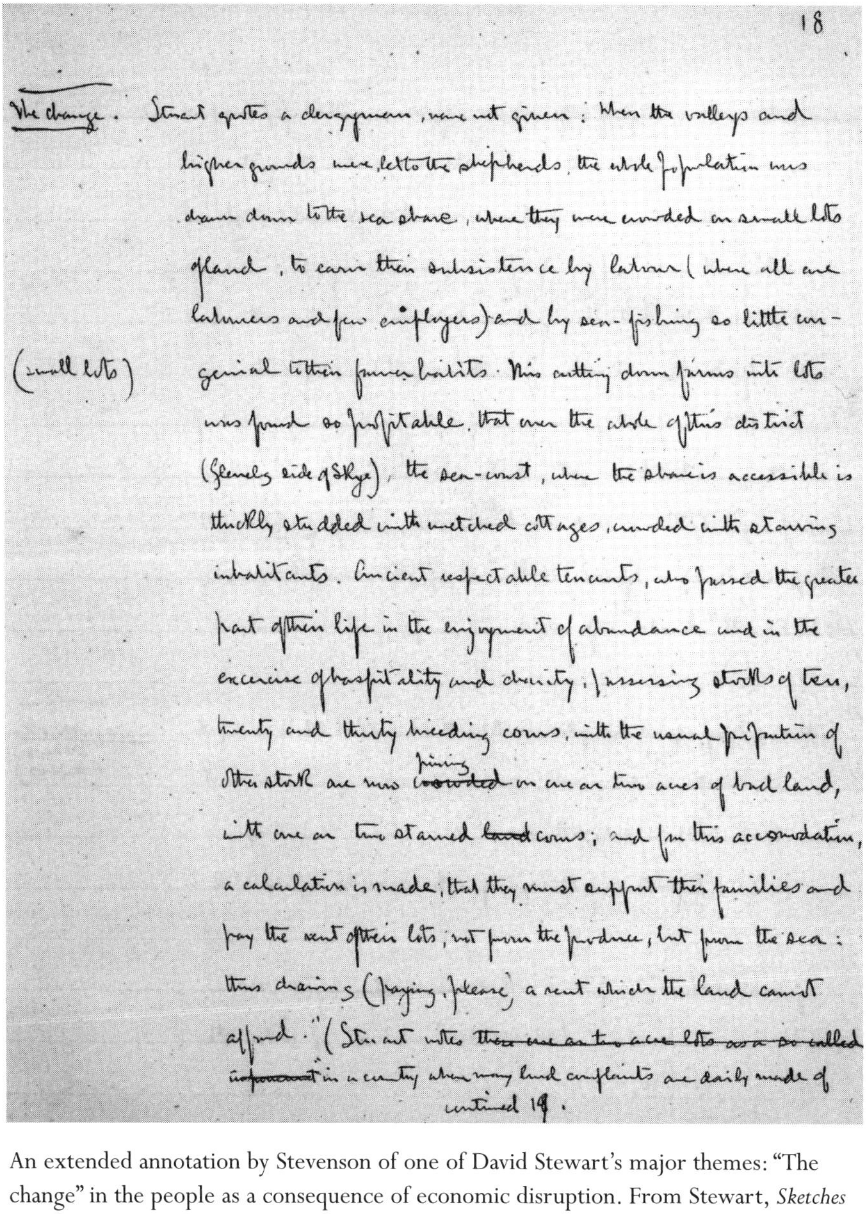

[handwritten manuscript page, numbered 18]

An extended annotation by Stevenson of one of David Stewart's major themes: "The change" in the people as a consequence of economic disruption. From Stewart, *Sketches of the Character, Manners, and Present State of the Highlanders of Scotland*. Reproduced from the original in the Henry E. Huntington Library and Art Gallery, San Marino, Calif.

wonderful,' said he, 'where the tenants find the money, for their life is mere starvation'" (*K,* 16:141). In his notebook Stevenson records an entire page and a half of Stewart's discourse on the depopulation of the fertile farms in the Highlands (the land was turned over to sheep raising) and the herding of people into small lots.

The Change. Stewart quotes a clergyman, name not given: When the valleys and higher grounds were let to the shepherds, the whole population was drawn down to the sea shore, where they were crowded on small lots of land, to earn their subsistence by labour (where all are labourers and few employers) and by sea-fishing so little congenial to their former habits. This cutting down farms into lots was found so profitable, that over the whole of this district (Glenelg side of Skye), the sea-coast, where the shore is accessible is thickly studded with wretched cottages, crowded with starving inhabitants (HN, 18; cf. ST, 1:160–61).

The subtitle Stewart gives to his section is "poverty followed by demoralization." The title for the immediate discussion is "change of tenancy." Stevenson's transcription, of which this is roughly one third, is quite extensive; this poverty is clearly one of the issues he was keenly aware of. The conditions of Highland life were largely the conditions of agrarian life—one that had been aggravated by a traditionally feudal system that was inefficient in providing a sustainable standard of living and that had even further deteriorated in the wake of the Jacobite defeat. The traditional clan system, which at least had ensured a connection between the tenant farmers and their chiefs, was no longer operative. In its place was a new agrarian model that displaced the tenants and offered them no surety of either work or arable land. It is this period that forms both the setting and context for *Kidnapped*. Thus Stewart's commentary finds its counterpart in Stevenson's language. "Their life is mere starvation," Stevenson's depiction, echoes Stewart's "starving inhabitants." This is a practice that Stevenson resorts to regularly. He is so steeped in his sources that their language is often repeated as his own, his vocabulary and phrasing echoing directly or indirectly that of the original text.

One of the first features to strike David on his landfall in the Highlands is the dress of the inhabitants.

The Highland dress being forbidden by law since the rebellion, and the people condemned to the lowland habit which they much disliked, it was strange to see the variety of their array. Some went bare, only for a hanging cloak or greatcoat and carried their trousers on their backs like a useless burthen; some had made an imitation of the tartan with little parti-coloured strips patched together like an old wife's quilt; others, again, still wore the highland philabeg, but by putting a few stitches between the legs, transformed it into a pair of trousers like a Dutchman's. All those makeshifts were condemned and punished, for the law was harshly applied, in hopes to break up the clan spirit; but in that out-of-the-way, sea-bound isle, there were few to make remarks and fewer to tell tales (K, 15:128–29).

The law suppressing the Highland dress "was a blow," as Stevenson remarked in his notebook, "singularly well directed against a race both proud and vain" (HN, 14). It was extraordinarily difficult for the Highlanders to accept: "The abolition of the feudal power of the chiefs, and the disarming act had little influence on the character of the people in comparison of the grief, indignation and disaffection occasioned by the loss of their garb" (ST, 1:121n). The Highlanders' attachment to their own dress was matched only by their dislike for the Lowland styles. The result was a form of sullen resistance and ingenious subterfuge.

> Instead of the prohibited tartan kilt, some wore pieces of a blue, green, or red thin cloth, or coarse camblet, wrapped round the waist, and hanging down to the knees like the *fealdag*. The tight breeches were particularly obnoxious. Some who were fearful of offending, or wished to render obedience to the law, which had not specified on what part of the body the breeches were to be worn, satisfied themselves with having in their possession this article of legal and loyal dress, which, either as the signal of their submission, or more probably to suit their own convenience when on journeys, they often suspended over their shoulders upon their sticks; others, who were either more wary, or less submissive, sewed up the centre of the kilt, with a few stitches between the thighs, which gave it something of the form of the trowsers worn by Dutch skippers (ST, 1:122–23).

Stevenson drew the details from Stewart, but he compressed them into half the space, added sharp and telling images ("like an old wife's quilt"), and framed the description within two sentences that provided the reader with general information that had an extraordinarily wide context. Thus in the final clause of David's last sentence—"but in that out-of-the-way, sea-bound isle, there were few to make remarks and fewer to tell tales"—Stevenson inserts a note that catches something of the period. For all the travelers remarked on the remoteness of the western islands and Highlands, on their being virtually sequestered areas detached from civil and governmental control. Stevenson calls attention to the remoteness and isolation that gives the place so much of its strangeness to the outside world, and David, as a Lowlander, is as much an outsider as any English traveler. It has always been recognized, particularly by David Daiches, that *Kidnapped* is a book about topography, or place, as much as anything else ("Where is the map of *Kidnapped*? I must have my map . . . a book of mine without a map, ye Gods!" [*L*, 6:40]).[21] In his compound phrasing—"out-of-the-way, sea-bound isle"—Stevenson compresses all his sources' repetitive commentary about the distance and inaccessibility of the islands, a motif heightened by the references to the remote captivity of Lady Grange on St. Kilda, and with David's own sequestration on the

Stevenson's long notation on the Highlanders' dress ("The Highland Garb" is Stewart's chapter heading). Reproduced from the original in the Henry E. Huntington Library and Art Gallery, San Marino, Calif.

Bass Rock. His task in this scene, as his protagonist sets foot on Mull, is to transform Stewart's nineteenth-century historical commentary into David's eighteenth-century contemporary history. Thus David does not mention any precise years in the course of his account; in this way he never appears as a self-conscious historian of events but rather as an innocent observer whose first impression is the one transmitted to the reader. The method is further complicated by the fact that the entire narrative is retrospective, told by David Balfour as a grown man with four children. But this aspect of the text is little noticed, possibly because it depends upon reading *David Balfour* to be fully aware of it—and possibly because David is embedded in the popular imagination as a young man.

The proscription of the Highland dress was an issue that could not be made to disappear easily. When David is in Mr. Henderland's house the subject is introduced again.

> He seemed moderate: blaming parliament in several points, and especially because they had framed the Act more severely against those who wore the dress than against those who carried weapons (*K*, 16:140). It is odd that the dress was proscribed with greater rigour than the carriage of arms; for in the latter offence, there was the alternative of a fine on a first conviction (HN, 14).

The inequity in punishment was clearly considerable. For wearing the dress, upon a first offense, the punishment was imprisonment for six months. Upon a second offense the punishment was transportation for seven years.[22] Stewart comments: "Considering the severity of the law against this garb, nothing but the strong partiality of the people could have prevented its going entirely into disuse" (ST, 1:120n). And Burt had remarked earlier: "The whole People are fond and tenacious of the Highland Cloathing" (EB, 2:191). Of course, in the figure of Mr. Henderland, Stevenson introduces an observant commentator on English rule in the far reaches of the kingdom. The acts that were passed after the rebellion were designed to pacify the Highlands and prevent any further uprising. Their effects were not only personally harsh but disruptive of the entire social and economic structure.

Stevenson, while never intending to argue these issues in the text, was nevertheless determined to signal them to the reader. He does so with subtlety and under the guise of an innocent neutrality. David merely reports Mr. Henderland's views on the effects of English policies on Highland life, and they are visibly tough. By proscribing the dress, parliament aimed at cracking the spirit of the Highlanders. And there was a curious kind of rationale in the motive. For the Highlanders' dress—particularly the philabeg, or kilt—was perceived by the Lowlanders as well as the English as the visible sign of an alien and barbaric people. Jamieson notes how the very sight of the Highlanders' kilts was confirmation enough for their neighbors of their *"barbarity"* (RJ, xxxviii–xxxix). Burt himself remarked on the "indecency" of the kilt, even though he was a sympathetic observer and a primary source for the Highland dress of the eighteenth century.

The common Habit of the ordinary Highlands is far from being acceptable to the Eye; . . . This Dress is called the *Quelt,* and for the most part they wear the Petticoat so very short, that in a windy Day, going up a Hill, or stooping, the Indecency of it is plainly discovered (EB, 2:185–86).

Burt's further commentary indicated just how deep an irritant this feature of Highland life was to the English.

It distinguishes the Natives as a Body of People distinct and separate from the rest of the Subjects of *Great Britain,* and, thereby, is one Cause of their narrow Adherence among themselves to the Exclusion of all the rest of the Kingdom; . . . the Plaid (or Mantle) . . . is calculated for the Encouragement of an idle Life in lying about upon the Heath in the Day-time, instead of following some lawful Employment; that it serves to cover them in the Night when they lie in wait among the Mountains to commit their Robberies and Depredations, and is composed of such Colours as altogether in the Mass so nearly resemble the Heath on which they lie, that it is hardly to be distinguished from it until one is so near them as to be within their Power, if they have any evil Intention.

That it renders them ready at a Moment's Warning to join in any Rebellion, as they carry continually their Tents about them (EB, 2:187–88).

In this description we see an antagonism so deep as to be almost irrational. The dress is responsible for the Highlanders' laziness, it hides and abets them in their lawlessness, and it aids them in their natural bent toward rebellion. But the core hostility was toward the clannishness of the people, so that the dress became the visible sign of all those characteristics of Highland life that were alternately despised and feared. Even the colors of the plaid were seen as a clever device for concealment, further justifying its complete suppression.[23] The Highland dress was a mark of separation, an emblem of that defiance of governmental authority most dramatically expressed in the late rebellion. As an innocent abroad, David carries with him the prejudices (albeit not the hostility) of his own country: "It was strange to see the variety of their array."

When David first sees Alan Breck Stewart on the *Covenant* he is struck by his clothes: "A hat with feathers, a red waistcoat, breeches of black plush and a blue coat with silver buttons and handsome silver lace: costly clothes, though somewhat spoiled with the fog and being slept in" (*K,* 9:73–74). The clothes of the real Allan Breck Stewart were an important part of the evidence in the trial of James Stewart. At one point, Allan was declared to have been wearing "a blue coat, scarlet vest, and black breeches of shag or velvet, which were believed to have been brought by him from France, and which was a remarkable or distinguishing dress

"The Highland Dress consists of a Bonnet without a Brim, a short Coat, a Waistcoat . . . short stockings and *Brogues* or Pumps without Heels." From Edmund Burt, *Letters from a Gentleman in the North of Scotland.* Reproduced from the original in the Henry E. Huntington Library and Art Gallery, San Marino, Calif.

in that part of the country."[24] Of course, the clothes of the fictional Alan are traditionally taken as a characteristic mark of the man's vanity. In actuality, they served to identify him by class and background. Even James More, who had none of Alan's elegance, shows up in Leyden in "an extraordinary big laced hat."[25] Stewart remarks several times on this aspect of the Highlander's dress:

> The waistcoat and short coat were adorned with silver buttons, tassels, embroidery, or lace, according to the fashion of the times (ST, 1:79).
>
> The silver buttons were frequently found among the better and more provident of the lower ranks (ST, 1:80–81).
>
> The serjeants had silver-lace on their coats, which they furnished, however, at their own expense (ST, 1:373).

Officers and non-commissioned officers always wore a small plume of feathers, after the fashion of their country (ST, 1:372n).

Stevenson joins these details into a sentence of his own in his Highlands notebook: "The men of the Black Watch bought Ostrich feathers for their own caps; and the sergeants silver lace for their own coats. I.348-49" (HN, 28). Clothes were not merely a distinguishing mark of dress but a sign of status and condition. Throughout *The Trial of James Stewart*, Allan's "cloaths" are presented by the prosecution not simply as physical evidence designed to prove his presence in the vicinity of the murder but as if they symbolized a dress that was not only costly but immoral, one associated with an enemy country and a profligate court.

In "The House of Fear" Stevenson uses the clothes to engrave Alan's vanity on the reader's mind and, in a more subtle way, to echo their real role in the historical trial: "Bury my French clothes!" cried Alan. "Troth, no!" (*K,* 19:164). The color, plush, and delicacy of Alan's dress give him a distinction that is apparent to all. It marks a stark contrast between his condition and the impoverishment of the general population. When David arrives on Mull he asks after his comrade: "'Was there one,' I asked, 'dressed like a gentleman?'" He is told that there was one who "wore breeches and stockings, while the rest had sailors' trousers." "'Ah,' said I, 'and he would have a feathered hat?'" (*K,* 15:126). Stevenson lifts the particularities of dress from his sources in order to fill out the characterization and create the social texture. Indeed, it would be difficult to say which comes first, the character or the social detail. For the detail is the character, and the character is fashioned from the detail. And the silver button, which Alan inherited from his father and was so prodigal with, is passed on to David as a kind of talisman. It signifies David's entry to the Highlands and marks his true position (hence the original subtitle for the novel, "The Lad with the Silver Button").

The general color of the dress in the two novels is drab, in keeping with the description of the travelers. Alan Breck's colors, on the other hand, are not only a social statement that adheres to the contemporary reality but a graphic contrast to the bare life of the country. His determination to hold on to his clothes may be a mark of willfulness and obstinacy, but it is also indicative of a desire to retain a sense of dignity that defeat in war has not conquered or diminished. The clothes themselves—"somewhat spoiled with the fog and being slept in"—are none too pleasant to look at or smell, as David recognizes. Yet they define the man and, by extension, the race of warriors that bears a king's name. The truth is that the impoverishment of the Highlands was so pervasive that any distinguishing quality was noticed and admired. Whether Stevenson was critical, or amused, at the idea of the officers of the Black Watch buying ostrich feathers for their hats and lace for their coats is beside the point. The fact is it distinguished them for their pride as well as for their vanity. In Alan Breck's work, the pride and the vanity are joined, and in that joining the character of the Highland officer is revealed.

The conditions of Highland life that David encounters are evident everywhere, beginning with his first house on Mull: "It was low and longish, roofed with turf and built of unmortared stones" (K, 15:126). After supping with the old couple who lived there he remarks: "And the house, though it was thick with the peat-smoke and as full of holes as a colander, seemed like a palace" (K, 15:127). Of course, David was so delighted to find something to eat and a friendly reception after the hunger and cold he endured on the islet that he would have felt princely anywhere. But the reality of the old couple's hut was not lost on other travelers. Burt repeatedly comments on the Highlanders' "miserable" shelter: "One may go a hundred Miles an end without seeing any other Dwellings than the common Huts of Turf" (EB, 2:205). These primitive shelters offered scant protection from the climate;[26] the inhabitants burned peat (or turf)[27] for fuel—in a space barely large enough for five or six people:

> They have no Diversions to amuse 'em, but sit brooding in the Smoke, over the Fire, 'till their Legs and Thighs are scorched to an extraordinary Degree; and many have sore Eyes, and some are quite blind. This long Continuance in the Smoke makes 'em almost as black as Chimney-Sweepers; and when the Huts are not Water-tight, which is often the Case, the Rain that comes through the Roof, and mixes with the Sootiness of the Inside, where all the Sticks look like Charcoal, falls in Drops like Ink. But, in this Circumstance, the Highlanders are not very solicitous about their outward Appearance (EB, 2:127).

Stevenson's picture is not as unrelievedly bleak as Burt's. He takes pains to draw attention to the authentic hut with its turf construction, the home of poor people, but he is at equal pains to focus on the kindness and generosity of the inhabitants. When Mr. Henderland, the other catechist, offers David sixpence for his journey, which he removes from "the turf wall of his house" (K, 16:144), it is the generosity of the gesture, rather than the meanness of the hut, that strikes David. From the beginning Stevenson builds a case for the Highlanders that focuses on their character rather than on their possessions. And part of that case is an unambiguous declaration that the most generous are those with the least to offer, just as the stingiest man in Kidnapped is the one with the largest estate. It would be too obvious to remark that the impoverished hut as a place of hospitality and friendship is a decided contrast from David's earlier visit to the house of Shaws, where his food was parceled out and the fire was kept low. There are to be many fine houses that David Balfour sleeps in before he comes to his journey's end; but he will find no

"A Highland Town . . . is composed of a few Huts for Dwellings, with Barns and Stables [that] are built in Glens and Straths . . . near Rivers and Rivulets." From Edmund Burt, *Letters from a Gentleman in the North of Scotland.* Reproduced from the original in the Henry E. Huntington Library and Art Gallery, San Marino, Calif.

warmer welcome than in the turf huts of the old couple on Mull, and the good minister on Morven.

Most of these conditions of dress and housing are part of the general pattern of Highland life that reflects the pervasive impoverishment of the people. Stevenson also recorded incidents describing the scarcity of livestock and the meagerness of food, including the rarity of any kind of condiment. In "Cluny's Cage" David noted the chief's status by commenting on his pantry: "As soon as the collops were ready, Cluny gave them with his own hand a squeeze of a lemon (for he was well supplied with luxuries)" (*K,* 23:205). And lemons were indeed a luxury, according to Burt: "I had always in my Journeys a *Pocket-Pistol,* loaded with Brandy, mix'd with Juice of Lemons (when they were to be had)" (EB, 2:25–26). But beyond the food, one of the inescapable conditions of Highland life was the ubiquitous dirt and filth. Burt commented constantly on this matter, which was endemic through-out Scotland and which he describes first in Edinburgh. The food was repellent because of the cook ("too filthy an Object to be described" [EB, 1:21]) and the preparation ("a Breast of Mutton . . . looked like the Glew that hangs up in an Ironmonger's Shop" [EB, 1:18]). David's language graphically reflects Burt's atti-tude toward Scottish public accommodations: "The inn at Kinlochaline was the most beggarly, vile place that ever pigs were stied in, full of smoke, vermin and silent highlanders" (K, 16:139). And the filth of the kitchens and bedrooms has its counterpart in the extreme dirtiness of the people, which leads Burt to volunteer that "strict laws against low fornication" are probably unnecessary. Stevenson, conscious of this aspect of the Highlanders' personal hygiene, has David use it as a biting rebuke to Alan during their quarrel: "'O!' says I, 'I ken ye bear a King's name. But you are to remember, since I have been in the Highlands, I have seen a good many of those that bear it; and the best I can say of them is this, that they would be none the worse of washing'" (K, 24:220). But if David's insult is a bit of clever satire, it more seriously underscores the recognition that the dirt and filth of the Highlanders was largely a consequence of their extreme poverty. Burt him-self reflected that it takes a certain amount of money to be clean, and the servants in the Highlands had neither the resources nor the motivation to practice cleanli-ness. Many reviewers of these eighteenth-century travel accounts realized that the Highland conditions were all bound together, that the clothes, the dirt, and the hovels were of a piece. As one wrote of Buchanan's *Travels in the Western Hebrides,* "Such a union of oppression, poverty, and nastiness, is scarcely to be found among the native Siberians . . . groaning under the Russian yoke, as is to be found in the Hebridean huts."[28]

Stevenson's aim in much of *Kidnapped,* particularly the chapters that form the second part of the novel, is to reveal and capture life in the Highlands through the refracting lens of his young and open-eyed narrator. Almost every detail that David notices in the course of his wanderings is a picture of contemporary cus-toms or manners. As we have seen in the case of the Highland chapters, these are drawn most heavily from Burt's *Letters* and Stewart's *Sketches.* But these texts were not exclusive. As we will see, *The Trial of James Stewart,* the only text publicly alluded to by Stevenson, provided an enormous amount of material. Indeed, as a class of documentation, criminal trials are among the richest repositories of social detail, almost unequalled in their graphic authenticity. Of course, not everything that Stevenson entered in his notebook found its way into the novel. The notebook was kept as a work product for Stevenson's planned history, but since the history never materialized, he cannibalized the notebook for incidents that would give his fictional narrative the factual reality of his source narratives. And the process was a painstaking one.[29] From the start, Stevenson was determined to be faithful to his documentary texts because that was his way of being faithful to the history. Thus the creation of a novel that was in actuality a fiction was problematic from the start. Stevenson had always been an avant-courier when it came to literary gen-res. His early experimental work in *New Arabian Nights* was so advanced that reviewers could do nothing but praise the style and be mystified by the form.[30] And his essays and travel writings were themselves old forms that he had made new. *Kidnapped* presented another challenge, an exercise in fictional truth—or as Stevenson memorably put it in his autograph introduction to the manuscript, the opportunity to construct a "narrative of fact." But for whatever reason, Stevenson believed that the fact of that narrative must never be called to the attention of the reader. In a way, that was his grand hoax: to pretend to create a fiction from whole cloth, but in reality to make nothing up. Even his hero, David Balfour, was not completely made up, since he was put together from Stevenson's own family—whether modeled on his cousin Willie Traquair or, more simply, dependant upon "Balfour" as a matrilineal name and "David" as a patrilineal one. This is not to make the absurd statement that Stevenson invented nothing in *Kidnapped* and *David Balfour*. But what he imagined was set within a frame of historical reality so meticulously charted that it was almost impossible to separate the invention from the history. At some point the question of how Stevenson's text is a fiction becomes an important one. But there is no doubt that he was committed to creating, or recreating, a world that had existed in the past and a people who inhabited that world. What made his experiment so intriguing was that he was not writing a nonfiction novel about a topical event but a factual narrative of an incident—and a way of life—that had ended nearly a century and a half earlier.

Chapter 3

COUNTRY OF THE BRAVE

The Highlands

Their character and history [lies] betwixt the heroic
and the common ballad.
—*Trials of Three Sons of Rob Roy*

The conditions of Highland life that David Balfour responded to most immediately were mainly physical—the houses, the dress, the dirt, and the poverty. He
was also keenly aware of the profound difference in language, a difference he first
realized when trying to communicate with the fishermen on the islet, and which
he encountered again after landing on Mull: "Few had any English and these few
. . . [were] not very anxious to place it at my service" (K, 15:129). Gaelic—or
Irish, as it was then called—was the common language of the Highlands, and to
some observers it was the only language, one "whereby the Natives are Strangers
to the World, being incapable to converse but in that Language."[1] But David (contrary to the Lowland chauvinism of the society) quickly discovers that the Highlanders' ignorance of English is often nothing more than a ploy. When he discloses
that he has money to offer for a night's lodging, "The man of the house, who had
hitherto pretended to have no English . . . suddenly began to speak as clearly as
was needful" (K, 15:130). The next day David's recalcitrant host balked at guiding
him to Torosay, for which he had already been paid. David, ever mindful of money,
remonstrated with him: "The impudent cheat answered me in the Gaelic that he
had no English. 'My fine fellow,' I said, 'I know very well your English comes and
goes. Tell me what will bring it back? Is it more money you wish?'" (K, 15:131).

This pretense of linguistic ignorance was drawn from two incidents in Burt,
although David's sarcasm and disdain are the novelist's own rendering.

Very often, if you ask Questions of the ordinary People here, and here-
abouts, they will answer you by *Haniel Sasson Uggit i.e.* they have, or speak,
no *Saxon* (or *English*). This they do to save the Trouble of giving other
Answers (EB, 1:132–33).

> In our Way we enquired of three several Highlanders, but could get nothing from them but *Haneil Sasson Ugget* (EB, 1:181).
>
> Burt says when he asked for a chief's castle by his name, not knowing the patronymic, none understood him. This seems very strange. They pretended. I.157 (HN, 5).

The unwillingness of the Highlanders to use their English, when they did have it, was a means of keeping themselves separate from Lowlanders and outsiders, of retaining their distinctiveness. Language, unlike the proscribed dress, was a feature controllable by the population. Stevenson could not write in Gaelic, but he was intent upon demonstrating the way that language functioned as a separating and identifying cultural instrument. In the criminal trials that Stevenson appropriated, the term "Irish" regularly describes the common tongue, and the word more vividly characterizes the people and joins them to their Celtic past. Stevenson was always conscious of the ways in which a people maintained their cultural integrity through the retention of their own language, even (or especially) when that language was subject to the hegemony of a more powerful tongue or more powerful state. Yet the Highlanders held on to their language against the pull of the English. At the end of *David Balfour* James More declares that the beauties of his native land—and the heroism of lost battles—can only be sung in the Gaelic. "But if you had only some of this language, you would weep also because the words of it are beyond all expression, and it is mere mockery to tell you it in English" (*DB*, 26:346). His countrymen prized their facility at poetry and song—Alan breaks out into verse after the victory of the round-house—a skill or a gift they viewed as a characteristic, if not a consequence, of their language.

Without question, the most prominent element of Highland life was the clan system. It defined the nature of Highland culture, and it was the clan system that was defeated and destroyed with the collapse of the Jacobite army. The complexity of that system was recognized as early as 1724 by General Wade, who condemned it yet found it strangely powerful at the same time.

> I Presume also to Represent to Your Majesty, that the Manners and Customs of the Highlanders, their Way of Living, their Strong Friendships, and Adherence to those of their own Name, Tribe and Family, their blind and Servile Submission to the Commands of their Superiors and Chieftans, and the little Regard they have ever paid to the Laws of the Kingdom, both before and since the Union, are truely set forth in the Lord Lovat's Memorial, and other Matters contained in the said Paper, which Your Majesty was pleased to direct should be put into my Hands to peruse and Examine.[2]

At the basis of the clan system was the relationship of the individual to his chief; it was a patriarchal structure that elevated loyalty and fidelity to the chief and the

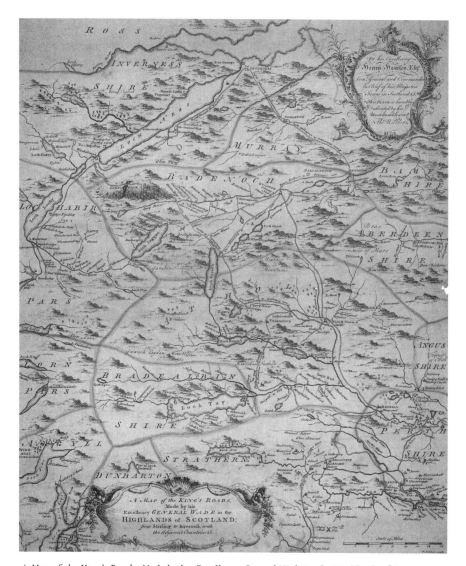

A Map of the King's Roads, Made by his Excellency General Wade in the Highlands of Scotland (London: Thomas Willdey, 1746). Courtesy of the National Library of Scotland.

clan above all else. "Each tribe or clan formed but one family, and the chief was the father of that family."[3] Thus members of individual clans felt themselves more attached to their own brothers than to any state or governmental authority. "The bond of union created by this singular institution was so strong, that the duty of the members of the clan towards their chief, superseded all other obligations" (*Sons,* xii). What they did they did for their chief and their clan, not for their country. Insofar as their country was identified with their chief, there was no problem.

But if there was no identification between chief and country, then there was no loyalty or commitment to any cause outside the clan. In fighting for Prince Charles, the Highlanders fought for their chiefs first; and the insurgent prince had to persuade the chiefs to come in and fight alongside his banner. Every major Highland regiment was associated with its clan first; and the clans were then associated with the cause. It is difficult, even now, for historians to decide whether the Jacobites were fighting first for Prince Charles or first for their chiefs. In any event, their loyalty and fidelity were primary virtues. As General Wade remarked:

> Their Notions of Virtue and Vice are very different from the more civilized part of Mankind. They think it a most Sublime Virtue to pay a Servile and Abject Obedience to the Commands of their Chieftans, altho' in opposition to their Sovereign and the Laws of the Kingdom, and to encourage this, their Fidelity, they are treated by their Chiefs with great Familiarity, they partake with them in their Diversions, and shake them by the Hand whenever they meet them.[4]

That the conditions of life in the Highlands were severe in no way lightened or mitigated the obligations of the people to their chiefs and their clans. Thus what Highlanders experienced were harsh physical lives marked by cultural or social values that virtually belied their living conditions. Rather than the barbarism that outsiders saw, there was a civility and hospitality that historians like Jamieson contrasted with the false civilization of the English. Of course, their loyalty to their chiefs exhibited itself in what was often viewed as the Highlanders' primary occupation—making war. And their renown as fighters—"Now the only remaining warlike Genious of the Scots is amongst the Highlanders"—was a central impulse in Stevenson's portrait of Allan Breck Stewart.[5]

For outsiders it was the clan system that identified the strong attachment that Highlanders exhibited toward each other in their social and familial patterns; and it was the clan system—"hostile to peace, and to settled habits of industry"—that outsiders perceived as the source of the rebellion against King George and the chief obstacle to civilizing the Highlands.[6] As early as Wade's *Report* after the first rebellion in 1715, the consensus was that "the Peace of the Kingdom" was threatened by the Highlanders' maintenance of arms and their refusal to obey the Laws.[7] And following the major rebellion of Prince Charles, the view was even more pronounced. An "Ignorant and Barbarious people" had to be made to recognize that their liberation from "a State of Slavery and Misery" could only come from their rejection of such a patriarchal system.[8] Unless the Highlanders could be weaned from their chiefs and their families—that is, unless their allegiance could be transferred from their Highland fastnesses to the government authorities situated in another country—there would be no success in pacifying the area.[9] Indeed, the central event in *Kidnapped* and *David Balfour*—the murder of the King's factor, Glenure, and the trial of James Stewart—concentrates these issues of Highland life. The defeat of the Jacobite rebellion brought an end to the social and economic structure of Highland life and even to the relationship of Highlanders among themselves. This is a major subject in Stevenson's epic. He does not present it directly but, rather, slant. Thus David is exposed not only to the harshness of Highland life—to "the 'enslaved' and poverty-stricken estate of the commons: the extreme dirt and destitution" (Lang, ix)—but to the virtues of that life as well. The virtues are perhaps not as easily recognized, but they are nonetheless an important part of David's education as he journeys through the wild lands of an alien people.

One of the first things David discards when he spends the night at a poor man's house is his Lowland prejudice that all Highlanders are thieves: "I slept uneasily that night, fearing I should be robbed; but I might have spared myself the pain; for my host was no robber, only miserably poor and a great cheat" (*K*, 15:130).

> The Lowlanders . . . regarded their neighbours of the mountains as a law-less banditti . . . [Yet] instances of theft from dwelling-houses scarcely ever occurred (ST, 1:37).
>
> *Virtue.* / Internal Highlands. Theft from dwelling house unknown, high-way robbery 1st case 1770. I.35. (HN, 8)

Jamieson supports Stewart's observation in his introduction to Burt's *Letters:* "Private *robbery, murder,* and *petty theft* were hardly known among them" (RJ, xliv). This is not to say that lawlessness and violence were not aspects of Highland life. But Jamieson and Stewart shared a common purpose—to put the Highlanders and their history in the best possible light and to soften the harsher judgments of their customs wherever possible. For example, cattle theft, or "lifting," and blackmail were major problems in the Highlands. So was the violence that Stevenson dis-closes in both novels—kidnapping, forcible abduction, and murder. What Jamieson and Stewart are talking about, however, concerns the individual and his relative safety or security. They argued that the Highlanders were not prone to petty theft, and those crimes for which they were notorious—cattle theft and blackmail—were essentially agrarian crimes that were a consequence of aggravated economic conditions. Thus Stevenson's calling attention to the host's poverty and predilec-tion for cheating, as opposed to his being a "robber," signals an important distinc-tion. He may be dishonest, but he is no thief.

But the distinction is possibly a fine one for outsiders. More telling, perhaps, is the nature of the clan relationships that reveal the qualities of the Highlanders. David meets Cluny MacPherson, one of the great rebel chiefs. MacPherson, "thanks to the affection of his clan" (*K, 23:203*), is secure from being discovered by the British troops searching for him. Stewart remarks how Cluny managed to avoid capture.

> Upwards of one hundred persons knew where he was concealed, and a reward of £1000 was offered to any one who should give information against him; . . . yet so true were his people, so strict to their promise of secrecy,* . . . that not a trace of him could be discovered, nor an individual found base enough to give a hint to his detriment.

> *In a character of the Highlanders, drawn near 300 years ago, the author says, "As to their faith and promise, they hold it with great constancie" (ST, 1:62–63).

The loyalty expressed in this anecdote is a shadow of the storied refusal of the Highlanders to reveal the presence of Prince Charles during his wanderings in the Highlands after the defeat of his army. Clan ties were valued above possessions; Highlanders preferred to keep their conscience rather than improve their purse. As Alan says to David, "I would go down to Koalisnacoan whatever, and trust my life into these people's hands as lightly as I would trust another with my glove" (*K, 21:184*). What made this attitude so remarkable was that it was exhibited in a people who were so poor that one might have thought their price would be quite cheap. If their hospitality to strangers was revealed by the old couple's treatment of David, their loyalty was expressed in Cluny's ability to live safely for years in the very center of a general and widespread manhunt.

Clan loyalties are also revealed in the Highlanders' attitude toward outsiders and particularly toward Lowlanders. On two occasions Alan charges David with being a Whig. The first time is shortly after they have met:

> "And so you're a Jacobite?" said I, as I set meat before him.
> "Ay," said he, beginning to eat. "And you, by your long face, should be a whig?" (*K, 9:78*)

Although David's question sounds the merest note of hostility, in actuality it is an innocent one. He has never met a live rebel before—and he is, in fact, awestruck before such a fancy if not flashy figure. Alan's response is craftier. He knows that David is a Whig, so he is not really asking him about his politics but rather injecting a sly comment on them. Stevenson glosses the term "Whig" on the holograph —"Whig or Whigamore was the cant name for those who were loyal to King George"—and although the gloss offers the smallest shred of information, there is a sense that the word is more than a definition of political allegiance. "By your long face," Alan says, and the reader understands his summing up of David upon a first glance—that he lacks the open, easy countenance of someone identified with the Highlands, or the Jacobites, or anything other than the dour Lowland allies of

the German king. Later, during the flight in the heather, when the two are em-
broiled in a quarrel, Alan goads David: "He spoke a good deal, and never without
a taunt. 'Whig' was the best name he had to give me. 'Here,' he would say, 'here's
a dub for ye to jump, my Whiggie! I ken you're a fine jumper!' And so on; all the
time with a gibing voice and face" (K, 24:218).

At this point it is clear that Alan is not sneering at David's politics. And it is here
that Stewart (quoting from Mrs. Grant's *Superstitions of the Highlanders*) provides
us with an extensive definition of Alan's meaning:

> The term WHIG was not applied by the Highlanders in a political sense. It
> extended generally to their neighbours on the plains, and a "*Lowland Whig*"
> comprehended the Puritan, Covenanter, and all those whose "dark, domi-
> neering spirit" and fanatical gloom were in essential opposition to the more
> striking traits of their own character and feelings. According to Mrs. Grant,
> it "was by no means among them a term appropriated to political differ-
> ences" (ST, 1:267n).

For Alan, then, chiding David with being a Whig was a means of deriding his background and his heritage. It was a way of scorning an aspect of Lowland life that
was particularly obnoxious to the Highlanders. Driven as they were by their ideas
of family kinship, they were repelled by what they considered the lack of familial
affection and loyalty among the Lowlanders. Thus the term "Whig"

> "might, perhaps, mean, in a confined sense, the adherents of King William,
> by far the greatest caitiff in Highland delinquency. But it meant more; it was
> used to designate a character made up of negatives, who had neither ear for
> music, nor taste for poetry, nor pride of ancestry, nor heart for attachment,
> nor soul for honour: one who merely studied comfort and conveniency, and
> was more anxious for the absence of positive evil, than the presence of rel-
> ative good. A Whig, in short, was what all Highlanders cordially hated, a
> cold, selfish, formal character."
>
> The Highlanders never forgave King William for Glenco; and for placing
> troops and garrisons in their country, and turning his arms against his
> father-in-law. I have already noticed the strength of parental affection among
> the Highlanders. Living at a distance from the seat of government, they
> were ignorant of the political and religious distractions which occasioned
> the Revolution; and looking, therefore, to the single circumstance of King
> William and Queen Mary depriving their father of his kingdom, and driv-
> ing him into exile and poverty, they considered them as monsters of filial
> ingratitude (ST, 1:268n).[10]

Alan's use of the term "Whig" draws on Stewart's extensive commentary. It comprises his sense of David, whose "long face" summarizes all those negatives that Mrs. Grant comments on; and it implicitly calls attention to the issue of filial loyalty for which David is certainly not responsible. But David *is* without a father (in both novels he continually attaches himself to surrogates), and he is therefore suspect to Highlanders whose identification is so completely bound up with their families. He overhears Robin Oig "telling Duncan that I was 'only some kinless loon that didn't know his own father'" (*K*, 25:227) and smarts at the remark. To the Highlander, that is the worst insult—to be bereft of a family. As Burt relates in an anecdote, to be a Chiefless Highlander is one of the greatest shames, and the provocation given to such a one—"Name your Chief"—is all that is required for the Highlander to do battle to defend his honor (EB, 2:221). David (talking to himself) dismisses the slur with sarcasm, thinking how odd it is that a man who is an outlaw should be so nice about the lineage of passing acquaintances. But David's clever remark aside, the issue is not so easily dismissed. For Stevenson here provides within the briefest of colloquies an opening into larger issues of Highland life—of family identification and the very question of self-definition. For so much of clan loyalty depended upon a definition of the individual within a social context. The self was not the center of all being but a rod connected to the hub of the wheel. David is not only a geographical and political outsider in the Highlands, but as a man without a family he stands outside the social matrix of Highland life. His wanderings in *Kidnapped* and *David Balfour* are efforts not merely to recover his lost estate but to discover his true identity—to give the lie to Robin Oig's snide remark. David's loneliness is not resolved until he marries Catriona. Then he establishes his own family while retaining a loyalty to the larger kinship network of friends that he made in the course of his adventures. Thus the Highland experience and the Highland values, far from being lost on David, were integrated into his life.

The Highlanders were legendary for their skill as warriors. Indeed, their ferocity in battle was partly responsible for their reputation as savages. Only uncivilized people could fight so fiercely and with such apparent disregard for their own lives. Alan Breck is Stevenson's portrait of an exemplary Highland soldier skilled in warfare. An incident in *Kidnapped* illustrates how Stevenson appropriates a historical anecdote in Stewart and weaves it into his text. In "I Hear of the Red Fox," Alan is haranguing David about the treachery of Colin Campbell, the king's factor, in wresting land away from the tenants. David, by way of argument, suggests that Alan is not one to judge matters of business, considering how wasteful he is of his silver buttons. Alan replies:

> "Ah!" says he, falling again to smiling, "I got my wastefulness from the same man I got the buttons from; and that was my poor father, Duncan Stewart,

grace be to him! He was the prettiest man of his kindred; and the best swordsman in the Hielands, David, and that is the same as to say, in all the world. I should ken, for it was him that taught me. He was in the Black Watch, when first it was mustered; and like other gentleman privates, had a gillie at his back, to carry his firelock for him on the march. Well, the King, it appears, was wishful to see Hieland swordsmanship; and my father and three more were chosen out and sent to London town, to let him see it at the best. So they were had into the palace, and showed the whole art of the sword for two hours at a stretch, before King George and Queen Car-line, and the Butcher Cumberland, and many more of whom I havenae mind. And when they were through, the King (for all he was a rank usurper) spoke them fair and gave each man three guineas in his hand. Now, as they were going out of the palace, they had a porter's lodge to go by; and it came in on my father, as he was perhaps the first private Hieland gentleman that had ever gone by that door, it was right he should give the poor porter a proper notion of their quality. So he gives the King's three guineas into the man's hand, as if it was his common custom; the three others that came behind him did the same; and then they were on the street, never a penny the better for their pains. Some say it was one, that was the first to fee the King's porter; and some say it was another; but the truth of it is that it was Duncan Stewart, as I am willing to prove with either sword or pistol. And that was the father that I had, God rest him!" (*K*, 12:101–2)

In the midst of his tirade against the Red Fox, Alan pauses to interpolate a story about his father, a story about Highland technical skill and largess—or, at least, the largess of "Hieland gentleman" officers. And in this story wastefulness is not a sin, just as parsimony is not a virtue. David, true to his pecuniary habit, remarks that Alan's father is not the man to leave his son an inheritance. But as Alan observes, he left him something else: his skill and knowledge as a swordsman. Stevenson thus contrasts the open, broad display of arms, technical skill, and pride in that skill with the crimped and confining relish in husbanding money. There is an abandon in the father's gesture—"So he gives the King's three guineas into the man's hand, as if it was his common custom"—that has its reflection in the style of the son. And just as the son admires the father for his virtuosity with a sword, he reveres him for the open gesture: "And that was the father that I had, God rest him!"

Stevenson lifted the anecdote from Stewart's discourse on the establishment of the Black Watch as an independent company whose role was to police the High-lands. Since the companies were formed during the prohibition against carrying arms, large numbers of men from respectable families were anxious to join. Barred from the practice of arms—their traditional pursuit—they sought to train and develop their skills through the legal sanction of the independent companies. But the men believed they would be stationed in the Highlands. When they were formed into regiments and transferred away from their homes, they were told they were going to perform before the king in London in order to prevent them from defecting—since the Highlanders' love for their land and their unhappiness at being removed from it were equally well known. Stewart then offers the following anecdote:

> The King, having never seen a Highland soldier, expressed a desire to see one. Three privates, remarkable for their figure and good looks, were fixed upon and sent to London a short time before the regiment marched. These were Gregor M'Gregor, commonly called Gregor the Beautiful, John Campbell, son of Duncan Campbell of the family of Duneaves, Perthshire, and John Grant from Strathspey, of the family of Ballindalloch. Grant fell sick and died at Aberfeldy. The others "were presented by their Lieutenant-Colonel, Sir Robert Munro, to the King, and performed the broadsword exercise, and that of the Lochaber axe, or lance, before his Majesty, the Duke of Cumberland, Marshal Wade, and a number of general officers assembled for the purpose, in the Great Gallery at St James's. They displayed so much dexterity and skill in the management of their weapons, as to give perfect satisfaction to his Majesty. Each got a gratuity of one guinea, which *they gave to the porter at the palace gate as they passed out.*"[11] They thought that the King had mistaken their character and condition in their own country. Such was, in general, the character of the men who originally composed the Black Watch. This feeling of self-estimation inspired a high spirit and sense of honour in the regiment, which continued to form its character and conduct, long after the description of men who originally composed it was totally changed (ST, 1:258n).

The core of Stewart's anecdote is drawn from a contemporary account. He adds interpretive commentary to ensure that the reader fully understands its significance. At the center is the character of the Highlanders. They do not accept money as if they were needy or in the position of living by their trade. They are gentlemen, and as such they are not in the habit of accepting gratuities. Stevenson enforces their position—perhaps even their class status—by citing the gillies who carried their rifles for them. This detail was first noticed by Burt and then quoted by Stewart (with slight inaccuracy) earlier in his same chapter: "I cannot forbear to tell you, before I conclude, that many of those private gentlemen-soldiers have *gillys,* or servants to attend them in quarters, and upon a march to carry their provisions, baggage, and firelocks" (ST, 1:250n; cf. EB, 2:116).

Stevenson is sculpting a small incident into a form that fits his dramatic text. He transforms a dry, albeit informative, anecdote buried in Stewart into a compelling story that highlights the character of Alan Breck. Alan has his father's great skill with weapons as well as his indifference to money (pointedly Alan raises the tip given the porter from one to three guineas). Stevenson further keeps faith with his character by having Alan interject partisan remarks about his political antagonists—the Duke of Cumberland is "Butcher Cumberland," and King George is a "rank usurper." Such remarks are not in Stewart's version. But Stevenson's method has a broader significance than the elucidation of character. He draws upon an early nineteenth-century text which contains within it an eighteenth-century text; then (writing at the end of the nineteenth century) he places it in a text of his own that pretends to be contemporary with the original anecdote. In other words, he is appropriating for his own purposes a story with historical standing—that is, one which is accounted true. He removes the laudatory tone in Stewart's report; he alters one guinea in the Westminster Journal's eighteenth-century account to three guineas; he adds a fourth Highlander (Duncan Stewart, Alan's father) to the three of the actual episode; and he transfers the entire tale to Alan Breck. Thus a third-person story becomes a first-person account, one with all the vivacity and immediacy of that point of view. Alan's animosity toward the Hanoverian establishment is reported with his usual frankness and disregard for niceties, with the same anger and rage that generate his remarks on Colin Campbell, the ostensible subject of this chapter. Alan also dismisses (or does not remember) others who were present—like the second officer of the regiment, Lieutenant Colonel Sir Robert Munro or Marshal Wade ("and many more of whom I havenae mind")—and inserts others of whom there is no record ("Queen Carline"). And by giving the account to Alan there is no need to identify what would otherwise be unknown allusions. Thus "the Black Watch, when first it was mustered," is not identified or dated; the "gentleman privates" with their "gillies" are not explained (Burt, as a contemporary traveller writing to an English reader glossed "gillys" as "servants" while Alan, as a Highlander talking to a Lowlander, either does not have to explain his language or is retaining the authenticity of speech, which would seem artificial if he were to gloss his own talk); and, of course, the sobriquet "Butcher Cumberland" is neither glossed nor explained.

Stevenson's silence serves to sustain the integrity of his own text—that is, as an authentic account of David Balfour's adventures, an eighteenth-century text with references that would be familiar to contemporaneous (i.e., eighteenth-century) readers. Stevenson follows this general method in both novels; there are allusions to contemporary incidents and writers (Pope, Burns, Defoe) that are part of the fabric of the composed text and that give the book its eighteenth-century bearings. But, of course, the actual readers are not those of the novel's presumptive date. Stevenson actually defies rather than helps his real reader. He forces him to uncover the allusions for himself, but nothing is lost if he does not. For the surface prose is sufficient unto itself; the literal meaning of the text can be followed with no difficulty whatever. Stevenson is writing at least two stories: the one the reader follows that is delivered by the narrator, David Balfour, and (in this case) by Alan Breck via David Balfour; and a submerged story of Stewart's anecdote, Burt's detail, the Westminster Journal account, and hovering over them all, Stevenson's controlling fabrication. And what is the point? Alan, who elevates his father in the story *he* tells and thus elevates himself, declares that what he is saying is true: "Some say it was one, that was the first to fee the King's porter; and some say it was another; but the truth of it is, that it was Duncan Stewart, as I am willing to prove with either sword or pistol." Naturally, this is the most glaring untruth in the entire tale. For if anything is known, it is that Alan Stewart's father is unknown, and Duncan Stewart, whose name can be found in the *Sketches* (ST, 1:309), is virtually Stevenson's invention. Further, the source of Alan's tale is unknown. Where does he get it? Presumably it was passed on to him orally by his father. In Alan's telling, however, the personal voice and the easy, idiomatic manner, contrast sharply with Colonel Stewart's formal, almost stilted declamatory style. Yet for Stevenson's readers (and all subsequent readers) the entire tale that Alan tells is a fabrication; and Alan's declaration that he will defend the truth of his tale by his sword only serves to make the reader believe that it is another one of Alan's flights of fancy, a story that may have a grain of truth to it but that is clearly embellished in Alan's regular style. Yet going over it all, we can see that Stevenson has covered his tracks so well that we must inevitably consider the interpolated story nothing more than a revelatory glimpse into the character of a fine swordsman and cavalier Highland gentleman. But the history remains. The core of the actual incident is there. Stevenson has indeed preserved it for his readers—and future generations of readers—a detail about Highland life and Highland character that was in fact true, that was in truth a reflection of Highland martial skill and Highland generosity. By transmuting and placing a buried historical anecdote in a fictional frame, Stevenson preserved both the anecdote and the history—and, by so doing, the life which that history records.

One of the more striking incidents in *Kidnapped* occurs when David is crossing Mull and encounters the blind catechist.

> In about half an hour of walk, I overtook a great, ragged man, moving pretty fast but feeling before him with a staff. He was quite blind, and told me he was a catechist, which should have put me at my ease. But his face went against me; it seemed dark and dangerous and secret; and presently, as we

began to go on alongside, I saw the steel butt of a pistol sticking from under the flap of his coatpocket. To carry such a thing meant a fine of fifteen pounds sterling upon a first offence, and transportation to the colonies upon a second. Nor could I quite see why a religious teacher should go armed, or what a blind man could be doing with a pistol (*K,* 15:132).

Stevenson's catechist is drawn from Buchanan's *Travels in the Western Hebrides,* a text that served as the source for the subject of religion in the chapters set on Mull and Morven. He had written to his father in late January 1886: "Many thanks for a letter quite like yourself. I quite agree with you and had already planned a scene of religion in *D. Balfour;* the Society for the Propagation of Christian Knowledge furnishes me with a catechist whom I shall try to make the man. I have another catechist, the blind, pistol-carrying highway robber, whom I have transferred from the Long Island to Mull" (*L,* 5:182).[12] Stevenson simply moved the man Buchanan had found in the western Hebrides to the island of Mull:

> *Questars,* in the Hebrides, on which I have already touched, that go about from house to house, teaching the children the Creed, the Commandments, &c. by rote, in the evenings, they are not only useless, but many of them worthless drunkards.
>
> There is a blind bully of this order in *Uist,* who, in order to escape contempt, and secure respectful attention both to his person and his doctrines, carries about with him, wherever he goes, loaded pistols. As he is remarkably strong, as well as full of courage, though blind, few people are fond of grappling with him.[13]

Buchanan's term "questars" is not easily identified. It appears to be an epithet, used in derogation of a class of men who subsist solely on the basis of handouts from the poor or by the patronage (or charity) of a gentleman. In one example cited by Buchanan, such a patron offered twelve pounds a year for a native of Harris to teach "the illiterate to repeat the creed and Lord's prayer, and to answer theological questions by rote, in Gâlic, and explain their meaning" (*TH,* 240). Stevenson made sure to cite the appropriate chiefs in moving his catechist from the Long Island to Mull. In Buchanan, the blind beggar's benefactor was named Macleod, since the island of Harris was traditionally the base of the clan Leod;[14] but in transporting him to Mull, the principal seat of the clan Gillean, Stevenson was obliged to place him under the authority of another chief. "It was MacLean of Duart gave it [i.e., the sinecure] to him, because he was blind" (*K,* 15:135). Stevenson knew which clans occupied the different territories in the Highlands ("Maclean of Dowart has generally been considered as the chief of all the Macleans").[15] Such information was available in a variety of sources but was most

Castle Duart, Isle of Mull, by John Clerk. From *Series of Etchings Chiefly of Views in Scotland* (Edinburgh: Bonnatyne, 1855), Yale Center for British Art, Paul Mellon Collection, New Haven, Conn.

accessible in Stewart's *Sketches,* which included a large color map of the territories of the islands and Highlands and also identified the clans who occupied them. This is most evident when Alan instructs the captain of the *Covenant* where he wishes to be landed. But it can be seen very simply at the beginning of chapter 16: "Both shores of the sound are in the country of the strong clan of the McLeans, and the people that passed the ferry with me were almost all of that clan" (*K,* 16:136). The reference relating to the clans on Stewart's map states: "MACLEANS, including MACQUARRIES. Morven on the Mainland, and part of the Isle of Mull, now the property of the Duke of Argyle, was formerly the inheritance of this clan" (ST, 1:xxii).

Returning to the catechists: "They are literally beggars; and depend for support solely on the alms of the poor people among whom they sojourn. This species of teachers is, in those parts, called *Questars*" (*TH,* 242). The closest definition of this word is in Jamieson's *Dictionary* (1880) under the term "quisteroun": "A scullion, cook: liter. a licensed beggar, O.Fr. *questeur,* 'one that hath a licence to beg.'" Jamieson comments that "*quaist,* a rogue, is still used in Mearns, as also the phrase 'a quaisterin body,' applied to a person who lives on his friends."[16] Stevenson discards the local term since it would have no meaning (it could not even be found in a contemporary dictionary) and substitutes the word "catechist." In the process, he elevated the blind robber into the higher category of "religious teacher." But he retains the decrepitude of Buchanan's model ("a great, ragged man") along with the alcoholism ("I will guide you to Torosay myself for a dram of brandy"). In other words, he draws on the characteristics of the questars that Buchanan describes— mendicancy, dirtiness, drunkenness—and conflates them into the single portrait of the blind catechist of Mull. Even the beggar's ostensible qualifications for the job are ironically called into question ("me that is a man of some learning"). Thus Stevenson succeeds in creating another vivid scene in which David is put in harm's way; but the scene is composed from a factual detail that is true to the period, although unknown to the novelist's audience. Moving Buchanan's questar from the

Long Island to Mull in no way bothers Stevenson. He is undisturbed by that kind of alteration of his documentary source. Rather, he is more concerned with the integrity of the historical detail. Thus he builds up a character where none exists in Buchanan. In the latter there is merely the anecdotal reporting of a type of person (blind bully, strong, full of courage) and a detail (the loaded pistols) that gives life to that anecdote. Stevenson takes this material and creates a voice that is inveigling and cunning. The voice, however, is belied by the visage, and David is quick enough to see that: "But his face went against me; it seemed dark and dangerous and secret." Frustrated by David's resistance to his demands for money, the "man of learning" becomes enraged and winds up swearing at David in Gaelic (although it is a nice question how David knew he was being cursed, since he knows no Gaelic). What is clearly intriguing is to see how Stevenson, within the space of three pages of his own text, transforms Buchanan's generalized description into a character with an altogether distinctive behavior. He individualizes both David and the catechist. And yet he is faithful, in his fashion, to the original. But it is a fidelity to the social reality of the detail, to the class of mendicant religious teacher that Buchanan introduces to his reader. Stevenson thus found in his guide's pages a figure that represented a peculiar aspect of social and economic life. The "blind bully" with the "loaded pistols" was a fortuitous discovery, a detail that struck the novelist's imagination and one he appropriated and amalgamated into his text.

Drawn as he was to elements of terror and violence, Stevenson was a master at creating fear. This fear was often one that depended for its effect upon the dominance of a larger force over a smaller one, an adult world preying on a young boy or young man. The kind of dread that we associate with the dark side of Dickens's London—the dread of arbitrary violence, of dislocation, of an inhospitable landscape, and the impenetrability of an alien tongue—is figured as well in Stevenson's earlier Scotland. The blind catechist is an image of the worst the Highlands had to offer a stranger from another land. But this figure that strikes fear in David's bones and nearly does him in is in actuality a creature of Stevenson's invention. By borrowing a figure set in ink, the novelist satisfied himself that he kept faith with the period. At the same time, he gave himself free rein to enliven what was essentially a historical mannequin. Stevenson ceded nothing to the originating text, which offered no style, no discourse, that could compete with his own: "We were now upon a sort of green cattle track which crossed the hills towards Torosay, and we kept changing sides upon that like dancers in a reel" (*K,* 15:134). Stevenson's gift for simile—for envisioning the desperate highwayman and the frightened (yet sturdy) David warily circling each other—has no counterpart in Buchanan, who provides the skeleton to be fleshed out by the fictionist. David continues:

Then I told him that, sure enough, I had a pistol in my pocket as well as he, and if he did not strike across the hill due south, I would even blow his brains out.

He became at once very polite; and after trying to soften me for some time, but quite in vain, he cursed me once more in the Gaelic and took himself off. I watched him striding along, through bog and briar, tapping with his stick, until he turned the end of a hill and disappeared in the next hollow.

The simplicity and apparent calm of David's speech is suddenly transformed into a bold and shocking final statement: "I would even blow his brains out." Even the catechist is stunned by David's aggression, and he decides that the better part of valor is to withdraw, though not without some final cursing. The picture of the thwarted blind man, tapping away, concludes the scene, and he disappears from the text—and the reader's eye—almost as suddenly as he had appeared.[17] This is a novelistic pattern. People are regularly carried over from the pages of other books; people who at one time had real lives are given a role to play in Stevenson's new-made pages and then vanish into the "next hollow" round the hill. Where do they go? Back into history? Do they return to their original sources? Or have they become reincarnated in the new text, transferred from Buchanan to Stevenson, given a moment's new life, and then made to disappear from that text-life forever? Stevenson breathes fictional life into his factual relics, restoring people who have long since been relegated to the bewildering labyrinths of libraries. In fact, he gives them lives they themselves never had (he acknowledges as much for Alan Breck in the dedication). Clearly it is unimportant to him to reproduce precisely their actual lives; in most cases, this is simply not possible because the information is unavailable. But more telling is its irrelevance. Stevenson's primary aim is fidelity to the period—to the customs and manners, to the social, political and economic realities of the time. The specifics of individual lives are secondary and of minor importance. What the individuals do provide are names, behaviors, and a physical existence that enables the novelist to claim factuality as a rationale for incorporating them into his fiction. In the process of unearthing these people from their buried texts, Stevenson—the archeologist of historical personages—gives them an importance they never had in their allotted pages and a permanence they were incapable of achieving on their own.

In a sense, Stevenson's practice can be likened to that of film in the twentieth century, which cinematizes people whose existence is known only to a small, dedicated group of scholars or historical investigators. (Oskar Schindler is a household name because of Steven Spielberg, not Raul Hilberg.) Setting biopics aside, film primarily cinematizes fiction, giving its characters an audience greater than any they could possess in print—Scarlett O'Hara in *Gone with the Wind* and

Dorothy in *The Wizard of Oz* are simply prototypical examples. But this is what
Stevenson was doing long before film, at a time when history was regarded as the
material for fiction in much the same way that fiction later came to be regarded
as the material for film. Scott, Thackeray, Eliot, Dickens, Charles Reade, R. D.
Blackmore, Conan Doyle, even Wilkie Collins and Rider Haggard—they all cannibalized history for their plots and often for their ideas. Historical events, or even
incidents, offered ready-made stories that could be refashioned for a large read-
ership, that would provide the bait to hook an audience and drive the sales. How
interested were the writers in the history as history? In instructing their readers
regarding the French Revolution and the Reign of Terror (*A Tale of Two Cities*)? Or
the legal system in seventeenth-century England (*Lorna Doone*)? Or the endless
Scottish question (*Waverley*)? It depends, of course, upon the individual novelist.
Certainly, Scott was ideological in a way that Dickens was not; Thackeray had personal prejudices about historical figures that he was determined to embed in his
pages (*Esmond*); and Wilkie Collins constructed early versions of movie docudra-
mas, sensationalizing crime in order to maximize an audience. If Meredith (*Vitto-
ria*) stands at one end of the historical novel game, Rider Haggard clearly stands
at the other. Where does Stevenson fall? Quite near the top, for he so completely
dissolved history into fiction that the fiction became transformed into myth. In
Scotland, *Kidnapped* and *David Balfour* are so much a part of the cultural mythology of the nation that the books' historicity is largely overlooked. Stevenson,
living in two ages (his real time and his imaginative time) was engaged in the
recovery and reconstruction of history, both as documentarian and fictionist, as
conduit of the past and creator for the future.

In Stevenson's letter to his father in late January 1886 he acknowledged that
the Society for the Propagation of Christian Knowledge furnished him with
his catechist for the "scene of religion" that the elder Stevenson suggested his
son should incorporate into *Kidnapped*. We have seen how he used John Lane
Buchanan's *Travels in the Western Hebrides* as a literal source for the blind catechist
in Mull. But the book was also the source for Stevenson's extended portrait of Mr.
Henderland, the good catechist. He simply adopted the author of the text, who
was in reality a minister who held a commission from the society, for his fictional
creation. Buchanan's disclosure of his role as a society missionary "from 1782
to 1790" provided Stevenson with an opportunity to create a counterpart to
the squalid and drunken catechist. He suddenly realized that he could convert
the author of the text into a fictional character as easily as he could convert the
author's real life questar. Writer and subject, historian and document, were
equally fit objects for the novelist's fictional tapestry. This is not altogether surprising since Stevenson had from very early used writers as subjects in his essays
and his fiction, the most notable example being François Villon. But Villon was a

well-known figure whose appearance in "A Lodging for the Night" was undisguised. Buchanan, on the other hand, was unknown to anyone other than Stevenson the researcher. The novelist appropriated the travel writer, along with his biography, for the sake of his own narrative. What the reader sees, however, is a seamless story of a decent man possessing strong religious values, a man who presents a strong counterweight to the ugly side of religion that David earlier encountered on Mull.

But Stevenson did not need Buchanan to use the Society for the Propagation of Christian Knowledge as a symbol for religion. By the middle of the eighteenth century the society was a venerable institution in Scotland. Its members included: James Boswell; Duncan Forbes of Culloden; James Erskine (whose wife, Lady Grange, along with her bizarre story, is repeatedly alluded to in *David Balfour*); Thomas Hope of Rankeilor (who was Lady Grange's champion, as well as David Balfour's advocate); Colin MacLaurin, professor of mathematics at the University of Edinburgh; and three men who were destined to figure prominently in the Stewart trial—Lord Advocate Charles Areskine, Lord Elchies, and Solicitor-General William Grant, better known as Prestongrange. Among the correspondent members in London were Edmund Burt and General Wade (who was in charge of building the roads in the Highlands after the rebellion in 1715, and for whom Burt worked as an engineer).[18] Robert Wodrow talks about the almost casual founding of the society in the *Analecta* (Stevenson painstakingly read Wodrow's *Correspondence*):

> Hou great a matter doth some times a litle good fire kindle! . . . and all as a litle weekly society for prayer and conference upon Christian purposes! There wer but eight or ten members, lauers; generally speaking, men of knouledge, solid piety, and estates: and, nou and then, some of the Ministers of Edinburgh met with them, and all they did was in concert with them, joyned with prayer, and flouing from great measures of a publick spirit—love to God, to souls, and abhorrence of sin; and the Lord wonderfully countenanced their honest essayes, and hath nou blessed and crouned them with great and publick success.[19]

The primary mission of the society was to establish schools in the widely separated parishes in the Highlands, "to have their Scholars instructed in the Principles of Religion, according to Holy Scriptures, and taught to read *English*."[20] David's description is blunter: "To evangelise the more savage places of the Highlands" (*K*, 16:139). But a political agenda was also a part of the mission. The society was chartered by the queen; it was Protestant, of course, and opposed to what was believed to be the prevailing Catholicism of the remoter regions of the Highlands. Further, it was felt that by reforming the Highlands—which meant displacing Catholicism and its perceived concomitants, the Stewarts and the Jacobite resistance—a side benefit would be the establishment of political stability.

> And therefore, the Commissioners are humbly of Opinion, no Method whatsoever is so likely to reduce the *Highlands* and *Islands* of *Scotland* to a profound Peace and Quiet, and to bring all the Inhabitants to a hearty and willing Subjection to Your Majesty and Your happy government, as that which Your Majesty and the Parliament have now in View; the affording them the Means of Knowledge of the Principles of the *Protestant Religion* and of *Virtue,* providing the Laws against Trafficking Priests and Jesuites be duly executed in these Parts.[21]

By adopting a society missionary as his primary religious figure, Stevenson drew on a strong tradition in Edinburgh history. Wodrow thought the founding of the society was one of Edinburgh's great achievements, and its history would "make a glorious part of our Biography in that period."[22] Although for Wodrow the religious reformation of the Highlanders was the principal mission, for others what seemed of equal if not greater importance was weaning the native people from their "Irish" tongue and converting them to English. Yet, paradoxically, the missionaries were successful to the degree that they were able to converse with the Highlanders in Gaelic. This was the case with Mr. Henderland: "As we went, he stopped and spoke with all the wayfarers and workers that we met or passed; and though of course I could not tell what they dis-coursed about, yet I judged Mr Henderland must be well liked in the countryside, for I observed many of them to bring out their mulls and share a pinch of snuff with him" (*K,* 16:140). With this detail Stevenson appropriates both the characteristic experience of Buchanan ("The Author . . . wandering about for nine years, where he very seldom heard or conversed in any other tongue than the Celtic") and a particular custom that the missionary commented on:

> Both men and women are fond of tobacco; the men commonly chew it, and beg a little from every gentleman; and there is no travelling through those countries without a certain quantity of that article in company. The gentlemen fill their nostrils with long quids of it, and these, when thrown away, are gathered carefully by the poorer sort, for a second turn. . . . In passing to and from the islands, tobacco is necessary to a gentleman, if he wishes to avoid both delay and imposition . . . any knowing man will deal his tobacco liberally, and in that event, he is sure of a speedy and very cheap passage, *or convoy,* through the different isles (*TH,* 10, 107–8).

The snuff provides Stevenson with a comic touch, almost a Dickensian tag, as Mr. Henderland continually asks David: "Ye'll no carry such a thing as snuff, will ye?"

It is a touch that David does not forget, for at the beginning of *David Balfour* he makes sure that his friend receives a small gift: "There's a Mr. Henderland, a licensed preacher and missionary in Ardgour, that I would like well to get some snuff into the hands of" (*DB*, 2:17–18). But comedy aside, the figure of Henderland is serviceable for other reasons. Stevenson uses him to provide David (and the reader) with a summary of Highland political news, a commentary on Alan Breck and the situation in Appin (prior to the murder of Colin Campbell), and a perspective on the unwavering, if futile, loyalty of the Highlanders to their defeated chiefs ("There's something fine about it; no perhaps Christian, but humanly fine" [*K*, 16:141]). In the persona of Henderland, Stevenson creates a composite of Buchanan and a prototypical society missionary, one who came to convert the Highlanders but stayed to become their champion. Henderland himself suspects this: "Ye'll perhaps think I've been too long in the Hielands?" he asks David, wondering if his political and religious sympathies have gotten distorted living away from his Lowland home. In a way, Henderland's fictional experience was Buchanan's actual life. Although the real missionary was born in the Highlands while Henderland was a Lowlander, there are remarkable similarities between the two: each was fluent in Gaelic; each was marked by religious sincerity and even zeal; each had spent a long residence among the "natives," living and conversing with the poor; and each had an intimate knowledge of the customs of the country. For Buchanan, these characteristics were commented on by the reviewers of *Travels in the Western Hebrides:* "Mr Buchannan is about sixty years of age, and a batchelor . . . a sincere and simple, though a very zealous man . . . and so ignorant of the world (having lived only like a hermit among poor people in remote islands and sequestered corners of the world)."[23] For Henderland, they were partly borrowed from the text, and partly intuited by Stevenson ("a simple, poor old man"[*K*, 16:144]). What is intriguing is how the figure in the fiction both reflects and embodies the writer of the documentary text. Buchanan as missionary was an agent of the Edinburgh Society in the Highlands; Henderland was the fictional representative of that historical person. In reading Buchanan, whose book is a plea for sympathy and understanding for the Highlanders, we see the inspiration for Henderland. Also, in reading Stevenson we see Buchanan exhumed from a buried text and made over in one with greater durability and appeal. Thus Stevenson discovers a historical personage, fashions for him a distinctive voice, and places him in a book that replicates his world. But the entire procedure, which pretends to factual representation, is actually a form of masquerade. For the fictional text is oblivious to its own factual reality. It was produced by a writer who was removed in time and space from the imagined world of the novel. And the late nineteenth century Highlands were nothing like the ones from Buchanan's time. For Stevenson, the dilemma (or paradox) of historical writing is inescapable: however well he recovers and assembles earlier experiences, the reconstitution of those experiences in a text outside their own time gives them an existence independent of their origins. In other words, the recreation of the past as a textual enterprise is, in fact, an imaginative one—partly because its subject no longer exists, and partly because invention is in the nature of fiction.

How should we assess the impact of these texts on Stevenson? Of Burt's *Letters*? Or Buchanan's *Travels*? Or Stewart's *Sketches*? Clearly he exploited and appropriated them for his own use. Frequently the source was so refashioned as to make it barely recognizable; often it was reworked but retained its original stamp; rarely was it transmitted with little or no alteration. Stevenson was profoundly affected by the tenor and import of these books. The first two were written in the eighteenth century, although sixty to seventy years apart. Yet the similarity between them is remarkable, in tone as well as in substance, in their depiction of life in the Highlands and in their view of Highlanders. Burt and Buchanan shared a common objective—to demythologize the picture of the Highlanders held by the English and, to a lesser degree, the Lowland Scots. In the process, they were making an appeal for greater sympathy and, by inference, for better treatment by the English government. The reviews of Buchanan's book, in particular, contained pleas for the government to offer economic assistance to the Highlanders.

One of the factors of Highland life that Buchanan emphasized and that Burt had touched on earlier was that of emigration. The economic problems were so intractable that the only solution seemed to be emigration to the colonies. One of the books that Stevenson read in preparation for his own Scots history specifically decried the absence of industries in the Highlands and proposed the establishment of fisheries as a partial solution to alleviating the Highlanders' economic distress.[24] Stevenson thought the book a genuine find: "Knox was most valuable; pure gold about the Highlands" (*L,* 3:134). Knox painted a grim picture of the enclosures, which forced people off the land in order to make room for sheep. The earlier depopulation of the south of Scotland was now being reproduced in the Highlands.

> The same causes have lately produced the same effects, in the Highlands, of which there is an example as late as the month of June, 1786, when 550 persons embarked in one ship for America, of whom 500 were from one estate only. A gentleman who happened to be present at the embarkation, declared, that the parting scene between the emigrants and their friends who remained behind, was too moving for human nature to behold.[25]

David observed this scene shortly after his arrival on Morven:

> But there was one melancholy part. In the mouth of Loch Aline, we found a great sea-going ship at anchor; . . . As we got a little nearer, it became plain

she was a ship of merchandise; and what still more puzzled me, not only her decks but the sea-beach also, were quite black with people, and skiffs were continually plying to and fro between them. Yet nearer, and there began to come to our ears a great sound of mourning, the people on board and those on the shore crying and lamenting one to another so as to pierce the heart.

Then I understood this was an emigrant ship bound for the American colonies (K, 16:136–37).

If Knox's description, unlike David's, is a bit restrained in its emotion. The sense of how much pain was involved in the Highlanders' forced removal from their homes was unmistakably expressed by Stewart, who viewed the entire issue of emigration as one of the central disasters of post-Culloden Scotland:

> The cruelty of removing the slaves on one West India estate to another, perhaps scarcely five miles distant, is frequently reprobated in the strongest terms . . . yet the ejectment or emigration of the Highlanders, their total ruin and banishment from their native land, is viewed with apathy, and their feelings of despair deemed unworthy of notice (ST, 1:154).

Stewart, continuing the comparison that Burt made and Buchanan amplified, discourses extensively on the analogy between the Highlanders and black slaves. This is important because the motif of slavery, although transmuted in its fictional form, recurs throughout *Kidnapped* and *David Balfour*.

Burt and Buchanan expressed common views of Highland life, and they also shared a common objective. Their primary aim was to describe the customs and manners of the people, apart from any utilitarian ends that might be entailed by that description. And Burt's aim was stated rather pointedly, for he was more concerned with ordinary people than he was with the great and the mighty: "For my own Part (who have already lived too long to be dazzled with glittering Appearances) I should be as well pleased to see a Shepherd of *Arcadia* (free from poetical Fiction) in his rustick Behaviour and little Oeconomy; or a Burgher of ancient *Rome* in his Shop, as to know the Character of a Consul" (EB, 2:290–91). This approach, essentially that of social history, was altogether novel and hardly applauded. Burt was accused of writing about low subjects, with the imputation that it was a kind of debasement: "These letters . . . abound with a variety of little stories and incidents, which, tho' they may seem low and trifling, give the reader a just idea of the uncultivated inhabitants of the northern part of our island."[26] Interestingly, Burt had anticipated just this kind of criticism:

> Writers, you know, for the most Part have not been contented with any thing less than the Characters and Actions of those whom Birth or Fortune had set up to publick View; or the Policy or Weakness of publick Councils.

The transition in Stevenson's notebook from Edmund Burt to David Stewart ("Stuarts Sketches"). Reproduced from the original in the Henry E. Huntington Library and Art Gallery, San Marino, Calif.

The Order and Event of Battles, Sieges, and such like, in great Measure dressed up in Habits cut out by themselves, but the Genius of a People has been thought beneath their Notice.

This, forsooth, is called supporting the Dignity of History. Now in this Case, who shall condescend to give a Detail of Circumstances, generally esteemed to be low, and therefore of little Consequence, and at the same Time escape the Character of a Trifler? (EB, 2:289–90)

Burt clearly argues for social history as a legitimate subject of inquiry. Further, both he and Buchanan wrote in the first person, as eyewitnesses, a method that justified itself on the basis of its unquestioned reliability. Reviews of both writers consistently remarked on their honesty, credibility, veracity, observation, fairness, and impartiality—in short, on the truthfulness of their reporting.

If we turn to Stewart, a third to two-thirds of a century later, we encounter a comparable situation. Stewart's themes were significantly different from Burt's and Buchanan's. He was not writing about the Highlands as an exotic locale where poverty and backwardness were curiosities for an alien audience. The major changes in Highland life had already occurred; for better or worse, the Highlands were integrated into British life. Stewart's text was, first, a history of the Highland regiments—a history of the clans and a commentary on the character of the Highland soldier; second, it was a discourse on the change in Highland life since the middle of the eighteenth century. Depopulation, forced emigration, the displacement of family with a capitalist mentality—all these changes led to what Stewart perceived as a deterioration in the Highland character. Stewart's loyalty to his clan and his native district led to the accusation by one reviewer of partiality to the cause of the Jacobites and the exiled Stewarts. Yet despite the charge, which was certainly justified, Stewart's book was an immediate success, at least in Scotland (the English magazines were apparently indifferent, judging by the absence of reviews in the major quarterlies). And the basis for that success was not fundamentally different from the virtues that were ascribed to Burt and Buchanan. The *Sketches* provided a mountain of seemingly irrefutable facts. Stewart quoted eyewitnesses for events as far back as the 1740s. His accumulation of original and singular anecdotes, his transcription of documents, his own minute knowledge of the period—all contributed to the conviction that his book was a veritable encyclopedia of information about the people and history of the Highlands. Furthermore, Stewart's style complemented his discourse. It was "clear, masculine, and free from all affectation or embellishment. 'He speaks plain soldier.'"[27] What was instantly recognized was the significance of Stewart's *Sketches*. This was no ordinary spring publication. The reviewer for *Blackwood's Magazine* said it best: "It must form a part of every library: the future historian must resort to it for materials: the heroes of a future age will look to it for bright examples."[28] Did the reviewer know he was foretelling the novelist? For Stevenson became that "future historian" who looked to Stewart for "bright examples," just as Stewart had drawn on those who went before him. The common thread linking Stevenson, Stewart, Buchanan, Knox, and Burt was their commitment to the concrete and verifiable reality of their materials. For all the writers, "facts" was the term that gave legitimacy to their reporting, their anecdotes, and their representation of customs and manners. Stevenson's use of David Balfour as a first-person narrator owes at least as much to this tradition as it does to his own predilection for the practice. Indeed, the eyewitness account of Highland life that David provides is itself a kind of factual reporting, reproducing the form that was its model. Stevenson's narrative of fact appropriates these earlier narratives of fact, thus ensuring that the facts survive even if their originating narratives have been displaced or have fallen into desuetude. He cannibalizes these earlier texts for their salient materials, those details that can be extrapolated and reconstituted in a new text that pretends to invert the aim of its originators and to create a fictitious narrative from a factual one. Yet Stevenson (unlike the reviewers of Burt et al.) was always aware that his predecessors' factual materials were embedded in discourses subject to individual interpretation, just as the reviewer critical of the *Sketches* argued that many of Stewart's facts depended upon a blend of truth and fiction. In his notebook, Stevenson consistently isolated factual details from commentary and interpretation. This is not to say that he was inattentive to Burt's and Stewart's commentaries. There is unquestionably a Highland bias that emerges in the novel, an attitude arrogated by Stevenson for David Balfour from all the source texts. From the perspective of Stevenson's own time—the late nineteenth century—there is nothing especially noteworthy about this. But within the context of the fictional text, it is quite dramatic. For David, as a Lowlander and a Whig, exhibits all the prejudices of his politics and his place. That he overcomes or sheds those prejudices is a consequence of his open mindedness and his experience. By disassembling the social realities of the Highlands from these contemporaneous narratives and reconstructing them in a fictional one of his own making, Stevenson re-presents those realities through the eyes of a character who is forced to encounter them for the first time. For David Balfour's reader, the Highlanders are demystified, seen for the first time as they are; for Stevenson's later reader, they are part of a vanished past, forever shrouded in romance.

Chapter 4

BROKEN SEPT

Criminal Law and the Clan Gregor

> The Highlands was a law unto itself until late on in
> the eighteenth century. . . . It was, so to speak,
> beyond the pale.
>
> —Stair Gillon

It is a commonplace to note the extraordinary connection between the law and history in Scotland, and perhaps even more particularly in Edinburgh. For the two constitute one of the strongest intellectual traditions in the country. It is surely no coincidence that the major library in Edinburgh was once the exclusive preserve of the Faculty of Advocates. And even after its incorporation into the National Library of Scotland, practicing attorneys continued to retain exclusive rights to the law materials in the original Advocates' Library. Scotland, after all, was justly famous for its fraternity of lawyers—for James Dalrymple and George Mackenzie, for John Maclaurin and David Hume and John Erskine.[1] What is particularly interesting about these legal scholars is how often they were engaged in writing their country's history. This may have to do with the early stages in the development of an ordered society, when there is a need to identify the sources upon which the laws of a country are to be founded. Are they to be based upon biblical tenets? Upon Roman practice and Celtic custom? Upon reason, common sense, and natural man? The major Scots legal figures, attempting to discover and codify the origins of their own law, were to a large extent involved in searching through their country's history. In the process, they had a compelling need for detailed information that would provide them with the requisite data for making decisions and passing judgments. And just as the juridical writers examined their country's records in order to establish fundamental legal principles, a non-juridical group of advocates also studied the law and Scotland's history.[2] Hugo Arnot, Cosmo Innes and John Hill Burton were among the most notable. Equally worthy, if more obscure, was William Kennedy, the historian of Aberdeen, who explicitly modeled his book on Arnot's *History of Edinburgh*.[3] This tradition of the advocate-as-historian was prominent in the nineteenth century and continued into the twentieth, in a somewhat popularized form, with lawyers like William Roughead, who made a career of reproducing quasi-popular accounts of episodes in Scottish legal history. In a very real sense, then, the Scottish lawyer was often the Scottish historian, particularly since studying the law invariably entailed studying the past. The civil law and the criminal law—land and property and inheritance; private and social behavior—were the twin pillars governing Scottish life. And the people best equipped to concentrate their attention on these issues were the professionals— the judges and advocates.

In 1774 John Maclaurin (later Lord Dreghorn) published the first abridgement and compilation of criminal decisions in Scotland. Maclaurin's aim, as he stated in the preface of his text, was to provide a sampling of the most famous Scottish trials, an objective subscribed to and followed by later writers.

> My original intention was to publish only some few remarkable and leading cases, which I had either argued, or attended to particularly. But it having been suggested, that I should extend my observation to a much greater number of criminal cases, I was soon convinced it would be proper to do so. In this country but few trials have been printed; no treatise of merit has yet appeared on its criminal law; and it is irksome to search the record of the court of justiciary, the only source from which a knowledge of this law can be derived: I was persuaded, therefore, that such a collection would contribute not a little to the advancement of jurisprudence, and be useful also to many gentlemen not bred to the law, who are called upon by the constitution to serve as jurymen.[4]

Maclaurin goes on to say that the original scheme ultimately led to the restriction of cases to criminal ones only, partly because they were more comprehensible for the general reader, and partly because they were more dramatic. "Criminal cases . . . may justly claim a more general attention; for no sum of money, no portion of land, can give rise to a judicial contest, equally interesting with that in which the life or liberty of a man is at stake" (iii). It is curious how, even in the late eighteenth century, with the most serious matters of jurisprudence before him, questions of what will most hold the interest of the reader are uppermost in the legal historian's mind.

Maclaurin then remarked on his transcription of the court records, something which posed major problems: "The notes of the opinions of the judges, on some of the later cases, were either taken by myself, or by other lawyers. They are all very imperfect, from our ignorance of short-hand . . . but I thought it more eligible to exhibit them in their rude and rugged state, as it in some measure proves their authenticity, than expose *that* to suspicion, by giving them a polish" (v). Here Maclaurin establishes a point of view that was reflected in the writing of all the later legal historians and adhered to as well by Stevenson—that authenticity was a primary consideration and matters of style or expression had to be subordinated to that fundamental value. Nonetheless, like the travel writers who insisted upon the higher claim of truth while similarly affecting an indifference to style, Maclaurin felt obliged to reproduce the "technical terms," "obsolete words," and ubiquitous "Scotticisms" he encountered in the trial records. It would be a mistake, he argued, for this language to be "weeded" and supplanted with "pure English," for that would give the entire enterprise "an air of affectation; which, in my apprehension, must be no less disadvantageous to a book, than it is to a character" (vi). Despite his disclaimer of any interest in "the style of the work," Maclaurin is acutely aware of the Scottish nature of the material—both its content and expression—and he exhibits a belief that language itself may be a critical determinant of authenticity. Finally, he confides to the reader, he offers this record of the past not simply for its own sake but in the hope that the knowledge will lead to the improvement of people's lives. In a sense, his attitude is that of a typical Enlightenment intellectual. He holds the belief that the general good can only be improved by an increase in the store of knowledge. Yet at the very moment he holds out that bright possibility he seems dubious about it, as he reflects upon his work and introduces, perhaps unwittingly, a peculiarly modern note at the end of the preface. For the indefatigable researcher discovered, in the course of poring over old records, that the history of his country's criminal law was one of unjust decisions, absurd arguments, and an uninterrupted series of trials whose only predictability resided in their endings. Maclaurin began his project as a bright lawyer who hoped to save his colleagues the time and trouble of searching for original documents in a disorganized court archive. He ended it as a captive of his own discoveries, the dark recording angel of his nation's Justiciary courts, "the *sad historian* of dooms and executions" (vi).

Eleven years after the appearance of Maclaurin's *Arguments,* Hugo Arnot (an advocate) published an abridged collection of criminal trials in Scotland. Arnot was the author of the comprehensive *History of Edinburgh* that was as "elegant and epigrammatic" in its style as it was dense and learned in its scholarship. His treatment of the trials compared favorably, as "a work of perhaps even greater research than his history of Edinburgh, and written in the same acutely metaphysical and epigrammatic style."[5] Arnot's writing was certainly more opinionated than Maclaurin's, and it was far more accessible. And the preface made explicit a subtler, more philosophical view of the function of such a compilation.

> The Criminal Records of a Country are an historical monument of the ideas
> of a People, of their manners and jurisprudence: and in the days of igno-
> rance and barbarism, they exhibit a striking, but hideous picture of human

nature. The records of Scotland, in particular, present such a frequent display of the extravagance of the human mind, as amuses the fancy after the wearisome detail of form, and the disgusting presentation of guilt.[6]

Arnot sustains his reputation for "causticity" in the Preface.[7] But interestingly he proposes to examine the criminal law in order to understand the people and the nation. He was convinced that criminal trials uncovered the elemental history of a people. Just as he had utilized local institutions and events in order to disclose the social and cultural history of the city in the *History of Edinburgh,* so in the *Criminal Trials* he exposed the larger history of Scotland.[8] Arnot, a "much admired lawyer," joined his technical skill to his scholarship in developing a text that provided useful information and also served as a moral beacon for his countrymen, reminding them of how far they had advanced from their earlier submission to religious authority and "tyrannical government."

Following Arnot came the most important writer on Scottish criminal law, David Hume, appointed Professor of Scots Law at the University of Edinburgh in 1786. Hume's work on the criminal law, considered "the text-book" in the field as early as 1838, was "constantly referred to as authority both by the Bench and the Bar."[9] While acknowledging Maclaurin and Arnot in his introduction, Hume nonetheless stated that the practicing lawyer "may almost be said to be without one printed authority" to consult on the subject of the criminal law.[10] Arnot himself had made a strikingly parallel point earlier: "There is no determined system of criminal jurisprudence in Scotland. It is a matter of doubt what is a crime in the eye of her law, and what not, also what is the punishment annexed."[11] Hume's object was to provide the young lawyer with the materials necessary to understand and practice criminal law.[12] He aimed for a commentary that would build upon the decisions of the justiciary court and would reflect the actual practice of Scotland with respect to crime. Criminal law was not looked at solely in terms of its technical principles but also from the point of view of its "general spirit," which Hume believed would always be "bent and accommodated to the temper and exigencies of the times."[13] He approached the criminal law (again with a parallel to Arnot) as a study in societal development, observing that practices that might have been objectionable in one period were tolerated in another. Thus an earlier juridical writer like Sir George Mackenzie would have little to offer Hume's contemporaries since the practices in Mackenzie's days were "utterly remote from what Scotland has since become."[14] Hume insisted upon an understanding of criminal law that openly recognized its intimate relationship to the life of the people. This particular characteristic was noted by Walter Scott, who attended Hume's lectures at the University of Edinburgh and remarked upon the way he traced "clearly and judiciously" the changes in the law from the past to the present, without ever becoming an antiquary or a technician. Hume's attitude was reflected as well in his skeptical view of the influence on Scottish practice of Roman law, which "never attained to a binding authority, like that of our own customs or statutes [which] are utterly remote from any thing that was known among the Romans."[15] If this was so for the civil law, how much more so for the criminal law, which bears a much closer relationship to and is more dependent upon the singular circumstances of the people. Thus there are inherent obstacles in attempting to transfer the criminal law from one country to another, from Rome, say, to Scotland. The effect of Hume's position was to base the principles of Scottish criminal law upon Scotland's experience, as that experience was documented in the records of the Court of Justiciary, otherwise known as the Books of Adjournal. Hume's position remained unchallenged in Scottish legal history:

> The importance of Hume . . . consists in the acceptance among all lawyers which his *magnum opus* has won, since it first appeared in 1797 down to the present day, and the fact that he brings us in direct contact with the sources and repositories. His sturdy nationalism was roused by the insinuating influence of English legal notions alien to those on which Scottish life had been built up. His historic sense rebelled against the loose generalities of Erskine and his references to the Roman Law. And so he resolutely turned to the records.[16]

From Maclaurin through Hume, then, there was agreement on a number of crucial issues relating to Scottish criminal law. First, that there was no systematic "treatise" (to use Maclaurin's term) defining the law;[17] second, that there were few printed authorities to draw upon for sources; and third, that any forward progress must start with the physical records themselves. Thus there is a strong tradition in Scottish legal history that runs from the late eighteenth through the early nineteenth century that emphasizes the importance, if not the primacy, of documentary evidence for establishing any rational system of criminal jurisprudence. In short, there is no law without documents and no history without records. In the absence of such documentation there is a spurious kind of justice, if indeed "justice" is even the appropriate word. Law is nothing more than power, and power is arbitrary and capricious. This theme runs through Hugo Arnot's work both in the *History of Edinburgh* and the *Celebrated Criminal Trials.* If crusaders like Arnot and magisterial scholars like Hume were attempting to wrest order from chaos, they were working against a long tradition of disorder.

> In tracing the development of the Criminal Law of Scotland the disturbed state of the country and the prevailing feudalism militate against anything like orderly progress. The Highlands was a law unto itself until late on in the

eighteenth century. The Crown administered the law then with armed forces or by letters of fire and sword, or left well alone. It was, so to speak, beyond the pale.[18]

Now for the project undertaken by the Bannatyne Club for the systematic publication of Scottish criminal trials from the earliest recoverable records. On November 19, 1827, with Sir Walter Scott presiding as president, the Bannatyne Club decided to support a multivolume publication of criminal trials based upon the original Books of Adjournal, to be edited by Robert Pitcairn, a member of the club and a writer to the signet. An extract from the minutes by the secretary, David Laing, offered the briefest possible justification: "A work of this nature would form a valuable accession to the Legal Antiquities of Scotland, and throw considerable light on the manners and opinions of the age to which they relate."[19] The project was arduous, protracted, and unremunerative, as Pitcairn repeatedly reminds the reader in the introductory notes and prefaces that he gathers at the front of each volume. But the major objectives and procedures were never questioned. The "ancient Records" were to be reproduced "in a scrupulously faithful and accurate manner, without using even the slightest liberty with the phraseology or structure of the original text" (xv). Like his predecessors, Pitcairn periodically refers to the authenticity of his documents and the fidelity of his transcriptions, particularly with respect to the "forcible vernacular" of the people, which is as much a part of the records as the practices and behavior that constitute the substance of the trials. But Pitcairn's main concern was to make available this wealth of original material—first to a professional audience and then to a wider public:

> To the lawyer, the historian, the antiquary, and the genealogist, especially, this compilation will be found to be of considerable practical utility . . . while, at the same time, the more general reader will at every turn meet with varied portraitures of national manners, customs, and the superstitions of bygone ages, which might in vain be searched for elsewhere (xx).

Pitcairn recognized that the appeal of the project was limited. He attributed its conception to Scott, whose antiquarianism was well-known, and then reported that Scott had considered doing it himself, selecting "the most remarkable of the ancient Criminal Cases of Scotland, combining the facts of each with all the correlative circumstances, worked up into a popular and narrative form" (xvi). It is not hard to understand Scott's interest, and of course the entire enterprise can be seen as furthering the larger objectives of the legal writers going back to Maclaurin (among the patrons listed for the edition was David Hume). But the project proved a severe strain on Pitcairn's finances, and the prospect of little if any return was an irritant he made no effort to conceal. Yet he persevered. For at some point he realized that the importance of the work was greater than any return he would ever realize from it.

> The grave nature of a work conducted on the plan of the present . . . entirely precluded the possibility of reducing any portion of it into a "popular" form, so as in any manner to compete, in point of interest, with works of fiction, or the lighter and more fascinating literature of the day. Such a work may indeed still be considered as a *desideratum;* but, in the Editor's humble opinion, it would require to be executed by a master-mind, such as his who suggested this publication (xix).

Pitcairn saw that the nature of the material might allow for a treatment that would appeal to a large popular audience, an insight that may have been sparked by his pressing need for money. At the same time he was clearheaded enough to see that writing such a book required the skill not only of the scholar-historian but of the fictionist as well. Fortunately, he knew his own limitations, and his suggestion that only Scott could execute such a work is sensibly plausible, even if it is couched a bit officiously. Although today his observation can be seen as remarkably prescient, Pitcairn certainly could not foresee that a writer would come along half a century after him and do exactly what he believed could only be done by the laird of Abbotsford.

Pitcairn had the shrewdness to see the potentially broad appeal of these ancient criminal trials. But what he understood intuitively was articulated or rationalized differently. That is, the justification for "patiently" collecting and annotating these "relics" of "obscure historical events" and "long forgotten superstitions" (xix) was to provide an accessible record of the past that would faithfully reveal "the public and domestic History of this country" (November 1, 1831, n.p.). Like Burt before him, Pitcairn was engaged in transcribing social history. And, indeed, that is how his massive work has been regarded, its great value deriving from the light it throws "upon the social and political history" of the late fifteenth through the early seventeenth centuries.[20] All this repeats a central thesis that has emerged from these editors and writers on legal history that the criminal records of a people are an index to their most intimate life, and whoever would discover that life must confront its documentary revelations. The most graphic language, the rawest descriptions of violence and sexual brutality, are inscribed in the ledgers of the court. Maclaurin drew the curtain on the past in order to inform a select audience and offer aid to practicing advocates; Arnot widened the curtain for the purposes of broad and vitriolic criticism of the abusive powers of the church and state; Hume systematically explored the records in order to establish a rational procedure for dealing with the inalterable reality of crime and punishment; and

Pitcairn gathered and printed the trials to provide a primary reference for the legal community.[21]

For all these legal scholars the advocate was bound up with the historian. They were conscious of their roles as recorders and interpreters of the past, as keepers of the records. And they were all, to a greater or lesser degree, Scots nationalists —or at least Scots cultural historians—as much as they were juridical writers and teachers. In chronicling the crimes of their country they were narrating the life and times of their countrymen, replete with everything from forcible abduction, rape, infanticide, and adultery—not to mention political crimes like rebellion and treason. And they all saw, and acknowledged, the powerful hold on the popular imagination of these stories that sprang, in Maclaurin's phrase, from the "passions or appetites of men." If Pitcairn realized that fiction could be made from them, then Maclaurin before him knew they had a certain value as entertainment, although for these sober Enlightenment types "instruction" would have been the operative word. And they were so committed to the importance of their primary task—a task that rested upon a base of accuracy, authenticity, and truth—that they insisted upon retaining the "forcible vernacular" of their sources, rather than "English" it and give the lie to the speech of their countrymen.[22] Thus, in a clear and unambiguous way they were preserving their country's cultural and linguistic history as much as they were preserving its legal history, and they were pursuing the same nationalistic path taken by missionaries in the Highlands like Knox and Buchanan. Like them, too, they brought hidden or concealed information into print, whether manuscript records or cultural practices, implicitly arguing for an openness and freedom of expression that celebrated the actuality of Scottish history, however terrible, just as Hume derided English criminal practice and Arnot railed against governmental tyranny. All these writers were part of a political as much as a legal tradition—indeed, the legal was political, even when some studiously sought to deny it—and that political tradition was as Scottish as Athole brose. Even in particular cases like the Macgregor and Stewart trials, where English power was a core issue, the discourse and forms of the proceedings ensured that those contentious events would live beyond their lifetimes in Scotland's criminal and documentary archives, and even longer in its popular imagination. Robert Louis Stevenson was certainly heir to a tradition of historical fiction that went back to Sir Walter Scott. But he was bound even more profoundly to a tradition of scholarship and writing that was centered in Scotland's legal fraternity— and more precisely in Edinburgh—among the men who pled and chronicled the most intimate and appalling stories of love, greed, and death in his country's turbulent history.

From the very beginning, when Stevenson conceived his scheme for a book about the Highlands, the Clan Gregor, commonly known as the Macgregors, held a central place in the design. In the letter to his father outlining the project, the first subheading under the first chapter is "Rob Roy."[23] A year later, when he again writes his father about an article he is proposing in support of his application for the university professorship, two of his five requests are for texts relating to the Macgregors.[24] Clearly, Stevenson viewed the story of the clan Gregor as a crucial element in a history of the Highlands. What accounts for this? Were the Macgregors universally regarded as critical to an understanding of Highland history? Had the legend of Rob Roy, widely absorbed through Scott's popular romance, contributed to the attraction of later generations for the outlaw's clan?[25] Or was there something about the Macgregors' history that illuminated the larger history of the Highlands? Whatever the case, Stevenson's texts served him well. Not only did they provide him with familiar figures whose personal lives could be incorporated in his fiction, but their collective histories enabled him to authenticate and embody some of the most fundamental issues in Scottish national life.

The primary and secondary materials relating to the Macgregors are voluminous.[26] In effect, writing about the Macgregors, even as early as 1817, was to write about a past distant enough to have taken on an aura of romance.[27] This is not to say that the historians were romantics but simply that the subject had receded far enough into the past to make many of the historic events appear more curious and problematic than real. Yet they all caution the reader that without written documents all tales and anecdotes are of questionable reliability. Indeed, if anything could be said to justify the integrity of the writers it is their determination to account to the reader for the accuracy of their reports. But, in fact, there is little they actually have to offer other than documents drawn from court records, occasional correspondence, and the supposedly good intentions of their oral informants. This does not deter any of them from narrating their story of the Macgregors, a history which by the early nineteenth century had something of a folkloric quality about it. For Highland history, now that it *was* history, had acquired a haze of nostalgia, and the Macgregors were the emblematic Highland clan upon whom that nostalgia devolved. It is a commonplace that Scott's novels glamorized the past, but it would be fairer to say that Scott was part of a larger group of writers who were independently sympathetic to the same issues and intent upon promoting similar attitudes. If yesterday was gone, and the Highlanders defeated, still the past could live on in the constructed fantasies of the present. No longer a physical threat, the Macgregors, like all Highlanders, could now be seen as an attractive ornament to the national culture, rather like the fashion for tartans and kilts. In a pattern that is all too familiar, the past was appropriated by the victors, who then proceeded to write its history.

But this is to get ahead of the story. Although the presumed history of the Macgregors, or one small branch of the clan, will be examined through Stevenson's meticulously constructed text, some preparatory observations are in order. The

Macgregors traced their lineage back to Alpin, King of the Scots, and considered themselves of royal descent. Surrounded by powerful neighbors, notably the Duke of Argyle in western Scotland, they achieved a particular notoriety through a succession of acts of parliament in the seventeenth century. These acts singled them out as an outlaw clan, proscribed the use of their name, and offered pardon from prosecution to anyone who killed them. A vivid illustration of the attitude toward the Macgregors can be seen in the "Act anent the Clangregor" adopted by the Scottish parliament on June 28, 1617:

> One act vpoun the third day of Apryill 1603 whereby It wes ordanit that þe name of m^cgregoure sulde be altogidder abolisched And þat the haill persounes of thatt clan suld renunce thair name and tak thame sum vther name And that They nor nane of thair posteritie suld call þame selffis gregor or m^cgregoure thairefter vnder þe payne of deade Ane vther act of þe date þe 26 day of Januare 1613 Quhairby It wes ordanit that nane of the Clangrego^r who wer at glenfrone the tyme foirsaid and who wer at þe fyir rasingis murtheris slauchteris and depredatiounes Committit vpoun þe Lairdis of glenvrquhie Lus and Coline Campbell of abiruquhill suld at no tyme thairefter beare nor weare ony kynd of armoure bot ane pointles kniff to Cutt þair meate vnder the said payne of Deade As alsua one vther act of the date þe 24 Junij 1613 Quhairby it wes ordanit that naine of [the] Clangrego^r nor na otheris who formerlie wer callit m^cgrego^r and hes renuncit thair names suld convene and meit togidder in onie pairt of this kingdome in gryiter numberis nor four persones vnder the said payne of deade.[28]

In 1633 another act "Anent the Clangregour" was passed, a consequence ostensibly of the clan's having "brokine furth again To the heavie oppressione of many of his Majesties good subjects," and this time the parliament went even farther than before:

> That the said name of Clan gregour and everie one of thame as they come to the aige of saxteine years Sall thaireftir yearlie give thair compeirance befor the lords of privie counsall vpon the tuentie fourt day of July. . . . And tak to thame some other surname. . . . And if it salhappin any of his hienes good subjects in taking any of the said Clan gregour being putt to the horne as said is To hurt mutulat or slay any of thame The pairtie quha sall happen soe to doe and thair complices sall nowayes be subject nor lyable to law thairfor nor incurre any paine or skaith in bodie or guides And sall be frie of all persuite criminall or civil.[29]

Finally, on June 15, 1693, the Scots parliament confronted the Macgregors again, this time as part of a general "act for the Justiciary in the Highlands."[30] Quite simply, having in 1661 cancelled the proscriptions against the clan, the parliament rescinded that statute and revived the act of 1633. From a legal point of view, the Macgregors were back where they had been sixty years earlier.

What these acts reveal both in their tenor and their stipulations (and they do not even skim the legal history of this clan) are the tough, even vindictive measures directed against the Macgregors by the Scottish parliament. One profile of the clan was captured in an eighteenth-century account of the Highlands: "CLAN GREGORE—Are a people very Remarkable for wicked Achievements . . . and Are rarely Absent from any Great Convocation whatever the Quarrell may be, Since plunder and Booty is their Bussiness."[31] The nineteenth-century historians were no less supportive of the earlier perceptions, but the depiction of the clan's barbarity was more forceful, partly because the language of cruelty and barbarism in old documents ("plunder" and "booty") often sounds quaint to a modern ear. The Macgregors "despised . . . laws," were possessed of "ferocious manners," engaged in "merciless depredations," had a "haughty spirit," were "unbending" in their "pride" and forever feuding.[32] They were beyond the pale of government, and even, to some, of human decency. The picture of the clan as a "tribe" resistant not only to the laws of a distant governing body like the parliament at Edinburgh but equally disdainful of neighboring lairds and competing clans is duplicated by all the writers. Thus the terms applied to them are repetitive and predictable: "violence," "ferocity," "warlike," "undisciplined," "desperate," "lawless," "wild," and "untamed." Clearly, there are enough accounts of heinous acts to warrant the characterization. But Highland crimes, as Maclaurin and others demonstrated, had more than its share of brutality, and it is doubtful that the Macgregors were singular either in their lawlessness or their cruelty. General Wade, in his first report on the Highlands in 1724, offered a list of scourges:

> The Clans in the Highlands, the most addicted to Rapine and Plunder, are, the Cameron's on the West of the Shire of Inverness, The Mackenzie's and others in the Shire of Ross who were Vassals to the late Earl of Seaforth, the McDonnell's of Keppoch, the Broadalbin Men, and the McGregors on the Borders of Argyleshire.[33]

All the commentators summarizing the Macgregors' history focus on the position of Highlanders in general and not just the particular clan that inspired these specific laws. For laws against the clans were passed regularly, and the 1693 act that revived the proscription against the Macgregors was primarily directed against "Depredations and Robberies frequently committed in the Highlands."[34] In point of fact, the laws against the clan Gregor were part of a historic pattern of legislation, hardly concerted but ineluctable nonetheless, and culminating in the clan acts of the eighteenth century that led to the demise of the whole system of clanship.

And it was the system of clanship that was the central issue for the historians. For although the raw and bloody history of the Macgregors made them a tantalizing subject, in actuality they functioned as a case study for a social system that was believed to be the crucial determinant of Highland history. All the writers on the clan Gregor comment extensively on this system, including Walter Scott in his review of the *Culloden Papers.* The connection between the chief and his clan was patriarchal.[35] But what this meant, in reality, was that each member of the clan felt like part of a family:

> The obedience of the highlander was paid to the chief of his clan, as representing some remote ancestor from whom it was supposed the whole tribe was originally descended, and whose name, compounded into a patronymic . . . was the distinguishing appellation of the sept.[36]

Disobedience to one's chief was tantamount to treason and akin to parricide (*Sons,* xvi). In the extensive list of violent and brutal incidents recorded in the long saga of Macgregor-Highland and Macgregor-government feuds, attacks on chiefs or heads of families were often the immediate trigger. For the clans, "the right of reprisal or revenge" was considered altogether justified if not indeed obligatory (*Sons,* xix). They were a "military" people with "arms" as "their common occupation" and "war their ordinary pursuit" (*Sons,* xxiv). They viewed the vigorous assault on them by the government as a determination "to destroy . . . their peculiar usages and institutions" and "to reduce them . . . to an equality with the low country, whom they despised" (*Sons,* xxxvii). All the important writers addressed the system of Highland clanship prior to assessing the Macgregors as a representative albeit most compelling case. Further, they stressed the necessity for understanding the nature of Highland culture (which for these writers largely meant history, which in turn reduced itself to narratives of feuds and small battles) as a condition for interpreting clan behavior and experience. Stevenson's immersion in Jacobite history was broader and his understanding of it more nuanced than that which appeared in many of these volumes. But like his predecessors, he could not isolate a seemingly self-contained subject like the Clan Gregor without first confronting the larger and more complex issues of clan culture. While he was certainly not reading Stewart's *Sketches,* Skene's *Highlanders,* or Burton's *Criminal Trials* for their notations on the Macgregors, like them he invariably placed his commentary on the clan within the larger context of eighteenth-century Scottish history and culture.

What Stevenson and the earlier writers were wrestling with was the relationship of the Highland clans to the law of Scotland. John Bartholomew articulated the problem with remarkable concision and clarity.[37] The patriarchal government of the chiefs was the system of law for the kinship communities that constituted clan life. But that system—indeed, the very principle of clanship—was never fully recognized by Scottish law, which preferred to use the clans as an instrument for the preservation of law and order rather than cede to them any legal authority. For their part, the clans simply disregarded the law of Scotland and utilized their own laws based upon their own custom, which differed considerably in areas like marriage and land tenure. And since revenge was a common motive for clan violence, feuds in the Highlands were endemic and seemingly uncontrollable. Therefore, the government came to view clans as societies that were collectively responsible for the acts of their members. "[The] policy of holding a whole clan as well as individual members of it responsible for crimes committed by these members reached its full development in the treatment of the clan Gregor at the hands of the Government."[38] And the Macgregors were not alone, as there were other attempts to eliminate whole clans, including "the Clanranald, the Macneills of Barra and the Clan Donald North."[39] But how was any person's membership in a clan to be ascertained? Bartholomew speculates that the name was determinant, since it was "one of the chief bonds of union," and that the proscription of the Macgregor name was a strategy for the annihilation of the whole clan. The tactic ultimately failed, as an inscription over Rob Roy's grave attests: "Macgregor despite them." Nonetheless, by the middle 1700s the law of Scotland had superseded the clan system and come to be the law of both the Highlands and the Lowlands.

Still, the Macgregors were a force to be feared in the seventeenth century. The acts proscribing their activities were not promulgated capriciously, and many of the anecdotes of brutal slaughter, vengeance, and decapitation that are recited in *Blackwoods* and *Sons* indicate that there was enough blood to justify the proscription. A number of writers take pains to picture the Macgregors as a clan surrounded by hostile enemies, like Montrose and the Grahams, and one as much interested in protecting itself as it was in marauding on others' territory. They are associated with the "inaccessible valleys" and "braes of Balquhidder," and with two prominent bodies of water, Loch Lomond and Loch Katrine.[40] Thus, not only are they given a history, but they are given a place, and a landscape, as well. If the Macgregors were marked by their "ferocity" and "violence" (which for some writers was mitigated by the fact that they themselves "were hunted . . . like wild beasts" [*Sons,* lix]), they were also identified by their fidelity. Indeed, they were attractive precisely because they were exemplary. The authority of the chief, the identifiable sign of the patriarchal structure, was writ large in the Macgregors' history. They fought for their chiefs, and they died for them. If this was the mark of the political and social system throughout the Highland clans, it was nonetheless in the Clan Gregor that the pattern was made most vivid to those outside.

By the early nineteenth century it was impossible to write about the clan with-out writing about Rob Roy, an outlaw of the preceding century who achieved notoriety as a cattle thief and blackmailer, whose exploits became the stuff of legend but whose actual experiences were harder to verify. Of course, Rob Roy achieved his greatest popularity with Scott's fictional portrait, one that John Hill Burton, in particular, disdained[41]—although the thumbnail sketch that Scott offered in his review of the *Culloden Papers* was a bit less generous.[42] For the *Blackwood's* and *Sons* writers, Rob Roy enjoyed the reputation of a "kind and gentle rob-ber," a latter-day Robin Hood who evinced no cruelty in the course of his raids. The physical description of Rob Roy emphasized his formidable strength and noted as well the extraordinary length or reach of his arms, a detail that Steven-son passes on to his son, James More, in *David Balfour*. Of course, no Highlander would need reminding that "roy" means "red," and red hair was a distinguishing mark of Highlanders in general, and the Macgregors in particular. This is another fact that Stevenson works into his text in a variety of ways. Finally, all the narra-tives that focus on the career of Rob Roy inevitably conclude with brief accounts of his sons, mainly James More Drummond and Robert Macgregor, alternately known as Robin Oig. In none of the accounts are the sons presented as positively as the father. But the sons went to trial, and the information about them in the court records, authentic or otherwise, is not duplicated anywhere for Rob Roy. In other words, there is no written record that will enable us to make a determina-tion as to Rob Roy's character, and all the writers who chronicle his career attest to the supposititious nature of the anecdotes and stories about him. Perhaps it is a measure of our belief, or our passion for myth, that legends rush in where all evidence fails. Stevenson would have no documents to rely upon were he to use Rob Roy as a personage in a text. Fortunately, Rob Roy's life ends before Steven-son's narrative begins, and he could only be brought into the pages of *Kidnapped* and *David Balfour* by allusion through his sons. Yet that may not be the relevant observation. Stevenson would have no qualm disputing any written record if he believed it was erroneous in its detail or skewed in its interpretation. A written account was material evidence, though, a tangible sign that somebody was an eye-witness to events or at least an unconscious scribe of history.

Although Stevenson derived his information about the Macgregors from a vari-ety of sources, some were clearly more authoritative than others. John Hill Bur-ton was one of the foremost Scottish historians whom Stevenson had written to when he had been contemplating his history of Scotland. Stevenson owned a copy of Burton's *History of Scotland* and carried it with him to Samoa. The *Narratives from Criminal Trials* that he had requested from his father when he was planning his paper on the Appin murder for the Edinburgh University chair had a long prologue on

"The Clan Gregor." Burton chronicled in a kind of mordant detail the savage and brutal history of the clan. Disinclined to romanticize the past or to idealize the Highlanders, he saw the Macgregors' history as part of a wider struggle between the Highlands and the Lowlands, between the people of the plains and the people of the mountains. Rather than focus on the savageness of some acts of the Highlanders, he stressed the incompatibility of the two peoples' views of life and the embittered attempts of each to subjugate the other. Burton did not neglect the "lawless" behavior of the clan Gregor, nor their "half civilized" mode of existence. But those descriptions were themselves attempts to place the clan within a social context and to contrast them with their antagonists to the south, "the Lowland Borderers, whom they regarded as a people of another nation, different in manners as in language."[43] The Macgregors viewed the Lowlanders with a "hatred and scorn" that could only be ascribed to the enmity which one distinct race feels toward another seemingly alien one. Burton saw the contest between the government and the Macgregors as a war that would not be satisfied, on the government's side at least, short of the extermination of the clan. Viewed from this vantage point, he judged the "predatory and sanguinary passions" that were passed from "generation to generation" as a response to the relentless vengeance with which the government persecuted the clan, a vengeance most forcibly expressed, as we have seen, in the successive acts "anent the Clangregour." It is a nice question, he concluded, as to who bore the most guilt in the long history of bloodshed and how one could determine the best way for punishing crime.[44]

Chapter 5

REBEL WITH A GRACE NOTE

Robert Macgregor

> His body . . . was cut down and delivered over to
> his friends, which they put into a coffin and con-
> veyed away to the Highlands.
>
> —*Caledonian Mercury*

One of the remarkable qualities of *Kidnapped* and *David Balfour* is the way the texts are interleaved, the one folding into the other, so that incidents in the second appear as if they were continuations of the first. Of course, this ought to be obvious to any reader of *Kidnapped,* since David Balfour is left alone at the end of the novel in front of "the very doors of the British Linen Company's bank." The final paragraph, inserted by the "present editor" and enclosed within brackets, only enforces the point that *Kidnapped* is incomplete, perhaps even unfinished. But history or tradition have tended to blur, if not dispel, that perception. The common printing practice of dropping the bracketed paragraph further contributed to the idea that the novel was finished as it stood. *David Balfour* was indeed a sequel, but it was one that picked up the action and took it in new directions. The central point, however, was that *Kidnapped* lost nothing without *David Balfour.* In other words, it was a text planted firmly on its own merits, sufficient unto itself. Nothing could be further from the case. Not only is the story in *Kidnapped* incomplete, but, more importantly, the central issues that Stevenson raises are left standing at the end, just like David Balfour "cooling his heels" before the bank. If it is true that the two books have distinguishable styles, it is equally true that they are of the same cloth. Stevenson had not completed his larger story by the summer of 1886, and when he returned to it six years later he was determined to make it appear as seamless as possible so that a reader years later would not even recognize that there was a hiatus between the books.

One of the simplest examples of the interleaving of both texts can be seen in the role played by the Macgregors. Stevenson does not deal fully with the Macgregors until the second volume, where James More Drummond makes his appearance as a leading figure. But chapter 25 in *Kidnapped,* "In Balquidder," serves as a telling prologue. David Balfour has already undergone a number of adventures in the Highlands. He has met wild Highlanders, good and true, impious and thieving. He has visited the hideout of an important Jacobite chieftain and traveled through the countryside accompanied by an instructive, if not always accommodating, follower of the Chevalier, Alan Breck Stewart. Now, just before crossing the Forth and returning to the Lowlands, David and Alan pass through Perthshire, and the country known as Balquidder. The following paragraph opens the chapter:

> At the door of the first house we came to, Alan knocked, which was no very safe enterprise in such a part of the Highlands as the Braes of Balquidder. No great clan held rule there; it was filled and disputed by small septs, and broken remnants, and what they call "chiefless folk," driven into the wild country about the springs of Forth and Teith by the advance of the Campbells. Here were Stewarts and Maclarens, which came to the same thing, for the Maclarens followed Alan's chief in war, and made but one clan with Appin. Here, too, were many of that old, proscribed, nameless, red-handed clan of the Macgregors. They had always been ill considered, and now worse than ever, having credit with no side or party in the whole country of Scotland. Their chief, Macgregor of Macgregor, was in exile; the more immediate leader of that part of them about Balquidder, James More, Rob Roy's eldest son, lay waiting his trial in Edinburgh Castle; they were in ill-blood with Highlander and lowlander, with the Grahames, the Maclarens and the Stewarts; and Alan, who took up the quarrel of any friend however distant, was extremely wishful to avoid them (*K,* 25:224).

Stevenson has condensed complex historical material into a fluid narrative line. It serves as instruction, provides suspense, and prepares for subsequent events. And the history is not merely located in the referenced details but embedded in the diction. The novelist introduces his readers to the past through direct narrative statement and the use of linguistic terms reflective of historical culture. Although "sept" has no special Scots origin, in practice this word was consistently applied to the Highlanders: "The Clan Gregor . . . had become a formidable sept in prosecuting all the evils which arose from feudal manners and hereditary antipathies" (*BW,* 75); "The devoted sept, ever finding themselves iniquitously driven from their possessions, defended themselves by force" (*RR,* 3). The term conveys two fundamental ideas—family and tribal unit—and each complements and reinforces the other. Thus the word emphasizes the strong familial connections among the members of the unit, or clan, expressing in itself the powerful adherence of the members to each other. In a similar vein, the term "broken"—

Balquidder Churchyard, designed by George Cruikshank, from the *Rob Roy* title page of Sir Walter Scott's *Waverley Novels* (New York: G. Routledge, n.d.). Reproduced from the original in the Henry E. Huntington Library and Art Gallery, San Marino, Calif.

which *is* Scots—is rich with historical meaning. It shows up in a late sixteenth-century criminal trial ("brokkin men") and Pitcairn proceeds to gloss it: "*Broken men,* outlaws, separated from every clan by their crimes, and depending upon plunder for their subsistence."[1] This phrase might almost be said to have assumed something of the character of a flash word for historians, for they use it repeatedly in describing those men who operate outside the law. Jamieson uses it in his introduction to Burt's *Letters,* Scott does so in his review of the *Culloden Papers,* and Burton glosses it as late as 1852: "'Broken men' was an expression applied generally to all the Border and Highland depredators; but in its limited sense it applied to those who had no chief or other person to stand surety for them."[2] In all these examples the historians felt compelled to define the phrase in order to enable the reader to understand its meaning. Stevenson uses the term "broken" in an original way, coupling it with "remnants" and adding a touch of pathos to the picture of small, surviving bands of men, dispossessed of their land and existing outside the law. As a writer, he certainly knew that the term would be Greek to his own audience. But he is at no pains to inform his readers of the word's meaning—and not because he desires to conceal knowledge or because he prefers them to be ignorant about what he is saying. As we know, in the margins of the holograph Stevenson regularly glosses the Scots diction that would be inaccessible to English readers. But, on a microcosmic level, the example of "broken" exhibits his method in this epic. He is so steeped in the terminology of his primary sources that he often uses their language as if it were his own. Of course, he is aware that "broken" has a special historic meaning that requires definition. But he is often content to allow the meaning that his linguistic context conveys to suffice ("broken"= "shattered, torn") rather than to provide a traditional gloss. To a large degree, this tactic is determined by the nature of the historical narrative. To define terms (and identify allusions) that were contemporaneous would only highlight the text as a nineteenth-century construction and would diminish its posture as an eighteenth-century memoir. Thus Stevenson opts, invariably, for the artistic solution, for burying the linguistic context rather than calling attention to it for his reader's sake.

Finally, Stevenson's quoted reference to "chiefless folk" completes his trinity of the classes of people who occupied the "wild country" in Balquidder. This, too, has a context that draws upon clan culture. Burt tells of encountering members of a clan, "the only one I have heard of, which is without a Chief; that is, being divided into Families, under several Chieftains, without any particular Patriarch of the whole Name." And he then remarks: "For the Chiefless Highlander . . . the Words [*Name your Chief*] were to one of that Clan, the greatest of all Provocations" (EB, 2:221–22). Scott cites this anecdote in his first reference to Burt: "A clan without an acknowledged head was considered as an anomaly among them. To use to any member of a clan which chanced to be in this situation the expression, '*Name your chief*,' was an insult which nothing but blood could avenge."[3] Stevenson thus compacts in one sentence the fractured and separate groups inhabiting the braes of Balquidder, none powerful enough to dominate and all victims to a greater or lesser degree of internecine warfare. In a sense, the septs and the broken and chiefless men are nothing more than the remains of a system that has fallen apart, the vestiges of a patriarchal social and political structure that survives only in the form of mean and petty combats between individuals or small groups.

Stevenson then continues with his history: "Here were Stewarts and Maclarens, which came to the same thing, for the Maclarens followed Alan's chief in war, and made but one clan with Appin." This is a plain compression of an elaborately detailed footnote in the *Sketches* describing how the Appin Stewarts and the Maclarens joined forces.[4] Stevenson's ability to cut to the heart of the issue—in this case by identifying accurately the clan alliances—is exhibited simply by having David Balfour state the connection between the two families, a point that is reiterated shortly after David's discovery that he and Alan are among friends: "For it was a household of Maclarens that we found, where Alan was not only welcome for his name's sake but known by reputation." Stevenson proceeds: "Here, too, were many of that old, proscribed, nameless, red-handed clan of the Macgregors." In a single, direct sentence he incorporates all the salient features of the Macgregors that a knowledgeable eighteenth-century person would have been aware of and that a nineteenth-century reader ought to know—that they traced their ancestry back to Alpin, King of the Scots; that the laws against the clan forbade them to use their name or baptize male children with the name Macgregor; and that they were known equally for their red hair, as exemplified by their leader, Rob Roy, and by their bloody violence. In the final two sentences Stevenson constructs a portrait of the clan that is both historically accurate as to details (they *were* enemies of the Grahams, their chief *was* in exile in France, and James More *was* imprisoned) and psychologically shrewd. Stevenson depicts the Macgregors —traditionally viewed with hostility because of their incessant feuding with rival clans and their perennial border raids—as a people isolated from all others, with no allegiances and defined by images of imprisonment, exile, and violence.

Having concluded the summary comments on the whole clan, Stevenson has David disclose the significance of his experience in this chapter:

> There was but one thing happened worth narrating; and that is the visit I had of Robin Oig, one of the sons of the notorious Rob Roy. He was sought upon all sides on a charge of carrying a young woman from Balfron and marrying her (as was alleged) by force; yet he stept about Balquidder like a gentleman in his own walled policy. It was he who had shot James Maclaren at the ploughstilts, a quarrel never satisfied; yet he walked into the house of his blood enemies as a rider might into a public inn (*K,* 25:226).

Stevenson now makes direct reference to one of his primary sources, and a seminal document in Scots legal history, the trial of Robert Macgregor before the "High Court of Justiciary held at Edinburgh, Dec. 24, 1753." The defendant, or pannel, is introduced as follows: "ROBERT M'GREGOR, *alias* CAMPBELL, *alias* DRUMMOND, *alias* ROBERT OIG, son of the deceased Robert M'Gregor, who was commonly called, and known by the name of *ROB ROY.*"[5] Of course, the episode is identified in the sparest declarative terms, as befits a contemporary like David Balfour who could not be expected to know anything more than the merest outline, or perhaps the notoriety, of the incident. Robin Oig and the principal conspirator, James More Drummond, his brother, were charged in the forcible abduction and forcible marriage of Jean Key, a young widowed heiress from Edinbelly in the parish of Balfron.[6] These charges, only two of four, formed the basis for one of Scotland's important cases in criminal law, although it was a case that had implications as well for Scottish political history. Also, it is significant that there was more than one trial. James Macgregor was tried first, and his brother, at large and "sought upon all sides," was tried later. In *Kidnapped,* Stevenson does not address either the criminal or political issues in the trials of Rob Roy's sons for the abduction of Jean Key; he reserves that for the subsequent volume, *David Balfour.*

But he does have David remark upon an apparently tangential matter ("It was [Robin Oig] who had shot James Maclaren at the ploughstilts, a quarrel never satisfied") and one about which his narrator can hardly have been aware. This offers an interesting example of the way a historical fiction is forced to balance the aims of accuracy and plausibility with the necessity for introducing relevant information. The detail about Maclaren's murder is critical because "In Balquidder" draws upon the historic enmity between the Maclarens and the Macgregors. At the same time, it provides an insight into the younger Rob Roy's temperament. "Rob Oig, who was then between 16 and 17 years of age, went deliberately with a loaded gun to a field where M'Laren was ploughing, and approaching from behind, fired upon the unfortunate man, and wounded him so severely that he died the same evening" (*Sons,* civ). Maclaren's murder resolved nothing, but the intensity of the tribal hatred can be gleaned from the reaction to the crime:

> Robert, after perpetrating the deed, retired to his mother's house in the neighbourhood, where he boasted that he had drawn the first blood of the M'Larens.—That James M'Gregor and Callum M'Inlister afterwards expressed their warm approbation of the crime, and their wish that one Donald M'Laren, a friend and kinsman of the deceased, had shared the same fate;—and that they threatened vengeance on the M'Larens if they should dare to bring the murderer to punishment (*Sons,* cvi).

All this clan rivalry is submerged in Stevenson's phrase, "a quarrel never satisfied." Certainly, the animosity driving the Macgregors cannot be conveyed in this briefest of expressions. In fact, Stevenson's Robin Oig is a good deal more attractive than the one revealed in the actual trial. But that is not the point. Stevenson's first objective is historical accuracy. He draws on aspects of Robin that are in line with the known figure: "He is said to have been rather of a slender and feeble make" (*Sons,* civ) becomes (with the inclusion of Alan Breck) "They were neither of them big men" (*K,* 25:228). In a sense, Stevenson's seemingly casual phrase about the Maclaren homicide might appear of insufficient interest to dwell upon let alone analyze. Yet it is anything but casual. It summarizes a salient detail of profound historic interest—that the murder of one clan member by another did nothing to alter or end clan rivalry. If anything, it only served to continue the cycle of violence and vengeance.

Turning to the question of fictional plausibility, it is inconceivable that a young man of David Balfour's experience would be aware of an event in Robin Oig's biography that occurred in 1736 and would be unknown to any but the parties involved. The case of Jean Key is another story. Those events occurred in 1751, which is one reason Stevenson changed the date of his novel from 1752. The Macgregor trial was a current affair, and it makes sense to have David aware of it. But the Maclaren murder is inserted by Stevenson for the reader's benefit, to amplify the story that he, the novelist, is telling. After all, no reader is going to care whether David Balfour could plausibly know about James Maclaren because who (other than Andrew Lang) would ever have heard about the incident in the first place? For if the story about the Macgregors and Jean Key is history, and buried history at that, except for the legal commentators, the tale of Robin Oig and James Maclaren is archeology.[7] Stevenson's attitude here is similar to that expressed later in his letter to E. L. Burlingame on historical fiction. As long as the integrity and historicity of the events are not compromised, the writer must be granted some freedom to manipulate his dates. Stevenson utilizes historical materials without ever losing sight of his artistic objectives. He is ever the historian and always the fictionist.

"In Balquidder" begins with a brief account of the wild countryside and broken clans, moves toward a dramatic encounter between David Balfour and Robin Oig, and then turns into a battle of the bagpipes between Robin and Alan Breck Stewart. But the chapter is more than a diverting description of two ferocious "fire-eaters" (the term that Stevenson applied to Alan in the dedication) who are soothed by the charm of their music. It begins with a brief history of the clans of Balquidder and ends with an account of the demise of one particular clan member of that country—Robert Macgregor/Robin Oig. Stevenson constructs a portrait of a historic figure, and in the process he augments a clan and its culture. Robin is a fugitive from the law, "yet he stepped about Balquidder like a gentleman in his own walled policy." Stevenson draws on source material ("It seems certain from several documents which have been preserved, that Rob Roy was a gentleman by birth") and language ("policy" is a Scots term for a small plantation or a gentleman's demesne) to capture the strutting pride of a son of Rob Roy.[8] Rob's arrogance is exhibited both in the style of his remarks ("'I am given to know, sir,' says he, 'that your name is Balfour'") as well as in their substance: "'I would give ye my name in return, sir,' he replied, 'but it's one somewhat blown upon of late days; and it'll perhaps suffice if I tell ye that I am own brother to James More Drummond, or Macgregor, of whom ye will scarce have failed to hear'" (*K,* 25:227). Rob treats David as if he were a mere nobody whom he, "with a great show of civility, but like a man among inferiors," nonetheless deigns to converse with. Hence he does not ask David his name but tells him that he has been informed of it, as if he were royalty to whom messages were delivered by underlings as a matter of course. Yet, ironically, Rob himself cannot use his own name, for "it's one somewhat blown upon of late days." The phrase, in context, might generally be understood by a reader to mean discredited, defamed, or perhaps exposed. But few would know that "*To Blaw out on one*" is "an old forensic phrase" that meant formally to be denounced as a rebel at the market-cross.[9] Insofar as the Macgregors were indeed rebels (having struck "a stroke for the good side"), the phrase is apt; insofar as they were outlaws, it is even more pertinent.[10] This is another example of Stevenson's incorporation of linguistic terms—often archaic or dialectal or technical, or merely obscure—to reinforce thematic issues in the text. Rob is proud to be the brother of Jame More Drummond, and he is equally proud to be a rebel. David Balfour grasps this immediately, and he admits to having heard of James More, as well as "'of your father, Macgregor-Campbell.' And I sat up and bowed in bed; for I thought best to compliment him, in case he was proud of having had an outlaw to his father" (*K,* 25:227). David's hyphenating "Macgregor-Campbell" is a sly way for Stevenson to introduce an important historic detail without elaboration or explanation. Since Macgregor was a proscribed name, Rob Roy had taken that of his protector, the Duke of Argyle.

> It was under the name of Campbell accordingly, that Rob was generally known out of the limits of his own country, and the society of his kinmen and retainers,—among whom however he was always recognized by his own surname of M'Gregor (*Sons,* lxvi).

It was not just Rob Roy who went by the name of Campbell. His younger son, Robin Oig, went by the name as well. This issue of names is played out in great and elaborate detail in the chapter;[11] it may even be said to be a central theme. All the sparring with names is one way to uncover much of the history that forms the background and drives the issues in the chapter. For the Highlanders, and for the clans, the patronymic was not simply a name but a mark of identity and a badge of honor. It was, in the deepest sense, one's whole being. Thus, upon a first meeting, each individual wants to establish the identity of the other. "What is your name?" is another way of asking, "Where do you come from?" Robin poses this to David when he addresses him upon learning that David's patronymic is Balfour. His first response is to connect the name Balfour to *his* or Robin's history:

> In the year '45, my brother raised a part of the Gregara', and marched six companies to strike a stroke for the good side; and the surgeon that marched with our clan and cured my brother's leg when it was broken in the brush at Prestonpans, was a gentleman of the same name precisely as yourself. He was brother to Balfour of Baith; and if you are in any reasonable

degree of nearness one of that gentleman's kin, I have come to put myself
and my people at your command (*K,* 25:227).

This small anecdote provides historical detail that fills out the political as well as
the physical portrait of the Macgregors. They fought for the prince, they were able
to call up six companies of men, they suffered wounds in battle, and they are
proud of their service. The sources for the anecdote—*Sons* (cxv) and *Blackwood's*
(256)—provide an even fuller background to the martial talents of James More
("He is said to have surprised the fort of Inversnait, and with 12 men only to have
made 89 of the garrison prisoners"). The surgeon, however, was lifted from another
text:

> Next day, Thursday, April 17th, he luckily fell in with one Balfour,* a
> young man, (who had been surgeon to the Macgregors in the Prince's serv-
> ice) . . .
>
> *Brother to James Balfour of Baith, near Dunfermline, who escaped the clutches of
> his enemies.—R. F.[12]

It was pure gold for Stevenson to find this detail. For one thing, he could build up
the picture of James More as a soldier with historical accuracy, and at the same
time he could utilize David Balfour's name in the context of the entire subject of
names. Stevenson (through Robin) uses David's name as a way of introducing a
detail from history that sheds light on the Macgregors; at the same time, he
acknowledges the importance of names as a way of establishing one's place in the
world, of indicating one's identity and one's connections with others. If David is
kinsman to Balfour of Baith then Robin will acknowledge him, even follow him,
in recognition of the surgeon's standing as a gentleman and his previous service to
the Macgregors.

But David, of course, never heard of the man: "I knew no more of my descent
than any cadger's dog; . . . and there was nothing left me but that bitter disgrace of
owning that I could not tell" (*K,* 25:227). Although as a Lowlander David should
hardly have cared about Robin's attitude ("I could scarce keep from smiling that a
man who was under the lash of the law . . . should be so nice as to the descent of
his acquaintances" [*K,* 25:227–28]), in fact he is particularly attached to the idea of
patriarchy. David is in search of a father, as every reader quickly recognizes, and
throughout both volumes he is continually adopting surrogates. It is a humiliation
not to be able to identify his patrilineage. At the same time, it must be said that
Stevenson can handle the idea in a comic vein, as he does in *David Balfour,* when
James More meets David and assumes that he is kinsman to the surgeon.

> "And now that I call to mind, there was a young gentleman, your namesake,
> that marched surgeon in the year '45 with my battalion."

"I believe that would be a brother to Balfour of Baith," said I, for I was ready for the surgeon now. . . .

"I think he was a very far-away cousin," said I, drily, "and I ought to tell you that I never clapped eyes upon the man" (*DB,* 5:56).

Stevenson was never so tied in with his characters and their issues that he could not see the comic—or seriocomic—side to them. The poise with which David waits for the "surgeon" to be dropped on him; the witty ambiguity as to the connection ("a very far-away cousin"); and the final blunt denial of any interest or association whatever ("I never clapped eyes upon the man")—all testify to Stevenson's ability to mock or ridicule an idea that is taken very gravely by the Macgregor brothers. The colloquy in *David Balfour* is as funny as the line in *Kidnapped* where David remarks to himself about the absurdity of an outlaw worrying about the "descent of his acquaintants." But if Stevenson (through David) is capable of ridiculing the Macgregors' commitment to their patronymic, it does not imply that the issues dominating the Macgregors' thinking are therefore superficial or amusing. The clan name was at the heart of one's identity. To be deprived of that name was equivalent to being deprived of one's family. One fought for one's clan, for one's name, before one fought for any cause. Indeed, when the Highlanders came out in 1745 for the Stuart cause they in fact came out as individual clans in obedience to their chiefs. If the chief did not follow the prince, the clan stayed behind as well. It is one of the features of the Jacobite rebellion that the clans followed their chiefs first, and with their chiefs the prince. Thus, to know your clan's name, or rather to herald your patronymic, was not to be boastful but rather to reflect your pride in your father, your family, and your clan. Hence, when David cannot satisfy Robin as to his name, or rather where he comes from, Robin dismisses him as "only some kinless loon that didn't know his own father" (*K,* 25:227), thus likening David to the "chiefless folk" cited at the beginning of the chapter.

But the issue of naming does not end with David and Robin. There is the contest between Robin and Alan Breck Stewart, a man who has made abundantly clear his pride in *his* patronym, which translates into pride of lineage. And it is here that the battle of names and clans is joined. The Macgregors and the Stewarts were old enemies. They contested the same territory: "'I did not know ye were in my country, sir,' says Robin. 'It sticks in my mind that I am in the country of my friends the Maclarens,' says Alan" (*K,* 25:228). And Alan reminds Robin of an earlier battle between a Stewart and a Macgregor:

"I am not the only man that can draw steel in Appin; and when my kinsman and captain, Ardshiel, had a talk with a gentleman of your name, not so many years back, I could never hear that the Macgregor had the best of it."

"Do ye mean my father, sir?" says Robin.

"Well, I wouldnae wonder," said Alan. "The gentleman I had in my mind had the ill-taste to clap Campbell to his name."

"My father was an old man," returned Robin. "The match was unequal. You and me would make a better pair, sir."

"I was thinking that," said Alan (*K,* 25:228).

Stevenson here utilizes a minor anecdote describing this contest. I quote from *Sons,* but versions of the story can be found in *Blackwood's* and *Sketches.* "When far advanced in years, [Rob Roy] had another affair of the same kind with Stewart of Appin, which was decided near the church of Balquhidder. Rob was worsted in this instance also, and declared that he should never make another experiment of his skill" (c–ci). Of course, Alan's recital of the story is tantamount to throwing down the gauntlet. He first attacks Robin by referring to his father's spurious name, which was the son's as well. It was a name particularly noxious to Alan, and his hatred for it gives resonance to his gibe ("the ill-taste to clap Campbell to his name"), echoing, as it does, old and deep-seated clan enmities.[13] It is at this point, the moment of mortal combat, that Stevenson introduces a wholly original idea: he has Duncan Dhu intervene and persuade the two "fighting cocks" to battle it out with bagpipes instead of swords. From the point of view of realism, the idea is ludicrous. Two of the fiercest, hottest-tempered Highlanders (Robin was known for his volatile temper) are going to resolve their bitter rivalry by blowing bagpipes. Does Stevenson believe this an imaginative solution to an otherwise irresolvable dilemma? There is no historic evidence that Robin Oig and Allan Breck ever met. But the fictional meeting enables Stevenson to sketch a portrait of Robin Oig that is, in some respects, more compassionate than documentary history might otherwise provide. There is no question that the crime for which he was charged, and hanged—the Jean Key affair—was instigated by his brother James.[14] There is also no question that he was guilty of the murder of James Maclaren.[15] But there is another picture of Robin, both in the trial account and in contemporary sources, that suggests a young man who was more caught up in events than a principal mover of them. Newspapers noted especially his profession of faith and the calm and grace with which he met his death.[16] Stevenson's chapter is both an elegy and a memorial for the man—recovering him from the past and acknowledging his crimes while, at the same time, giving him a new place for the future and infusing forever his youth and passion into his music.

So we are left with the duel of the bagpipes. In a way, the scene is mock-heroic without the comedy. Two warriors are reduced to musicians, each admiring the other's skill. If swords have not been converted into ploughshares they have, for the moment, been exchanged for bagpipes. That Robin wins the contest is not surprising. His brother played the pipes (as Stevenson notes at the end of *David Balfour*),

Highland Piper, from the fifth volume of the Abbotsford Edition of Sir Walter Scott's *Waverley Novels* (Edinburgh, 1845). Reproduced from the original in the Henry E. Huntington Library and Art Gallery, San Marino, Calif.

and there is no evidence of Alan's musical ability. But what is more significant is that through the playing Stevenson creates a peaceful resolution of an intractable hereditary feud. When Robin plays "a piece peculiar to the Appin Stewarts and a chief favourite with Alan" the signal is given for an end to the clan warfare. Alan acknowledges Robin's superiority as a musician. The sentence concluding their dramatic confrontation begins: "Thereupon that quarrel was made up" (*K*, 25:232). The term echoes the "quarrel" that was left unsatisfied at the beginning of "In Balquidder" and brings to a close one chapter in a long history of violence. Of course, this is simply a fiction. In truth, as the final paragraph returns us to history, "the man came to be hanged." But, in the world of the imagination, Robin Oig was given another characteristic, that of an artist, of someone who could draw such beauty out of those bagpipes that Alan Breck could say, "I am not fit to blow in the same kingdom with ye." If Robin's name was blown upon by the authorities, it was nothing compared to *his* blowing, one that raised the spirit and put to rest the thirst for blood.

Chapter 6

PIPES AT DUSK

James More Macgregor

I play a little now and then
——James Macgregor

If the Clan Gregor was introduced in *Kidnapped* through the figure of Robert Macgregor in a single chapter, the situation in the second volume was far more complex. Stevenson integrated the Macgregors' history with David Balfour's. Rather than present the clan and the political and legal issues they raised as an isolated episode, in the manner of an interpolated story, Stevenson made the Macgregors a structural part of the novel. As an example, the spine of the narrative is the love story, with its proud and vivacious heroine, Catriona Drummond. Further, the last seven chapters adapt and reconstruct the final days of James Macgregor, the eldest son of Rob Roy. In *David Balfour* Stevenson uses both the details and the context of the *Trials of Three Sons of Rob Roy* to expand his treatment of this most famous of Highland clans. In the process he broadens the readers' exposure to Highland history and deepens their understanding of the complex factors that contributed to the emergence of modern Scotland.

Stevenson weaves the Macgregors into the narrative in small as well as large ways. On the simplest level, he uses the clan's characteristic red hair as a repeated device. Neil Duncanson, James Macgregor's gilly, or servant, was "a short, bandy-legged, red-haired, big-headed man" (*DB*, 1:10) who David first encountered with Catriona. Red hair is, of course, not specific to the Macgregors, and it is useful to remember that the color red functions as a powerful motif in both novels. In *Kidnapped* there are two chapters with "red-fox" in the title, and in *David Balfour* there are chapters titled "The Heather on Fire" and "The Red-Headed Man." What Stevenson is doing with this color is, of course, significant and interesting. The color not only characterizes Rob Roy and Colin Roy Campbell, the assassinated king's agent in *Kidnapped,* but it serves to distinguish the "red-coats" pursuing Alan and David as well as to describe the breeches that Alan wore and to give some color to his clothes. It also identifies the blood that is spilled during battles and murders, and it identifies the feuds that characterize the clan enmities. "Blood foes" or "blood enemies" are Stevenson's terms for deadly feuds, a concept that was specific to Scotland and was carried on with a determination that brooked all contradiction or attempts at conciliation. Absent an elaborate analysis of the color red, suffice it to say that, for David in *David Balfour,* "Neil of the red head" (*DB,* 10:114) was a convenient code for the Macgregors.

Another simple device for identifying the clan that played so prominent a role in David's life was to reference one of their chief activities, cattle theft. David has just told Alan that he believes he has shaken the Highlanders who have been trailing him. Alan, more conscious of his countrymen's ability to stalk their prey without being seen, is less certain:

> Ye see, David man, they'll be Hieland folk. . . . A man kens little till he's driven a spreagh of neat cattle (say) ten miles through a throng lowland country and the black soldiers maybe at his tail. It's there that I learned a great part of my penetration. . . . Now the Gregara have had grand practice (*DB,* 11:135).

The bit lecture that Alan delivers is an illustration of Stevenson's ironic if not quite wry humor and his deft presentation of historical information. The word "spreagh" and the phrase "to drive a spreagh" mean both cattle and the stealing of a herd of cattle. The *Scottish National Dictionary* quoted Pennant's *Tour* as early as 1771: "The Highlanders at that time esteemed the open theft of cattle, or the making of a spreith (as they called it) by no means dishonourable." Scott's *Rob Roy* was similarly quoted in 1817: "They take pride in it, and reckon driving a spreagh (whilk is, in plain Scotch, stealing a herd of nowte) a gallant, manly action." Scott, ever the guide and teacher in his fiction, defines the phrase within the sentence in order to ensure that his reader understands its meaning. This technique, which he employs regularly, is akin to the extensive notes he prepared for the Waverley novels. It is notable, as well, that he (like Pennant, although the travel writer could be excused given the nature of *his* book) not only defines the term but explains the attitude that lies behind it. Stealing cattle was not an illegitimate activity so much as a badge of honor, a way for Highlanders to exhibit their courage.[1] And it was well known that the Macgregors were among the most experienced of cattle thieves.[2] Indeed, they were familiar with all aspects of cattle raising: "They were accused of having, soon after the murder of John M'Laren, houghed and killed, under cloud of night 40 head of young cattle belonging to his kinsman Donald" (*Sons,* cvii). Stevenson uses his own knowledge of the Macgregors and history to introduce into the narrative the kind of information that Scott provides, but without the commentary or direct explanation. Thus, that cattle-stealing was a matter of pride (as Scott puts it) comes through in Alan's presentation. Stevenson makes the attitude his character's, thus dramatizing it rather than making it the author's direct statement. Of course, this is no more than the difference between late nineteenth- and early nineteenth-century artistic practice, but it is significant how careful the later Scots writer is not to impede the narrative through authorial intrusion. Further, Stevenson compacts more information within the sentence: "neat" and "throng," uncommon terms, convey the idea of well-shaped, trim cattle and densely crowded countryside. Alan's description is both an evocation and a remembrance of the excitement, perhaps even the romance, of cattle-stealing. It is capped by the chase of the "black soldiers," which many readers might identify as the Black Watch, although few would recall that the term echoed the "red-soldiers" in *Kidnapped* (16:139).[3]

While Alan is instructing David, who acknowledges that cattle theft was a "branch of education that was left out with me," Stevenson is demonstrating to his readers the difference between two kinds of knowledge: "But that's the strange thing about you folk of the college learning: ye're ignorant, and ye cannae see 't. Wae's me for my Greek and Hebrew; but, man, I ken that I dinnae ken them— there's the differ of it" (*DB,* 11:135–36). This theme always intrigued Stevenson, and it appears as early as *The Rajah's Diamond,* where a distinction is made between information gleaned from books as opposed to knowledge drawn from life. By having Alan discourse on the spreagh as a skilled activity Stevenson calls attention not simply to the physical courage of the Highlanders but to their mental acuity, their ability to determine upon a path of action when there are a number of variables to consider. Moreover Alan has the intelligence—which is nothing less than Socratic wisdom—to know what he does not know.[4] The larger point, of course, is that Stevenson subverts the image of the uncivilized Highlander (implicit in the predatory cattle thief) and substitutes an alternative picture of an individual whose behavior is calculated and deliberate, one who might even be summed up, albeit ironically, in Alan's repeated declaration that he is a man of "penetration."

By far the most detailed and comprehensive view of the clan Macgregor comes through Stevenson's adaptation of the historical figure of James More Macgregor, the eldest son of Rob Roy. If Robert Macgregor appeared in one chapter in *Kidnapped,* James More covers virtually the last third of *David Balfour.* His presence is important for highlighting the legal and political issues that are at the center of the novel; and Stevenson's dramatization of the documented person is extremely revealing of the novelist's methods and aims in the construction of historical fiction. Of course, all the characters (with the exception of David Balfour) are historical, although some are documented minimally by their names. In the case of the Lord Advocate, Stevenson developed a portrait so skillful in its depth and dramatic intensity that it has been uniformly praised as one of the novelist's great legal creations, matched (or surpassed) only by the superb portrait of Lord Braxfield in *Weir of Hermiston.* In each case, Stevenson constructs the personality with fidelity to the historical context, shaping it to fit the dramatic requirements of the narrative. Clearly, he has sufficient material from a variety of primary and secondary sources to factually authenticate the fictional James Macgregor. But these details alone are not enough to capture the character or meaning of the historical person. Stevenson's challenge was not simply to ensure that everything that appeared in the novel had a documentary or factual basis; rather, it was to reconstruct the James Macgregor that lay behind the documents. He had to be true to history and yet remain faithful to fiction, preserving his right as a magus to recreate the dead in order to make the living aware of the past.

Stevenson builds his portrait deftly, using details like James More's formidable physical strength ("the size of the man, his great length of arm in which he came near rivalling his father" [*DB*, 27:355]) to confirm commonly known characteristics.[5] But this aspect of the man, as well as his touch of vanity (he wore "an extraordinary big laced hat" [*DB*, 25:326] and "shrugged his shoulders with a very French air" [*DB*, 25:327]), is not nearly so interesting as the personality with which he is invested. And here Stevenson composes a portrait that is both imaginative in its originality and faithful to its milieu. To begin with, he draws on a detail regarding James Macgregor that was highlighted in the *Blackwood's* article and that is reproduced at the end of *David Balfour*—his extreme poverty. In the following example, James has just reached the Netherlands and David invites him to stay with him as his guest. James More accepts:

> "Sir," said he, "when an offer is frankly made, I think I honour myself most to imitate that frankness. Your hand, Mr. David; you have the character that I respect the most; you are one of those from whom a gentleman can take a favour and no more words about it. I am an old soldier," he went on, looking rather disgusted-like around my chamber, "and you need not fear I shall prove burthensome. I have ate too often at a dyke-side, drank of the ditch, and had no roof but the rain" (*DB*, 25:333).

Stevenson here illustrates James's habit of dramatizing himself at every opportune occasion, particularly when he has something to gain. He is not merely in need of a bed and a roof; he is, rather, owed the hospitality, as if everyone were obliged to recognize his position and his status in the world. His casual use of the term "gentleman" (just as Robin Oig in *Kidnapped* walked about like a "gentleman in his walled policy") signifies the way he perceives himself and how he demands that others see him. His lack of money is a point of pride rather than a sign of humiliation: "I think no shame of a poverty I have come by in the service of my king" (*DB*, 25:332). He is conferring a privilege on David by deigning to accept the offer of room and board, even though the rooms are not what he is accustomed to consider worthy. But he insists upon his position as an "old soldier," and he calls up, for David's benefit, the hardships he has endured in the course of fighting for his country. The style with which he delivers himself becomes Stevenson's means for commenting on him, for calling attention to the paradoxical tone of self-servingness and obsequiousness that David finds it almost impossible to bear. An example:

> "But, my dear David, this world is a censorious place—as who should know it better than myself, who have lived ever since the days of my late departed father, God sain him! in a perfect spate of calumnies? We have to face to that; you and me have to consider of that; we have to consider of that." And he wagged his head like a minister in a pulpit (*DB*, 27:351).

James is determined to coerce David to marry Catriona, ostensibly because they have been living together in Leyden. So the color he puts on it is moral: the world is a hard, unforgiving place, and everybody is judged harshly. Therefore it is best to marry and put to rest any tongues that might censure the immorality of David's and Catriona's recent living arrangements. Again, the rhetoric is Stevenson's way of mocking the sentiment; and by likening him to a minister (who is nothing better than a trained dog) delivering a sermon that nobody listens to or takes seriously, he is even further undercut. But perhaps the most revealing point is James's claim that he is a victim of the world's slander. Not only has James borne the travails of the old soldier, but he claims that since the death of Rob Roy (and "late departed father" works as a trite phrase that mocks both the speaker as well as the idea) he has been at the mercy of the world's slanders. The truth, of course, is far different. James Macgregor was tried for the murder of James Maclaren, and he was convicted most recently for the abduction of Jean Key. In the Maclaren trial he was charged, with others, "as being notorious thieves and resetters of stolen goods . . . not as substantive charges under the indictment, but as matter of evidence with regard to the general character of the pannels" (*Sons*, cvi–cvii). In other words, he was a habitual thief who had no credibility when brought before the court on any specific criminal charge. When he says "I make no secret that my affairs are quite involved" (*DB*, 25:332) he states the closest thing to a truth that he is capable of. That the trials of James and Robert Macgregor were the occasion for their troubles goes without saying. But Stevenson is intent upon drawing his portrait of James as closely as he can to the historical figure—hence the details serve as spokes directed to the hub, which is the trial for the abduction of Jean Key—while creating a fictional character who reflects the curious combination of bombast, courage, and opportunism that the novelist stitched together from the documented materials. It is important to note that not all the documents share the same perspective of the Macgregors. But there is unanimity with respect to one fundamental trait. James is given the habit of a liar and double-dealer, and David is the voice who repeatedly sings this refrain: "I think he was so false all through that he scarce knew when he was lying" (*DB*, 26:345). For David, James's "swaggering" or "prating talk" (26:344), which he likened to the "babbling of a parrot" (26:344), was itself a kind of lying. Perhaps the most vivid description comes from Alan Breck: "The man's as boss as a drum; he's just a wame and a wheen words" (29:373–74). The word "boss" is good Scots for "empty," and it conveys the picture of a big man who is full up, drunk even, on his own talk. At the end—at his death—David finally says, "You know the man already, what there was to know of him; and I am weary of writing out his lies." (*DB*, 29:380)

Yet even if everything about James was a lie, David nonetheless finds something positive (if not quite redeeming) to say about him. He is "a caressing parent" (26:343), kissing his daughter "with a good deal of tenderness" (26:338), and he appears to David to exhibit some genuine "feeling" (26:346). On one level this is an example of Stevenson's fundamental belief (translated into artistic practice) that some trace of virtue can be found in even the worst of men, and as Macgregor's chief says at the end, "There are worse folk than James More, too" (*DB*, concl.:403).

But this is to get away from the main point. Stevenson has created a fictional character who is—as he was in real life—physically powerful and imposing. He has given him a voice and a personality that emphasizes a number of features: his swagger, his sense of pride in his name and his ancestry, and his total preoccupation with his own interests and needs. Yet he is a man who, despite his size, his strength and his prowess as a soldier (note the five wounds), is nonetheless without any control over his life. There is even a kind of pathos in the discrepancy between the size of the man and his powerlessness. We meet him first in the house of his enemy, Prestongrange, who was the prosecutor in the Jean Key trial. When he reappears in the second half of the novel he is dependent upon David's generosity for lodging, and David even supplies him with small sums to keep him in liquor at the tavern. And at the very end he is beseeching his chief for any small employment, as he lives in extreme poverty in exile in France. All these details about James Macgregor's last days are to be found (as we would now expect) in *Blackwood's,* and the incidents are, as we shall see, lifted from the article for the final chapters. At this point, however, we can say that James is at the mercy of forces he is unable to control or manipulate, and neither his strength nor his swagger can alter the conditions or the prospects of his life.

We will now turn to his daughter, Catriona Drummond, and see how she fits into the triangle that Stevenson constructs with James Macgregor and David Balfour. James More had five daughters, according to the *Blackwood's* piece, although no names were given for any. The most remarkable detail concerns his escape from Edinburgh Castle, where he was held while on trial for the abduction of Jean Key. To assist in his escape, his daughter dressed as a man and James Macgregor dressed as a woman (a ruse Prince Charles used in a famous incident). Stevenson lifted the idea of this forceful and bold act employed by a young woman and used it as one spark in his full-bodied portrait of Catriona Drummond. It is an episode that makes readers view her with unabashed admiration, or as Prestongrange said to David: "Is not this Highland maid a piece of a heroine?" (DB, 18:233) The fictional text treats the historical incident humorously, even though the Lord Advocate was hardly amused by the turn of events. He has just informed David that Catriona has helped her father escape: "But I think you would like to hear the details of the affair. I have received two versions: and the least official is the more full and far the more entertaining, being from the lively pen of my eldest daughter" (DB, 18:231). Prestongranges's note to David of "two versions" is Stevenson's quiet reminder to his reader that all accounts of historical events are subject to bias. Indeed, there is even a self-reflexive reference in the note. Stevenson is aware of at least two sources for the incident, although he knows quite well that the reader will assume Barbara Grant's lively letter to her father is invented (just as James More's escape from Edinburgh Castle was undoubtedly invented) and will, therefore, view the issue of alternative versions as nothing more than a bit of verisimilitude, a pretty piece of realism.[6] Self-reflexiveness, however, is an important theme in the novel—as is the issue of bias in the reporting of events—but for now it is sufficient to observe how Stevenson artistically and dramatically transforms the most casual of historical incidents beyond anything it possessed in its original documentary form. To look at the passages in *Blackwood's* and *Sons* and compare them with the inspired epistolary paragraph in "The Tee'd Ball" (DB, 18:231–33) is to recognize immediately the difference between a lifeless source and its rebirth as timeless fiction. But the selected incident is a part of the legal and political entanglement that was the Macgregors' history. However charming the presentation of the escape, delivered in Barbara Grant's delightful mode of expression, the fact of the episode was part of a political intrigue that involved deceit, betrayal, and even the prospect of political assassination. Stevenson draws on these elements later in the novel, but they are there from the beginning. In a sense, every incident that involves James Macgregor is by its nature a part of the politics and the law of the period—that is, insofar as it relates to the Macgregors and the government. It is perhaps not so apparent to the common reader that Prestongrange, as Lord Advocate, is quite simply the government prosecutor moving against all those figures the government deems pernicious and disruptive, in short its enemies, including James Macgregor and James Stewart. Stevenson has the uncanny ability to lift from the historical sources those incidents that have some inherent interest for dramatic purposes and refashion them in order to make them more entertaining for the reader. And yet, by their nature, the incidents are inherently representative of important political and legal issues of which the novelist is keenly aware. The procedure might almost be called subtextual or contextual. Stevenson knows the full significance of these matters—that is, the background and meaning of James Macgregor's escape from Edinburgh Castle, the jailers who became the scapegoats and were sacked or demoted, and the possibility that the escape, however managed by the daughter, was in fact orchestrated with the connivance of the government, who had other uses for James Macgregor. That this was so can be seen in the passage that Stevenson added after he received the galleys for the work. In response to Sidney Colvin's asking him to be clear, he supplies a paragraph in which David delivers an interpretation of James's escape: "It might please the authorities to give to it the colour of an escape; but I knew better—I knew it was the fulfilment of a bargain" (*DB*, 18:231). This entire paragraph of fifteen lines was a device to explain what James Macgregor's escape signified. Stevenson was so saturated with his knowledge of these events that he clearly lost sight of the fact that it was Greek to his readers. For them, the escape was simply a wonderful incident pulled off by the bonny lass, whom Preston-grange refers to (in a word applied to her father) as "this rogue of a Katrine—or Cateran, as we may call her" (*DB*, 18:230). (The play on her name calls up the image of a Highland brigand.) When he reviews the galleys in response to his literary overseer's comments he decides to elucidate the complex political intrigue that governs the incident. Whether the reader is aware that this explanation was indeed historical, and as close to the reality as it was possible to get, is quite beside the point. The novelist was unconcerned with that aspect of the reader's response. As long as the reader was held by the narrative and captivated by the suspense, the characterization, or even the style, then Stevenson was content. The deeper implications of the text remained. Its truth to history and law was unassailable, and that meaning would give it lasting value. We must never forget that Stevenson sustained a paradoxical or contradictory attitude with respect to his writing and his audience. He had the highest regard for his readers—in the sense that he believed he owed them a book that they wanted to read, that would give them pleasure—and he was always at pains to make everything he wrote serve the reader's interest. At the same time, he had a limited regard for his reader's ability to understand what fiction was about or to recognize anything beyond the surface story in a narrative. In a sense, Stevenson might even be said to have been disdainful of the average reader. But he never exhibited that attitude in the text itself. What I have called the subtextual or contextual meaning is, from one point of view, a kind of self-reflexivity. That is, its meaning is one Stevenson himself is aware of, and one he occasionally refers to in the course of the narrative, but it is not a meaning that the reader could be expected to know. It is simply unavailable on a surface reading of the novel. That it exists in the text, and that Stevenson places it there, is undeniable. The question of its retrieval, however, is the genuinely interesting one.

Stevenson uses the incident of James Macgregor's escape from Edinburgh Castle for specific ends. For historical purposes, he is determined to keep the record straight; for narrative purposes, he needs to effect the escape in order to bring James back for the dramatic final chapters; and for thematic purposes, he wants to deepen the character of Catriona Drummond, augmenting both her courage and her filial loyalty while at the same time highlighting David's love for her. The novelist runs so many things simultaneously that it is almost astonishing to separate them out: the use of Scots diction to distinguish Barbara Grant's style from the styleless prose of the periodical and *The Scots Magazine;* the wit and humor that are such hallmarks of Barbara's expression, and which serve as a means for characterization as well as a stylistic feature in its own right; and the ability to move an interpolated narrative forward (which is essentially what Barbara's letter is) without superfluous and retarding descriptions. Stevenson manipulates the documentary incident to create art while keeping faith with history.

In part 2 of *David Balfour,* during David and Catriona's voyage into Holland, when they are getting to know each other, Catriona delivers a two-page narrative of her life ("It is only a girl I am, and what can befall a girl at all events?" [*DB,* 21:275]) that is interesting both for the voice and the history.[7] Catriona begins her memoir with the rebellion ("I went with the clan in the year '45" [*DB,* 21:275]) and continues through the defeat and the pursuit of the rebels by Cumberland's soldiers: "It went what way you very well know; and these were the worst days of all, when the red-coat soldiers were out, and my father and my uncles lay in the hill, and I was to be carrying them their meat in the middle night, or at the short side of day when the cocks crow" (*DB,* 21:276). It is a narrative marked by its movement and vivacity, for Catriona is nothing if not a colorful narrator, who adds a touch of drama to every point; it is a narrative that mixes romance and folklore with history in much the same way, albeit without the humor, that Catriona mixed (and confused) the history of Scotland in an earlier colloquy with David. It is also a narrative delivered in a manner that stands in stark contrast with David's presentation of his own story, which he insists upon as nothing more than a "plain tale" (*DB,* 21:277), a point of view he maintains through the length and breadth of the novel. Of course, the contrast between vivid writing and the plain prose that David is committed to, or perhaps is capable of, is a central one in the text, just as it recurs in Stevenson's fiction throughout his career.[8]

For now we turn to a crucial segment of Catriona's personal narrative—her description of the Jean Key affair. I quote the passage in full:

"Next there was my uncle's marriage, and that was a dreadful affair beyond all. Jean Kay was that woman's name; and she had me in the room with her that night at Inversnaid, the night we took her from her friends in the old, ancient manner. She would and she wouldn't; she was for marrying Rob the one minute, and the next she would be for none of him. I will never have seen such a feckless creature of a woman; surely all there was of her would tell her ay or no. Well, she was a widow, and I can never be thinking a widow a good woman."

"Catriona!" says I, "how do you make out that?"

"I do not know," said she; "I am only telling you the seeming in my heart. And then to marry a new man! Fy! But that was her; and she was married again upon my Uncle Robin, and went with him awhile to kirk and market; and then wearied, or else her friends got claught of her and talked her round, or maybe she turned ashamed; at the least of it, she ran away, and went back to her own folk, and said we had held her in the lake, and I will never tell you all what. I have never thought much of any females since that day. And so in the end my father, James More, came to be cast in prison, and you know the rest of it as well as me." (*DB*, 21:276–77)

With this characteristically brisk and partisan description, Catriona brings forward one of the central episodes that lay just behind the visible pages of the novel—the forcible abduction of Jean Key and the subsequent trials of the Macgregor bothers for that and its associate crimes, including forcible marriage, rape, and hamesucken. Stevenson had first referred to this incident when he introduced Robin Oig in *Kidnapped*: "He was sought upon all sides on a charge of carrying a young woman from Balfron and marrying her (as was alleged) by force" (*K*, 25:226). In that chapter, neither the name of the woman nor the details of the episode were divulged (although we see in the quoted sentence how precisely Stevenson inserted two of the formal Scottish criminal charges). All the reader learned was that Robin was hanged—the reasons for the hanging were never disclosed. In *David Balfour*, however, with James Macgregor a major character and Robin a mere passing reference (as befits their respective historical roles in the episode), the crime and its implications (or meaning) occupy a larger part of the text. Stevenson utilized a minor historical incident the significance of which proved greater than the incident itself, although there is no question that the actual events were as painful as they were tragic. The Macgregor trials served a variety of purposes for Stevenson's study of Scottish history: they contained all the ingredients of a sensational drama; they revealed much about the character of domestic and social life in the Highlands; and they illustrated the roles played by government and politics in the manipulation of the law. On the most profound level, however, the trials of the Macgregors, and of James Stewart, symbolized the complete subjugation of the Highlanders that formally had been achieved by their military defeat at Culloden. Unlike the treason trials immediately after Culloden, these were ostensibly criminal as opposed to political in their motivation and juris-diction. But as Stevenson demonstrates, they were at bottom political, and their motives were parallel with those that convicted Balmorino and Lovat for their parts in the rebellion.

Before turning to the actual circumstances of the Jean Key affair, it is worth noting how deeply ingrained its traces became in Scottish history, which is replete with partisan interpretations and misrememberings. It is cited in the *Blackwood's* memoir of Rob Roy, which is marked by a bias wholly on the side of the brothers and even more defensive of Robert Macgregor than Catriona Drummond:

> [Robin Oig] was arraigned for having carried away, by force, a young widow, who had voluntarily eloped with him and became his wife; and although she declared this to be true, he was taken, at a market in his own country, by a party of soldiers from Inversnaid, carried to Edinburgh, where he was con-demned, and executed on the 6th of February 1745 [*sic*] three years after his wife's death.[9]

The affair even shows up as local history in a geographical dictionary of Scotland under the place-names Balfron ("Edinbellie was the scene of the forcible abduc-tion of Jean Key [Dec. 3, 1750] by Rob Roy's sons, for which Robin Oig, the prin-cipal, was three years after hanged at Edinburgh") and Balquhidder ("Robin Oig, Rob's fifth and youngest son, here wedded the widow whom he had ravished . . . and hither three years later his corpse, after execution, was brought by a large company of sorrowing kinsfolk").[10] But aside from the absorption of dubious nar-ratives into local legend and folklore, not unlike the history of Rob Roy, the most profound legacy of the Jean Key affair can be found in the area of legal history, where the trials of James and Robert Macgregor were cited regularly as illustra-tions and precedents in Scottish criminal law.[11]

Catriona Drummond's description of the episode exhibits the liveliness and directness that we would expect from her character; at the same time, on Steven-son's part, it is a deliberate summation and compression of an extraordinarily complex sequence of events. Obviously, Catriona's tale retains the bias of the Macgregors, as she assumes the viewpoint of her uncle, if not indeed of her father; but in her brief telling of the story she reproduces, in miniature, the disputes over fact and interpretation that are reflected in the actual trials themselves. In the process, she becomes the unwitting counter for Stevensons' more probing argu-ment on the nature of truth as it is revealed (or mis-revealed) in the course of sub-jective reporting.

But let us look first at Catriona's narrative: "[Jean Key] had me in the room with her that night at Inversnaid, the night we took her from her friends in the old, ancient manner. She would and she wouldn't; she was for marrying Rob the one minute, and the next she would be for none of him." The phrase "the old, ancient manner" refers to forcible abduction, one of the crimes listed in the indictment against James and Robert Macgregor. Catriona's phrasing softens the harsh reality of the formal charge and gives it a kind of dignity, as if the practice were one that time and custom had smoothed into a lofty ritual, one that almost conferred a virtue on its practitioners. Furthermore, if the forcible abduction was accompanied by a (forced) marriage—which was often the cause for the abduction in the first place, and which was indeed the case with Jean Key and Robert Macgregor—then everybody would live happily ever after. The reality, of course, was quite different. Stevenson was well aware of the criminal law and the social history with respect to these practices. In one sense, Catriona's phrase was an innocent reflection of a particular kind of attitude in the Highlands, one that Sir Walter Scott tried to place in the context of Highland history, after citing the famous case of Simon Fraser's notorious rape-marriage of the dowager of the Lovat estate.

> Even in ordinary cases, the bride was expected to affect some reluctance; and the greater or less degree of violence did not, in these wild times, appear a matter of much consequence. The Scottish law-books are crowded with instances of this sort of *raptus,* or, as it is called in their law, "*forcible abduction of women.*" . . . And we remember a woman on the banks of Loch Lomond, herself the daughter of such a marriage, who repelled, with great contempt, the idea of its being a real grievance on the bride, and said that, in her time, the happiest matches were always so made.[12]

In the introduction to *Sons,* the Simon Fraser incident is also the occasion for addressing the question.

> It has been contended in palliation of this frightful outrage, that the *forcible abduction,* as it is called, of women, was in these times a crime of almost daily occurrence; and that the records of Scottish criminal jurisprudence are filled with discussions on this odious breach of the laws. . . . The alleged frequency of such legal discussions, while it may shew the turbulent and unprincipled character of a part of the population, proves no less distinctly the horror with which their crimes were viewed, and the jealousy with which they were avenged by the laws (xxxiii–xxxiv).

It is important to reiterate that forcible marriage was tantamount to rape, and that forcible abduction and marriage were often cited together, although (as in the case against the Macgregors) they constituted separate charges in a criminal indictment. Hume describes the offense: "Forcible abduction and marriage . . . is alleged to have been the proper *crimen raptus* of the Roman law, and to have been punished with death, even when it was not attended with a violation of the woman's person. . . . Indeed the abduction must ordinarily have been accompanied with a rape, which could not be the less criminal for having taken place under the pretence of a marriage."[13] And Alison: "Forcible abduction and marriage constitute a crime punishable with the highest arbitrary pains. . . . In the case of the Macgregors, July 1752, forcible abduction and marriage were charged along with other offences of a capital nature." Alison further states that "The offence of abduction, if committed without any intention of marriage or rape, belongs to another class of crimes."[14]

What is the significance of all this law? Obviously, it is crucial to Stevenson's text. James Macgregor decided that Jean Key, a young widow with a small fortune, would make a suitable wife for his brother. That she neither knew the Macgregors nor cared to be connected with them, that she had been widowed only two months, was of no consequence to James More, who was later viewed as the principal behind the action rather than Robert, who was (apparently) a willing agent but not nearly so determined as his older brother. The Macgregors, along with other men, broke into Jean Key's house on a winter's night, terrorized her mother and family, and violently carried her away. According to one witness, James Macgregor "spoke in the Irish language, the deponent does not know what it was, but immediately after the three men, mentioned to have been in the room, laid hold of her, and carried her off, putting her head over a man's shoulder, and her feet as high at least as her head: That they carried her off when she was shrieking and crying like a woman in labour" (*Sons*, 62). She was thrown over the pommel of a horse, and removed to a village called Ruindennan in the Macgregors' fastness in the country of Balquhidder. This brief description does not begin to convey the sense of terror that comes through the testimony delivered by the witnesses for the government. The "cries and shrieks" (*Sons*, 36) emitted by Jean Key in her house were only the audible signs of an experience that would affect her mind and, in the end, destroy her body.

The story continued with enormous complication and great pain. In order to secure her inheritance, the motive behind the abduction ("Here is Rob, my brother, a young fellow that wants to push his fortune" [*Sons*, 62]), it was essential for Robert Macgregor to marry her. So Jean "was led or brought into a house, and held by the waist by the pannel [James Macgregor] until a man pronounced some words without any questions asked at her, or consent given, which they called a marriage" (*Sons*, 63). It only remained to consummate the form. Annabell Mitchell, a witness for the prosecution, testified to what she saw and what Jean Key told her:

That that night she told the deponent, they had married her, and bedded her before the deponent came: But the night was so bad, and Jean Key was so distressed, that they could not stay long without doors. Depones, That after they came into the house, there were two women who took off her cloaths, and put her again to bed, which women the deponent did not know. Depones, That the deponent in going to her bed, was obliged to pass by the said Jean Key's bed, and then saw Robert Campbell, the pannel's brother, in naked bed with her (*Sons*, 37–38).

In the trial of Robert Macgregor the ceremony was described as follows: "That when the pretended marriage was celebrated at Ruindennan, in the Highlands, James, the pannel's brother, held her by the middle, while one, who called himself Smith, said some words over them, and then declared them married persons; . . . That thereafter, the said James and two women got her into a room with them, pulled off her clothes, flung her into bed, and then put in Robert to her" (*Sons*, 176–77).

This is merely to abstract the abduction and the marriage. It does not convey the fright experienced by the members of Jean Key's household, the threats by the Macgregors to "make doors of the windows" (*Sons*, 42), the swords and pistols and dirks they carried with them, the lamentation and wailing of the young woman— in short, the bare experience of suddenly being helpless and in the power of men who care nothing about using arbitrary violence in order to achieve their ends. The shock of the attack was all the more traumatic because it was so unexpected. Jean Key "could not imagine the M'Gregors would attempt any thing lawless . . . being now subdued by the laws" (*Sons*, 59). In a real sense, the boldness of the act was all the more dramatic because of the latent belief that behavior of that type was no longer possible, that the laws had eliminated that kind of lawlessness. Unfortunately, Jean Key was wrong. She was abducted forcefully and abused physically—suffering "a blue mark, or contusion on her arm . . . when they were putting her upon the horse" (*Sons*, 38)—and thrown into a room where she was undressed and put to bed for Robert Macgregor. It is interesting to see how Stevenson places Catriona Drummond in the bedroom, just as the trial records the testimony of women who were there, took off Jean Key's clothes, and put her to bed. This simply indicates the novelist's veracity in the general accounting of events. Two of the witnesses for the defense were Agnes and Mary M'Alpine, a mother and a daughter whose names identified them as Macgregors and aligned them with the pannel (James Macgregor). Thus Stevenson transfers the thrust of the historical figures' testimony to his fictional creation, Catriona, who is a member of the same clan. Agnes M'Alpine testified that "Jean Key having taken off her own clothes without any assistance from those present, was put to bed: That the deponent, with the above mentioned two ladies took Jean Key's clothes from her as she threw them off, and laid them by" (*Sons*, 68). The daughter, Mary M'Alpine, testified even more dramatically: "That Robert Campbell and Jean Key were sitting by one another; and Jean Key had her hand about his neck, and he his hand on her breast: That Jean Key seemed to be in very good humour, and no way displeased, but very merry" (*Sons,* 72–73). And Mary M'Illeaster, "*alias* M'Gregor," testified "she saw Jean Key go to bed, and which she appeared to do with as great willingness as any woman ever she saw: That she herself threw off her clothes . . . That after the said Jean Key was in bed, she saw Robert Campbell, the pannel, and some other gentlemen, come into the room, and throw off his clothes, and go to bed to the said Jean Key: . . . That the said Jean, about the usual time of going to bed, turned drowsy and fell asleep, leaning her head upon the said Robert Campbell, who at the same time had his hand upon her breast" (*Sons,* 76).

And so Stevenson has Catriona saying, "She would and she wouldn't; she was for marrying Rob the one minute, and the next she would be for none of him. I will never have seen such a feckless creature of a woman; surely all there was of her would tell her ay or no." With these two sentences Stevenson conflates the two opposing sides of the issue as they were presented at the trial. For the government, the marriage was forced and the woman had no control over it. Her clothes were taken off her by the attending women, and she was put to bed to await the pleasure of Robert Macgregor. For the defendants, Jean Key "was willing to adhere to her marriage with Robert Campbell, which was voluntary, and not forced" (*Sons,* 91). In effect, this last point became the key to their argument. If they had indeed abducted her, which they did not admit, and if they had conducted a marriage by force, which they also denied, it was still the case that after the fact Jean Key had agreed to "adhere"—the term appears repeatedly—to her husband. Thus a substantial portion of the testimony turned on whether she was forcibly married or whether she consented to the marriage, whether she was physically taken to bed or whether she went voluntarily to enjoy her own pleasure. From a reader's point of view, the trial record is an instructive picture of how one story can be presented through two completely different lenses, with two alternative perspectives—hence Catriona's confusion about Jean Key. The fictional character, supporting the position of the historical defendants, can make neither head nor tail of the entire situation. Her recourse was to call Jean Key "feckless" and attribute this fecklessness all to widowhood ("well, she was a widow, and I can never be thinking a widow a good woman"). Widows cannot be expected to be like maids—loyal and virtuous—presumably because they are sexually knowledgeable. Indeed, there is even a revulsion at the idea of sex with someone else ("And then to marry a new man! Fy!"). That, ironically, was Jean Key's own position, since she had been widowed only two months. In a curious way, Stevenson has shifted to the fictional Catriona the historical woman's unwillingness to enter into a new and unwanted sexual liaison. However, David finds wanting in logic the argument that a widow cannot be a good woman. So Catriona resorts to intuition: "I am only telling you the seeming in my heart." And with "seeming" Catriona reflects another feature of the trial record. Part of the defense strategy, particularly in Robert Macgregor's trial, was to argue that the entire abduction was a staged event, a conspiracy between Robert Macgregor and Jean Key to circumvent her mother's opposition to their proposed marriage. Therefore, "Jean Key was seemingly to oppose and resist, in order to deceive and impose upon her mother," and "Robert Campbell . . . should seemingly carry her off by force" (*Sons,* 230). In other words, the appearance of things was not the reality. Indeed, it was precisely the opposite.

From this point on, Catriona delivers a compressed summary of the rest of the events: how Jean Key was seen publicly with Robert Macgregor in order to present the appearance of a married couple; how she then "wearied" of the marriage or else was persuaded or reclaimed by her family and friends; and how, eventually, she declared that the Macgregors had held her captive "in the lake" (in *Sons* "she was held in bondage" [226]). Finally, as she tells David while wrapping up her small story, James More "came to be cast in prison, and you know the rest of it as well as me." We have come full circle, in a manner of speaking, because early in the novel, David met James More in the Advocate's house. But we are not completely caught up. For Catriona's summary is just that, a summary that conflates a number of crucial elements of a story that became even more complicated after the abduction and marriage. Although Jean Key's family attempted to secure her release by force, the law was unable to bring the Macgregors in from their country fastness. The family then obtained a "sequestration" of Jean Key's property from the Court of Session in Edinburgh. This effectively meant that all her assets were frozen. To counter this move, the Macgregors (through a "memorial") insisted that Jean Key "was under no constraint, and was willing to adhere to her marriage", and therefore the "sequestration of her estate and effects" should be removed (*Sons,* 91, 90). They even produced a document—a letter written and signed by Jean Key—attesting not only to her acquiescence but to her complicity in the abduction and marriage. The judges interviewed Jean Key privately, to determine whether she had voluntarily signed the document or whether she had been coerced into it. They decided to place Jean Key under the protection of friends (or as Catriona says, "Her friends got claught of her and talked her round"), and she then proceeded to retract the document which was written under duress (and only after the Macgregors discovered she could in fact write).

James More was captured first and put on trial. The complications (or complexity) of the case can be seen in the verdict. The jury declared "not proven" on the charges of forcible marriage and rape, and "proven" on the charges of hamesucken (or attacking, invading, and laying violent hands upon Jean Key) and forcible abduction. The jury also declared that Jean Key "did afterwards acquiesce in her condition," which was saying, in effect, that she had agreed to the marriage after the fact. David Hume states that in rape cases there must be resistance to the last, "so that it is by main force only and terror that the violation is accomplished. It was probably on this ground, that the jury acquitted of that part of the charge in the case of James Macgregor; while they found him guilty of the hamesucken and forcible abduction" (1:302). In the subsequent trial of Robert Macgregor, he was found guilty, "art and part, of entering with other lawless people armed, the house of Edinbelly . . . and in a forcible and hostile manner, within the said house, did attack, invade, and lay violent hands upon the person of the said Jean Key" (*Sons,* 205). In short, they were both acquitted of the forcible marriage and rape charges, and convicted of forcible entry and forcible abduction. In either case, the crime of hamesucken was a capital crime, and Robert Macgregor was hanged for it. There were extensive arguments by the defense as to whether or not hamesucken should be considered a capital crime, and the jury in Robert Macgregor's case went so far as to recommend to the judges that it not be considered capital, in order to save him from hanging. The judges rejected the jury's recommendation out of hand and delivered a stern rebuke on their interference in the judicial procedure.[15] Robert Macgregor was hanged, and as David Balfour says in *Kidnapped,* the rest is, in a manner, history.

There are aspects of this trial that cannot fail to have appealed to Stevenson quite apart from the trial's crucial importance in the history of post-Culloden Scotland: the isolation of a family in the wild; the nighttime setting; the violence and terror; the whole element of surprise and danger so threatening to a helpless young woman; the Macgregors rushing; "Glengyle in the muir with 100 men"; the physical abduction; Jean Key traumatized, almost driven out of her mind. And yet, at the same time, there are details that remind us of the mundane and ordinary: carrying Jean Key into the boat to prevent her feet from getting wet and letting her go into the fields to talk with Annabel Mitchell. There is a spareness to the details that is dramatic, even touching: "Jeany, come out"; "Don't you know your own daughter?"; "We are not come to rob your house." Stevenson emulates much of that homely or unaffected detail in his own style. It is a quiet, unobtrusive manner that stands in stark contrast with the barren, almost unadorned narrative that constitutes the trial. The small (and large) details in the trials are the perfect embodiment for Stevenson's fiction. They are both reality and adventure, the materials of past life heightened by the narrative mode, the eyewitness accounts of ordinary people testifying to extraordinary events, the drama emerging from their unmediated description of those events.

It remains to turn now to Stevenson's most imaginative and brilliant application of the Jean Key affair in *David Balfour.* During the voyage to Holland, in the second part of the novel, David assumed the role of protector to Catriona, who was virtually penniless and completely on her own. David secured their lodging in Leyden, and they both lived under the same roof, presenting themselves as brother and sister. Needless to say, there are suggestive implications in this turn of events, although the simplest and least controversial observation is that this sequence of chapters constitutes one of the most charming love stories in nineteenth-century fiction. Nevertheless, the condition of an unmarried young man living together with an unmarried woman under the same roof could hardly fail to raise questions. Indeed, David himself calls attention to those questions. Further, the device of having David buy Catriona new clothes—and her wearing them or not, depending upon the state of their friendship—introduces both an erotic note and a speculative inquiry on sex and on women as property.

For the moment, however, the central issue is the nature of the relationship between David and Catriona and how James More attempts to manipulate it. After his arrival in Leyden, where he was treated hospitably by David and invited to share his lodgings, it occurred to James More that something could be made of the fact that David and his daughter shared the same quarters. As a good father, therefore, he proposed to protect Catrona's reputation (a decision that followed naturally upon his discovery that David had come into an inheritance): "My daughter stands beyond doubt. So do you, and I would make that good with my sword against all gainsayers. But, my dear David, this world is a censorious place—as who should know it better than myself, who have lived ever since the days of my late departed father, God sain him! in a perfect spate of calumnies? We have to face to that; you and me have to consider of that; we have to consider of that" (*DB*, 27:350). Since David refuses to be taken in by James's sententiousness, the soldier drops all pretense and (asserting the compromised position of his daughter) lets David know precisely what his options are: "'Why, sir,' says he, 'I think I need scarce describe them to a gentleman of your condition; either that I should cut your throat or that you should marry my daughter'" (*DB*, 27:352). David is in love with Catriona, but he is convinced she does not feel the same for him: "I have told you that, upon my side, there is no objection to the marriage, but I have good reason to believe there will be much on the young lady's" (*DB*, 27:353). And, at precisely this point, we can see just how closely Stevenson fitted the Macgregor trials into the structure of his text:

"This is all beside the mark," says he. "I will engage for her acceptance."

"I think you forget, Mr. Drummond," said I, "that, even in dealing with myself you have been betrayed into two-three unpalatable expressions. I will have none such employed to the young lady. I am here to speak and think for the two of us; and I give you to understand that I would no more let a wife be forced upon myself, than what I would let a husband be forced on the young lady. . . . I will marry Miss Drummond, and that blythely, if she is entirely willing. But if there be the least unwillingness, as I have reason to fear—marry her will I never" (*DB,* 27:353–54).

The point is continued in the following chapter, when David confronts Catriona —who has called him a coward—and reveals what transpired between himself and her father:

> "He was to make you take me," I replied, "and I would not have it. I said you should be free, and I must speak with you alone; little I supposed it would be such a speaking! *'And what if I refuse?'* says he.——*'Then it must come to the throat cutting,'* says I, *'for I will no more have a husband forced on that young lady than what I would have a wife forced upon myself.'* These were my words, they were a friend's words; bonnily have I been paid for them! Now you have refused me of your own clear free will, and there lives no father in the Highlands, or out of them, that can force on this marriage" (*DB,* 28:362–63).

In these two paragraphs, and indeed in the scenes of which they form a part, Stevenson has folded in the central theme of the Jean Key affair. James More plays the same role in the fictional text that he acted in the historical drama. He is the principal agent behind a marriage for money, determined to coerce David into marrying Catriona just as he had spurred his brother Robert to the abduction and marriage of Jean Key.[16] The fictional situation replicates in its outline and language the criminal character of the historical incident. David repeatedly rejects the idea of a forced marriage for Catriona and insists instead upon the principle of free will, on her right to choose her husband rather than having one forced on her. His plea has both a fictional and a historical resonance. It is the dramatic declaration of a devoted lover, and at the same time it is a passionate defense and vindication for a wronged woman. Forcible marriage, as I said earlier, was a crime of rape (in Alison and Hume its description comes under that heading). The definition is clear and unambiguous: "The crime of rape . . . consists in the forcible carnal knowledge of a woman's person against her will" (Alison, 209). "The knowledge of the woman's person must be against her will, and by force" (Hume, 1:302). In the information provided by the government in the Macgregor trial, the phrase is virtually a refrain: "without her consent and against her will, and then, under colour of consummating that forced marriage, concurred together in causing her chastity to be violated by Robert M'Gregor" (*Sons,* 218–19). Or, "being guilty of the impious profanation of [marriage] by causing the form of it to be celebrated against the will, and without the consent of the woman" (*Sons,* 219). The question, put simply and pointedly, was "whether Jean Key was carried from her own house, married to Robert M'Gregor, and detained some weeks in his possession by force and compulsion . . . or freely and of her own choice" (*Sons,* 225).

In David's defense of Catriona's right to choose her own husband, and in his rejection of James More's scheme to force a marriage upon her, Stevenson not only reenacts the historical drama that served him so well, but he memorializes the forgotten woman who had no choice and who paid the highest penalty for her helplessness. In the legal and historical accounts of the Macgregor trials the figure of Jean Key was invariably subsumed under complex legal issues of guilt and punishment, of responsibility and complicity, even of clan culture and history. It is only in the actual trial documents that the tragedy of the real woman emerges, a tragedy best comprehended by an artistic genius who was also an acute legal scholar. Stevenson did not attempt to recreate the person of Jean Key; rather, he represented the condition that she was compelled to experience, of being forced to marry against her will. In a larger sense, he recreated and recalled within the fictional text the broad historical experience of *abduction* (the cognate terms used in the novel are "kidnapped" and "trepanned") that formed such a prominent part of Scottish life—and not just Highland life—in the eighteenth century. In the final chapter of *David Balfour,* for example, after James More has been thwarted from his mission of capturing Alan Breck Stewart for the government, a mission which would have enabled him to buy his freedom (he was still under conviction for the Jean Key affair), David Balfour acknowledges that Catriona has been separated from James More: "We had taken a daughter from her father at the sword's point; any judge would give her back to him at once, and by all likelihood clap me and Alan into jail" (*DB,* concl.:402).[17] Stevenson is not writing idly here:

> By the statute 9th George IV. C. 31, 20, it is declared, "That if any person shall unlawfully take, or cause to be taken, any unmarried girl, being under the age of sixteen years, out of the possession, and against the will of her father or mother, or of any other person having the lawful care or charge of her," he shall be punished with fine, imprisonment, or both (Alison, 226).

That Catriona is better off without her father, that he leveled a curse at her (censored from all the printed versions of the novel) when he was bested by Alan, that he was no better than a rogue—all these things are beside the point. Abduction is abduction, and both novels are vitally concerned with the issue. To take a more complex example, there are three references in *David Balfour* to the notorious abduction and imprisonment of Lady Grange on the distant western island of St. Kilda, an incident that Stevenson mirrors in the kidnapping and sequestration of David Balfour on the Bass Rock: "Ye're not to be tried then, and ye're not to be murdered; but I'm in bitter error if ye're not to be kidnapped and carried away like the Lady Grange" (*DB,* 9:111). One theory of the Lady Grange affair held that she was abducted for political reasons, because she possessed "certain secrets" that could compromise her husband and his friends by revealing their Jacobite associations.[18] David was also held against his will by agents for the government, whose motive was to prevent him from testifying for the defendant (James Stewart) at a trial which was criminal in form but fundamentally political in meaning.

And in the same way, the trials of the Macgregors were criminal in their indictments but profoundly political in their implications. At the conclusion of James Macgregor's trial, the government information referred to it as "a case of great importance . . . brought to vindicate . . . one of the most atrocious and scandalous violations of the public peace" (*Sons,* 242). It was a case brought against the "most barbarous of the tribe of M'Gregor" and the "enormities practised by the unruly part of that tribe" (*Sons,* 242). The government document called attention to the country of the Macgregors, "the mountains, lochs, and woods" where they managed to avoid the authority of the law, which was really the authority of the government. As the Macgregors were historically among the most notorious and visible of the clans, so the crime against Jean Key provided a convenient opportunity to strike a definitive blow against everything that the clans represented— their allegiance to nothing and nobody apart from their own members, their disdain for both the boundaries and the orderliness of Lowlanders, and their habit and willingness to operate according to their own set of laws, which amounted of course to nothing more than lawlessness. If they could maintain their autonomy and defiance before the rebellion, however, the situation after Culloden was quite different. The government in London simply would not tolerate it. We have already seen how Stevenson deployed the anti-Highland legislation in *Kidnapped;* in the second volume he focused on the way even criminal law could be used as political weapons. There is no question that the indictments directed against the Macgregors were targeted at a people considered both subversive and dangerous, a people whose criminal behavior was either misunderstood or translated into political terms. Yet the legal writers never raised the issue of politics in their citations of the Macgregor trials. For Maclaurin, Hume, Alison, and Burnett, the cases were of interest only insofar as they illustrated legal issues pertaining to the crimes of abduction, forcible marriage, and hamesucken, and to the question of the penalties (or punishments) applied to the pannels.

Stevenson's view was far broader and more deeply historical. As an example, he utilized the details about James More's role as a spy for the British government, and of his arrangement with Lord Holderness to capture Stewart and return him to Britain to stand trial for the murder of Colin Campbell. This entire episode, played out in the final chapters of *David Balfour* and drawn extensively from the *Blackwood's* article, was nothing if not political. Indeed, even the escape from Edinburgh Castle, which gave Barbara Grant such amusement, was believed to have been a setup by the government in order to enable James More to pursue Alan

Breck, whom the government considered its primary political enemy. What was in it for James was clear enough. He would be absolved from the conviction for the Jean Key affair, and clemency might be possible for his brother Robert. Of course, as we discover in Stevenson's accurate and telling detail, James failed and shortly after died in abject poverty in France, a bathetic end which nonetheless symbolized the final defeat of the clan system, if not Highland culture, as an autonomous and distinctive entity. But if the end was inevitable, it was still ambiguous, for in a strange way James More retained an attraction in the midst of his mawkish sentiment, playing his Highland pipes and singing his melancholy tunes: "But the notes of this singing are in my blood, and the words come out of my heart. And when I mind upon my red mountains and the wild birds calling there, and the brave streams of water running down, I would scarce think shame to weep before my enemies" (*DB,* 26:344). The image of the Highlander as poet, eulogizing the beauty of the landscape and memorializing the stories of the people in their own language, attaches itself to James, as it did earlier to Alan Breck, and later to Robert Macgregor playing the pipes in Balquhidder. We might recall that when David Balfour gave himself over to memories he too was prone to weeping—for his lost father, for lost friendships, perhaps even for lost innocence. In James More, Stevenson concentrated a historical culture that was both cruel and lovely, one in which pride and lawlessness contained the seeds of the culture's demise, yet one in which the primary values were love of family and country. That the Macgregors were unable to recognize the discrepancy between their beliefs and their behavior goes without saying. James Macgregor could see no contradiction between his brother's happiness and the abduction of an innocent woman to secure that happiness. Nor could he see a contradiction between his love for Catriona and directing her into David's arms. In a sense, the Macgregors were merely actors in a historical drama they dimly understood and over which they had no control. It fell to Stevenson, writing long after the events and blessed with the twin talents of the scholar and artist, to recover that drama and refigure its design.

Chapter 7

THE APPIN MURDER

This murder has been visibly the effect and consequence of the late rebellion.
—Lord Justice-General to James Stewart

This murder seems to be a complication of all guilt.
—Robert Mackintosh,
Counsel for James Stewart

Early in 1894, less than a year before Stevenson's death, when Sidney Colvin and Charles Baxter were planning the first collected edition of his work, the novelist proposed a series of prefaces for the projected volumes. He had already written a piece on *Treasure Island* (misleadingly titled "My First Book") for the inaugural issue of S. S. McClure's new magazine. Despite his unwillingness to write essays anymore, his mastery of the form was undisputed.[1] But the originality of his literary criticism was never clearly and universally recognized. Partly, this was because much of it appeared informally in letters to stimulating and encouraging correspondents like Henry James or to close and imperceptive ones like Sidney Colvin. Stevenson's comments on his own work survive solely in his letters, for he never wrote about himself for public consumption. "A Gossip on Romance" or "A Humble Remonstrance" might be considered covert defenses of his fiction. But short of acknowledging that all writers' manifestoes are apologias for their work, the central point is indisputable: Stevenson's published essays (with the exception of the *Treasure Island* piece) are not directly concerned with his own work—all the more reason to regret the absence of finished prefaces to his major texts. It could be argued that Stevenson's habits precluded the composition of these prefaces, that the existence of a fragmentary note to *The Master of Ballantrae* only confirms the belief that Stevenson had a tendency to begin more projects than he could complete. This is an old argument, and there are sufficient examples to demonstrate the point. Yet it is equally the case that Stevenson's passing remarks on his own texts often serve as iconic statements about fictional art. His assertion that a short story is a complete whole, whose end comes out of the beginning and cannot be suddenly or arbitrarily altered, is a remark frequently cited in commentaries on the short story and one that emerged from Stevenson's comments on "The Beach of Falesá." His remark on "Thrawn Janet" in a letter to Lady Taylor, the dedicatee of *The Merry Men and Other Tales and Fables,* is another case in point. Although the story is commonly considered one of his masterful achievements, he wonders whether it might not possess a purely local significance, and thus be limited in its appeal and ultimately its meaning. He raises questions about the fable as a form that exhibits an imagination working to define both the meaning and utility of the artistic vehicle as well as the nature of the content. Again, the issues are introduced in the context of his own reflections on the stories he was collecting for publication. The point is quite simple: Stevenson was one of the most acute theorists about the nature of fictional art in the last quarter of the nineteenth century. It is not mere chance that his volume of letters to Henry James constitutes one of the most illuminating discourses on the nature of fiction in the period. Stevenson was an inveterate experimenter in fictional form, and James was his most intimate confrère. It is especially lamentable that Sidney Colvin objected so strenuously to the idea of prefaces for the Edinburgh Edition (Swearingen, *The Prose Writings of Robert Louis Stevenson,* 193), because Stevenson could be extraordinarily revealing about his own work, especially work done in the past. Unlike James's later prefaces to the New York edition, which were models of indirection and implication, the Scots writer brought the same clarity and directness to his recollection of the genesis of the work as he did to the art itself. Moreover, with *Kidnapped* and *David Balfour* Stevenson was in the world of his great forebear, Sir Walter Scott—the world of Scottish history—and he was obliged, if not constrained, to commit himself to serious questions about the origins of the text in historical reality as well as any questions about the nature of the text's meaning as fictional art. In effect, the nature of the fictional text determined the composition of the preface. Stevenson was acutely aware of Scott's enormous effort in constructing his notes to the Waverley novels, notes that modern readers might incline away from. But if he was half-serious in his suggestion to Burlingame that he compose introductions and notes to a selection of his own texts, when he did compose a note to *Kidnapped* he was completely serious. For one thing, Stevenson knew that *Kidnapped* and *David Balfour* were, combined, his single greatest achievement. They stood apart from the totality of his work, apart from the individual brilliance of a short story or essay or poem. Partly, the achievement was a function of the historical importance of the material and, partly, it was a function of the originality and brilliance of Stevenson's execution. In any case, when he began his "Note to Kidnapped" he did not engage in the kind of deception that characterized the dedication to Charles Baxter in the first printed book edition. For just as David Balfour was impelled to tell the story of Robin Oig because, as he said, the man came to be hanged, so was Stevenson determined to tell the story of *Kidnapped* because it, too, was in a manner history.

As he tells us in the opening sentence of his "Note to *Kidnapped,*" Stevenson had prepared himself to write a history of the Highlands "from the Union to the Present day; social, literary, economical and religious, embracing the 15, the 45, the collapse of the clan system, and the causes and the growth of existing discontents." Fourteen years earlier his letters had provided a prospectus as broad in scope as it was detailed in coverage. Now, looking back over those years, he implicitly acknowledged the futility of this ambition and "bequeathed" the project "to a more qualified successor; I was myself debarred by the difficulties of the Gaelic language, and the state of my health which made me an exile from my native country; but I desisted with regret, having grown more and more convinced of the utility and interest of the work." The genesis of Stevenson's epic thus lay in a rich contextual world of language and history and culture, and his immense preparation for a social, political, and cultural history of Scotland had not been at all in vain.

> It was in the course of these Highland studies that I bought, in the city of Inverness, the printed trial of James Stewart, bound up with a critical examination of the evidence; I suppose the volume cost me a few shillings, and has proved certainly the best of my investments. I was taken with the tale from the beginning; no one so dull, but must have been struck with the picturesque details; no one at all acquainted with the Highlands, but must have recognised in this tragedy something highly typical of the place and time. Agrarian crime in Scotland had a color of antique and disinterested virtue; it was in the cause of the exiled chief, not of the tenant, it was for another, not for himself, that the murderer acted. Hence a part of the pleasure with which I considered this old trial; hence, I determined to found upon it a narrative of fact; and hence, in order to make certain of my local colour, I visited Appin in the early summer of 1880.[2]

Stevenson publicly acknowledged his indebtedness to the printed trial in the dedication to *Kidnapped,* and he did so privately in a late letter to Sidney Colvin, saying that he should have had the volume bound in velvet and gold for all the riches he derived from it (*L,* 8:160). Stevenson's note is like any writer's retrospective view of an earlier composition, recollected in tranquillity eight years after the fact. But he continued to use the printed trial during the composition of *David Balfour,* which was published in book form less than a year before he wrote the note. Although on one level the printed document is nothing more than the proceedings of a trial for murder, Stevenson immediately saw it as emblematic of his Highland studies. "For a long time after the Rebellion the state of the Highlands continued to be a source of grave anxiety to the Government. The strength of the Jacobites had been thoroughly broken at Culloden; but the baneful spirit of Jacobitism still survived, and the northern counties remained in a disturbed condition."[3] Stevenson viewed agrarian crime, the violence originating in land disputes between tenants and owners, as an act of fealty to the fallen or displaced chief. The consequences of that crime, suffered personally, were suffered proudly. Stevenson both admired and distanced himself from this behavior, for if it was "disinterested" and the actor derived no personal benefit from it, not even the pleasure of revenge, it was also of another time and place. Thus it bore no relation to the conditions and realities of current life. The single word "antique" might as easily describe the entire Jacobite cause as one man acting alone in the name of that cause. Stevenson could not but be taken by the printed trial, for all that he admired—loyalty in the face of duress, selflessness, commitment to a lost and hopeless cause that yet trailed a small cloud of glory—was contained within that bound volume. Reading the *Trial,* he conceived the plan to dramatize the nature and dissolution of the clan system, and became "determined to found upon it a narrative of fact," one that would reflect the realities of Highland life after the defeat at Culloden in 1746. Stevenson's history of the Highlands was destined to assume the form of fiction. His phrase is the first deliberate expression by an early modern novelist of a new fictional genre, the nonfiction or documentary novel.

In the April 1882 issue of the *Cornhill Magazine* there is a long article on "The State Trials," part of an irregular series under the casual and quite Victorian heading, "Rambles Among Books." The same issue carries Stevenson's "Talk and Talkers" (just as two months later the magazine printed the first installment of "The Merry Men"). This great collection of English and Scottish trials, beginning with that of Thomas Beckett, Archbishop of Canterbury, for high treason, was edited by T. B. Howell between 1809 and 1815 and thereafter by his son, Thomas Jones Howell. It is one of the great resources of English legal history. Sir Walter Scott naturally had a complete set in his home at Abbotsford, and although there is no record that Stevenson owned the volumes, he certainly would have access to them at the Advocates' Library. In any event, he could hardly have missed so extensive a piece in a magazine to which he had himself contributed. More to the point, the questions raised were very close to those that Stevenson was confronting in his own fiction. The *Cornhill* essayist, most likely Leslie Stephen, presented the *State Trials* as a welcome antidote to the unreality of contemporary literature: "We tire of the skilfully prepared sentiment, the pretty fancies, the unreal imaginations, and long for the harsh, crude, substantial fact, the actual utterance of men struggling in the dire grasp of unmitigated realities."[4] The trials offered the reader an alternative literature, built upon a foundation of solid facts and with the authenticity of witness testimony. There is even a charm in the brutal reality of these vignettes of life. It is as if the *Cornhill* writer had lifted that scene from *The Rajah's Diamond* where the Prince tells Simon Rolles to read Émile Gaboriau, the French originator of the police novel, if the young clergyman would learn something of the real world. For the state trials were nothing more than the police reports of the past, a minute verbal record that provided later readers with a curiously odd pleasure—the "charm of the State Trials," the "charm of their brutal reality" (457, 456). This word is even adopted by a subsequent editor of an abbreviated version of Howell's collection: "Far abler writers than I have frequently dilated on the charms attending a study of the State Trials. . . . I myself long ago discovered the charm of this anthology, and under the spell of long since defunct reporters . . . have been present in the imagination of the Assizes, the Sessions, and the Old Baileys of some two hundred years."[5] There is a curious aesthetic at work here. On the one hand, daily life is extremely difficult, as the police blotter all too readily indicates (Stevenson used a telling phrase for modern life in *The Suicide Club*—"it's a battlefield"—a phrase Graham Greene later adopted as the title for a novel, although he cites another source). Since the ordinary citizen can do nothing to alter the litany of calamities that fill the columns of the newspaper, he is left with a feeling of guilt at his impotence and retreats into a fantasy world of invention and romance. But the need for substantive reality in the form of literature remains. It is a need that can only be satisfied by unmediated or direct materials from the past: "I may be ashamed of myself when I read some hideous revelation of modern crime, not to stimulate my ardour as a patriot and a reformer, but to add a zest to my comfortable chair in the club window or at the bar of my favourite public house. But I can read without such a pang of remorse about Charles I. and the regicides" (456). The newspaper accounts of crime and punishment are beyond our power to ameliorate. Hence we turn to the past. Archival records of crime and punishment give us the satisfaction of confronting, intellectually and emotionally, the unremitting realities of life while enjoying the luxury of not having to do anything about them. Being drawn into the historical past through the direct testimony of living personages, we are made vividly conscious of the "ceaseless lapse" of time, and we see ourselves in its "ever closing scroll" (457). This idea was certainly congenial to Stevenson—that we are all bound in history, and by revisiting the past, in a manner of speaking, by living in it as if it were the present, all the while conscious of our imaginative act, we are exposed to the present, however displaced or transformed. Thus when the *Cornhill* writer talks about solid facts we are aware of Stevenson's desire to do something solid in his history, "solid" being another term for "substantive," "tangible," "material," even "durable" and "important." What the trials (or police reports) offer is a direct and unmediated representation of life, for the tough conditions and experiences of living people. The *Cornhill* writer focuses on the people and events, rather than on the legal arguments. It is not in plot so much as in character, in the "minute ver-bal record—vivid as a photograph," in the "vignettes of real life," that the "charac-teristic charm of the narrative" (458, 459) reveals itself. It is an easy step for the essayist to see why novelists were drawn to these trials for material, how the famous Annesley case provided both Charles Reade and Sir Walter Scott with inspiration for two of their most famous books, *The Wandering Heir* and *Guy Man-nering* respectively. Undoubtedly, it was coincidental that such an elaborate de-fense of this extensive collection of criminal trials as a form of pleasurable reading should have appeared in a magazine so closely associated with Stevenson, but in another way it is probably a perfect gloss on his own attitude. For the trials offered all those details that energized the novelist's imagination, bringing the past to life, offering an eyewitness account of events, and revealing an obscure and often archaic vocabulary as part of a fresh and living language. Then, too, there was the knowledge possessed by the present reader but unknown to the earlier one, knowledge that enabled us to view the past with perspective and even, on occa-sion, humility. For if we know today what the judges and advocates did not know yesterday, it is equally plain that future readers will know tomorrow what we are ignorant of. And they will surely view us through the same hard and unsparing optics that we use for our ancestors.

The first of the thirty-three volumes of *State Trials* contains seven prefaces col-lected from editions going back to 1719. In the preface to the second edition, published in 1730, Sollom Emlyn, a great barrister and champion of legal reform, argued at length on the justification for printing these antique documents.

> The Professors and Students of the Law will not be the only persons, who may receive benefit from this Work: here will be matter also of Instruction and Entertainment to all who are delighted with History, or inquisitive after the transactions of the former of present times; many parts of History will here be illustrated and set in a true light; the Reader may here see, as it were, with his own eyes, not reading to trust to the representations of oth-ers, which are often full of partiality or prejudice, according to the party and disposition of the Historians. But the nature of this Work admits not of such turns and disguises, as other general accounts are but too justly charge-able with; the following Trials being plain Narrations of Sayings and Facts, for the most part published by Authority of the respective Courts, or by in-different Hands; where it happens to be otherwise, the Reader is informed of it in the Title at the Head of the Trial.[6]

Stevenson could just as easily have written this, for the attitude is consistent with his own. The trials are informative and pleasing, satisfying the classical Horatian ideal for works of art. Further, their subject is of the broadest possible interest and presented without partiality or prejudice, since it comes to the reader through the voices of the actual participants rather than filtered through the partisan voice of an intermediary author.[7] In other words, what Emlyn is arguing for is the truth of the document, and, by implication, the truth of the history that the document records. And it does so through "plain Narrations of Sayings and Facts," for facts are indisputable, where interpretations are subject to passion and prejudice. Presented plainly and without ornamentation, they speak for themselves. Facts, in short, are the substance of trials and the anchor for history. "These Volumes will impartially transmit their memory to posterity . . . and this not by general characters which are scarce to be rely'd on, being oft according to the inclinations of the Writer, but by real Facts" (1:xxiii). As an advocate one hundred and forty-five years later, Stevenson shares with this English barrister some common assumptions: that a firsthand account of a criminal proceeding offers an entry into the past; a way of recovering small details; picturesque place-names; the terror and anxiety revealed in peoples' depositions, a terror and anxiety that is unstudied and even possessed of a kind of spontaneity. Of course from the vantage point of 1886, the assumption that mere facts could reveal the truth is, at best, naïve. Stevenson no more believed that than he believed that the truth was, in fact, penetrable. But he had no doubt that the facts were recoverable, and it was the facts that he determined to weave into a narrative. Rather than the court record of a criminal trial the reader would have in his hands a fiction, a "plain Narration of Sayings and Facts," and would be carried away into the world of James of the Glens, of the Lord Advocate Prestongrange, of the Duke of Argyle. In short, the reader would be taken to a world that converged at Inverary in the Highlands during the week of September 21 through September 25, 1752.

Just two years after the publication of *Kidnapped,* Augustine Birrell commented on it in "Notes about Books," a column he wrote for the new, quasi-nouveau magazine, *Atalanta.*

> Mr. Stevenson has made dexterous use of history in the construction of his plot and in the manufacture of his story. Like a wise man he has gone to the State Trials—that storehouse of good things, that seed-plot for the Shakespeare of the future. In the nineteenth volume of this collection may be read a full account of the trial of James Stewart. . . . It appears from the indictment, that both James Stewart and Alan Stewart, commonly called Alan Breck Stewart, son to Donald Stewart . . . were charged with the murder; and indeed the whole indictment reads very like a rough draft of one half of *Kidnapped.* . . . More goes to the making of such a book as *Kidnapped* than "dull fools" suppose.[8]

Since Stevenson provided the initial hint about the printed trial in his dedication to the novel, it hardly required a detective to uncover the truth of that revelation. But even as early as this, Birrell writes as if the common reader is unaware of the source for the story. Six years later, D. L. Cameron reiterated the point in the same magazine.

> Many people who have read "Kidnapped" and its sequel, "David Balfour," or, to adopt its new title, "Catriona," in the last volume of "Atalanta," have the vaguest ideas of the historical foundation of the story. In spite of the preface there are some who suppose that Mr. Stevenson invented the Appin murder even as the eminent scientist imagined that Mr. Matthew Arnold had invented Bishop Wilson. . . . "Kidnapped" and its sequel, are magnificent examples of historical novels, almost literally faithful to history, and yet so lighted up by the genius of the author that there is nothing slavish in their exactness. There is an epical completeness about the central fact upon which the books are founded. The Appin Murder was buried in old law books, or at the best lived in the traditions of the Appin district, but now Mr. Stevenson has made the world ring a second time with its fame. The authorities for the facts are neither many nor exceedingly difficult to get, and it would repay the students of the "Atalanta" School of Fiction to compare the plain tale told at inordinate length in the report of the Trial and elsewhere, with the artistic setting that Mr. Stevenson has given to the narrative.[9]

By this time the trial was so firmly linked with Stevenson that even legal historians were compelled to pay homage to the novelist when they wanted to call attention to the case. When H. L. Stephen omitted the Stewart proceedings in his pocket edition of *State Trials,* he felt compelled to apologize:

> I had hoped to place before my readers the true account, or what passes for such, of that murder of Colin Roy Campbell of Glenure which, as we now know, produced such romantic consequences for David Balfour. . . . But, alas! the lawyers on these occasions have been hopelessly beaten by the professed story-tellers; and the reports of the trials of Lord Lovat and James Stewart are as dull as the romances of *Waverley* and *Catriona* are entrancing.[10]

Although Stevenson clearly did not share Stephen's view of the dullness of these trials, it is equally obvious that Stephen does not mention the author's name because he assumes that everyone will know David Balfour.[11] And when the first modern edition of the trial was published in 1907, in the "Notable British Trials" series, the editor's opening sentence still invoked Stevenson: "The story of those strange doings in my native county of Argyll has attracted me since I first read about James Stewart in the great pages of 'Kidnapped' and 'Catriona.'"[12] Mackay's volume, which was reprinted in 1931, ran to nearly four hundred closely-printed pages, including almost one hundred pages of appendices. And he did not even include the complete supplement to the *Trial,* which was bound up with Stevenson's copy and upon which the novelist drew extensively. The point of all this is quite simple: after the publication of *Kidnapped* and later *Catriona,* the historical interest in the Appin murder was inextricably connected with Stevenson's dramatic treatment of the subject. But this connection was limited to a narrow band of readers, those who were drawn to the story either through their own history (as Mackay says) or as a consequence of their own background as lawyers or legal historians. Thus a Scots writer like William Roughead, who edited a number of notable British trials and made a career of retelling both famous and obscure accounts of criminal trials, mainly for murder, could easily allude to Stevenson's use of trial materials.[13] But few readers had any real knowledge of the crime itself, let alone any understanding of the political or legal issues that it highlighted. Or that Stevenson had constructed one text out of another, the original, historical document layered into the later, fictive one. Or that the *Trial* and its companion, the *Supplement,* served not only as a source for an imaginative novel of adventure but, in fact, became that novel. In short, Stevenson interleaved the printed trial within its fictive offspring, thus bringing to life the antique document along with its long dead personages, reviving the events in such a way that they became accessible to all rather than remaining the province of the scholar and the antiquarian. His task, a paradoxical one, was to fictionalize the history and, at the same time, to historicize the fiction. Hence the narrative of fact, where narrative means story, in the sense in which Hayden White might use the term, and fact means history, insofar as it identifies or can be confirmed by material documents or actual events.

On May 14, 1752, between five and six in the evening, in a wood near the village of Ballachulish, a party of five men, headed by Colin Campbell of Glenure, was passing through the wood of Lettermore on their way to the ferry at Ballachulish. Shots were fired from an elevated part of the woods; Glenure fell and died shortly after. Mungo Campbell, a relative, ran to where the shots were believed to have come from and later declared that he saw a man in a dark coat running away. On the simplest level, this was the homicide that became the subject for one of the most notorious criminal trials in Scottish history. The printed trial read as follows (italics and small caps have been converted to roman):

> The Trial of James Stewart in Aucharn in Duror of Appin, for the Murder of Colin Campbell of Glenure, Esq; Factor for His Majesty on the forfeited estate of Ardshiel; Before the Circuit Court of Justiciary held at Inverary on

Thursday the 21st, Friday the 22d, Saturday the 23d, and Monday the 25th
of September last; by his Grace the Duke of Argyll, Lord Justice-General,
and the Lords Elchies and Kilkerran, Commissioners of Justiciary. Edinburgh: Printed for G. Hamilton and J. Balfour. 1753.

This was the title of the document that Stevenson realized held a key to his documentary history of the Highlands. The title itself illustrates a number of the elements that were of historical significance. The names Stewart and Campbell are
juxtaposed—one the accused and one the victim, or perhaps each a victim. They
are thus representatives of two clans whose enmity towards each other was the
most widely known and deep-seated throughout the Highlands. The forfeited
estate of Ardshiel, which carried in its simple descriptor the whole complex history of passionate rebellion and absolute defeat—of loyalty to a chief who no
longer had control over his own lands and, by extension, over the people who
claimed fealty to him. Finally, there was the Duke of Argyll, Lord Justice-General,
head of the Campbell clan and titular head of the Justiciary Court in Scotland. His
role never required his presence in criminal cases, yet there he was sitting at the
head of the court in Inverary, the seat of the Campbells and the home of Argyll
himself. If the document's title is descriptive, there are layers of history that are
embedded in that title—not just in the trial itself—which became a part of history. Two of Scotland's acclaimed legal historians provided extensive summaries
of the case. In 1785, just thirty years after the trial, Hugo Arnot carried a long
review of it in *A Collection and Abridgement of Celebrated Criminal Trials in Scotland,*
and John Hill Burton included it as the first exhibit in *Narratives from Criminal Trials in Scotland* (1852). Stevenson requested both texts from his father when he
planned a paper on the case to accompany his application for the professorship in
law and history at the University of Edinburgh.

The *Trial* provided material for four complete chapters of *Kidnapped* (12, 17,
19, 21) and a portion of a fifth (18). Its purpose was threefold: to introduce the
historical personages and events, to recreate dramatically the Appin murder, and
to place both the people and their actions in the broadest possible historical context. The first of the chapters comes after Alan and David's successful defense of
the roundhouse and the captain's agreement to place them ashore in friendly (that
is, Stewart) country. The chapter title, "I Hear of the Red Fox," reflects Stevenson's initial purpose of providing introductory information. Alan and David are
enjoying a pipe and the morning's sail "in a bright sunshine" while waiting to be set
ashore. This seems the most appropriate setting for an exchange of confidences:

It was at this time we heard each other's stories, which was the more important to me, as I gained some knowledge of that wild, Highland country, on
which I was so soon to land. In those days, so close on the back of the great

rebellion, it was needful a man should know what he was doing, when he went upon the heather (*K,* 12:100).

Stevenson's use of the term "stories" is ubiquitous in both novels, and it is a good indication of his method and his meaning. For it is clear that stories are a form of communication, a means of connection (or bonding), and a source of both objective and subjective information. Thus "narrative" (another term for story) is the device by which meaning is conveyed, and as such it is a straightforward dramatic implement that makes no apology for itself. Knowledge, imparted by stories, is, as David says, "needful" or "important." Journeying into uncharted territory is risky and dangerous. David is a naturally shrewd lad, and he is well aware of the value of knowledge, a value that goes hand in hand with his love of books and learning, his respect and admiration for authors, his desire to study law, and (in the end) his own entrance into the ranks of authorship. The uncharted territory is figured in the absence of maps that would enable the captain to put Alan and David down in friendly country. Alan is content to rely upon his experience of the land, assuming that will get him through ("I have been often enough picked up and set down upon this coast, and should ken something of the lie of it" [*K,* 11:97]), although the shipwreck created an unforeseen disaster for David. A small lesson here is never to trust to your experience alone and to carry with you proper guides for your journey. One of the functions of Stevenson's dependence on maps for his texts is to reinforce the idea that they (like directories) are means for shepherding us along unknown paths; they are necessary devices that we give over at our peril. The disparity between David's acquiescence in such guides and Alan's preference for his own intuitive knowledge is, in part, a difference between the Highlander's seemingly boundless faith in his own experience and the Lowlander's close measurement in all things material (and possibly spiritual). It goes without saying that David, an untried youth, needs all the help he can get in navigating both an unmapped Highland wilderness as well as the mental traceries of assorted and diverse people along the way.

David begins the conversation and introduces the name of his minister, Mr. Campbell, which triggers Alan's visceral response to that name. "'I know nothing I would help a Campbell to,' says he, 'unless it was a leaden bullet. I would hunt all of that name like blackcocks. If I lay dying, I would crawl upon my knees to my chamber window for a shot at one'" (*K,* 12:100). In his argument against the pannel, Simon Fraser—the son of the notorious Lord Lovat, who was beheaded for his part in the rebellion—appears as the "council" for "Mrs. Campbell of Glenure, and her infant children, against James Stewart."[14] Fraser summarizes the enmity of the two Stewarts towards Glenure:

[21]

houfe : that Allan Breck Stewart faid, that he ha-
ted all the name of Campbell ; and the deponent
faid, he had no reafon for doing fo : but Allan
faid, he had very good reafon for it : that thereafter they left that houfe ; and, after drinking a
dram at another houfe, came to the deponent's
houfe, where they went in, and drunk fome
drams, and Allan Breck renewed the former con-
verfation ; and the deponent, making the fame an-
fwer, Allan faid, that, if the deponent had any
refpect for his . friends, he would tell them, that
if they offered to turn out the poffeffors of Ard-
fhiel's eftate, he would make black cocks of them,
before they entered into poffeffion by which the deponent underftood fhooting them, it being a common phrafe in the country : that John Stewart faid
he did not blame Glenure fo much as Ballieveolan
for taking thefe poffeffions, whereas Glenure was
doing the King's fervice ; and Allan Breck replied,
that befides that, he had another ground of quarrel
againft Glenure for his writing to colonel Craw-
furd, that he, Allan, was come home from France ;
but that he was too cunning for him ; for that,
when at Edinburgh, he had made up his peace
with general Churchill, and had got his pafs, which
he had in his pocket-book : that the deponent
afked a fight of it : that he fearched his pocket-
book, but could not find it ; upon which he tore
a leaf out of the book, and faid, there it was.
And depones, That he faid twenty times over he
would be fit-fides with Glenure, where-ever he
met him ; and wanted nothing more than to meet
him at a convenient place. Depones, That, at
this time, Allan Breck was not drunk, for he
could walk and talk as well as any man. But it
could

Stevenson's under-
scoring of Allan Breck
Stewart's threat to
"make black cocks" of
his enemies, from his
copy of *The Trial of James
Stewart*. Courtesy of the
Princeton University
Library, Princeton, N.J.

Both of them have many times threatened him with death, and both of them
have even gone beyond general terms; for Allan declared *he would, on the first
occasion, shoot him as he would a black cock;* . . . and James, still more inveterate, swore, in the fullness of his heart, *That he would shoot Glenure, even if he
himself was so disabled as to be obliged to go upon his knees to a window in order to
do it (T, 85–86).*

Prestongrange, the Lord Advocate, picked up the image in his summation:

Allan said, that if the deponent had any respect for his friends, he would tell them, that if they offered to turn out the possessors of Ardshiel's estate, he would make *black cocks* of them before they entered into possession, by which the deponent understood shooting them, it being a common phrase in the country (*T,* 176–77).

Both Fraser's and the Lord Advocate's summaries were drawn from the deposition of a witness, in this case from one Duncan Campbell, "change-keeper" or public house keeper: "Allan said, that, if the deponent had any respect for his friends, he would tell them, that if they offered to turn out the possessors of Ardshiel's estate, he would make black cocks of them, before they entered into possession by which the deponent understood shooting them, it being a common phrase in the country" (*T/A,* 21).

Stevenson has simply drawn upon the separate threats of Allan and James, compressed them into one, and given Alan Breck Stewart his own distinctive voice. Yet even in so simple an adaptation as this, he gives it an inimitable twist. "Blackcocks" is the exotic linguistic detail, but the transmitted threat of James Stewart, with its formal diction and bit rhetorical turn, is given a vivid hardness in Stevenson's translation.

that he would shoot Glenure, even if he himself was so disabled, as to be obliged to go upon his knees to a window in order to do it (*T,* 86).	If I lay dying, I would crawl upon my knees to my chamber window for a shot at one (*K,* 12:100).

The issue is not whether Stevenson is copying or borrowing from his source but how he transforms it in creating a text that is seamless in style and voice, yet one that registers a broad range of emotional tones as well as intellectual discriminations. What is always apparent is the novelist's appetite for detail, whether it be a linguistically exotic term, visually or aurally suggestive, historically rare, culturally and topographically specific, or a vivid image (crawling on your knees to the window) that bundles within itself the potential for conveying the passion of emotion.

After David asks Alan why he harbors such hatred for the Campbells, Alan presents a litany of reasons, providing, in effect, a mini-history of the long hostility between the clans—from the perspective of a passionate Stewart. David is aware that the harangue is partisan ("But I paid the less attention to this, for I knew it was usually said by those who have the underhand" [*K,* 12:100]) yet through the dialogue one sees Stevenson quietly introducing a major theme, namely, that power determines the law and possibly even the history that is passed along. Alan's concluding peroration reveals this, albeit unbeknownst to the brave warrior: "'There's more than that,' he continued, 'and all in the same story: lying words, lying papers, tricks fit for a peddler, and the show of what's legal over-all, to make a man the more angry'" (*K,* 12:100–101). Again we see the word "story," by which is meant the narrative history of the Campbell-Stewart feud, a history going back generations and delivered with all the passion and vivacity of something that happened only yesterday, as, indeed, much of it did. Since this is all preparatory to the murder of Colin Campbell, the passion that infuses a Stewart against the Campbells is conveyed to the reader as a living experience rather than as dead history. One of Alan's central complaints ("lying words, lying papers") reflects a major issue that Stevenson confronts: power derives from language or resides with the literate. The hand that writes the word rules the world. For the Campbells, aligned as they were with the king, enjoyed the power of the state, a power derived from the language of the law as embodied in the acts of parliament. Thus when Alan says "the show of what's legal over all" he is voicing the central issue in what came to be the trial of James Stewart. He is also expressing what was a central difference between the Highlands and the Lowlands, and between Scotland and England. For who controlled the law controlled the life, and the life of the Highlanders, of the tenant farmers that James Stewart tried to represent, was subject to the dictat of the legal system. And the legal system was in the employ of the Hanoverian government through its Scots ally in Inverness, the clan Campbell and its chief, the Duke of Argyll. What Alan Stewart is saying, and what comes to be said and dramatized in great detail in the second volume of David Balfour's epic, is that the law is not a grammar of justice but a system of power, and it resides in the hands of the strongest.

David finds Alan less than reliable as an interpreter of law, given his "wasteful" propensity in giving away his buttons.[15] Stevenson has Alan then narrate the episode of his father and the gentlemen of the Black Watch, and then come around to his own background again. Although the creation of Duncan Stewart as Alan's father is an invention, the episode itself (as we saw) is not. Stevenson stitches together factual material from disparate sources in his own consecutive narrative. Thus Alan informs David that he was originally in the English army and deserted at Preston Pans, a point David finds astonishing ("a condemned rebel, and a deserter, and a man of the French King's" [*K,* 12:102]) and one that is made repeatedly in the *Trial.* But Alan must explain to David, and the reader, why a man with his record would dare to show himself in the country. Of course, he misses the heather, and he picks up some money recruiting for the French king:

"But the heart of the matter is the business of my chief, Ardshiel."

"I thought they called your chief Appin," said I.

"Ay, but Arshiel is the Captain of the Clan," said he, which scarcely cleared my mind (*K,* 12:102–3).

If David is commonly viewed, by Alan and readers, as a bit dull with the touch of a prig about him, he often serves as the cat's-paw for Stevenson's very dry wit. David is here exposed to the kind of complexity and confusion that the clan system presented to outsiders, a confusion that, on the simplest level, has to do with names and patrimony. In the *Trial* James Stewart is identified as follows:

> He is a bastard brother of Charles Stewart late of Ardshiel, attainted, who, out of his own tenants, and those of Dougal Stewart of Appin, his chieftain, levied a regiment or battalion, at the head of which he went into the late rebellion, accompanied, among others, by this pannel (*T*, 157–58).

Stevenson marked this passage, and we can imagine him seeing the comedy in an outsider's attempt to distinguish the place-names from the chiefs' names and to keep them separate. In a sentence that he deleted in the manuscript, he first wrote, in response to David's query ("I thought they called your chief Appin"), "He *is* Appin." But he substituted the more oblique and ambiguous response that suggests there are two people, Appin and Ardshiel, rather than just one. But Alan goes on with a long account of Ardshiel's misfortunes, and it is an account that carries a sentimental tinge and is in fact untrue in significant details. So in addition to the picture of poor Ardshiel, reduced to the life of buying his own "butter in the marketplace, and taking it home in a kale leaf" (*K*, 12:103), Alan adds: "There are the bairns forby, the children and the hope of Appin, that must be learned their letters and how to hold a sword, in that far country" (*K*, 12:103). Now Stevenson knows that "Ardshiel himself, the attainted person, made his escape into foreign parts, leaving at home his wife and a family of children" (*T*, 158). In fact, before Glenure was appointed factor to the estate Ardshiel's wife managed the collection of the rents: "Alexander Stewart of Innernahyle, who hath deposed, 'That, before the factory, as he believes, the tenants paid their rents to the lady of Ardshiel, and that she again employed the pannel to deal with them'" (*T*, 159). This passage about the collection of the rents was marked by Stevenson in his copy of the *Trial*. Alan is creating sympathy in David's mind for the plight of the exiled chief, adding the children to the figure of poor Ardshiel doing his own small shopping, the sad decline of a once proud chief who bears a king's name. David is the perfect straight man, asking exactly the question that enables Alan to drive home the main point—that the tenants pay two rents, one against their will to the factor who administers the forfeited estate and the other out of loyalty to the exiled chief. And now James Stewart is introduced into the story: "But that's the handiwork of my good kinsman and my father's friend, James of the Glens: James Stewart, that is, Ardshiel's half brother. He it is that gets the money in, and does the management" (*K*, 12:103). At this point Stevenson reverts to the retrospective mode, as David says, "This was the first time I heard the name of that

James Stewart, who was afterwards so famous at the time of his hanging" (*K*, 12:103). He was famous because his dying speech was printed and committed to the minds and hearts of Highlanders everywhere, as he became one of the last patriots and martyrs to the Jacobite cause.

David is suitably impressed, not with James Stewart but with the nobility of the tenants paying two rents. Alan then brings up the name of his enemy again: "'Now, if ye were one of the cursed race of Campbell, ye would gnash your teeth to hear tell of it. If ye were the Red Fox'. . . . And at that name, his teeth shut together and he ceased speaking. I have seen many a grim face, but never a grimmer than Alan's when he had named the Red Fox" (*K*, 12:104). The trial is replete with witnesses' depositions as to the attitude on the part of both James Stewart and Allan Breck Stewart toward Glenure.

> That the said Allan then gave the said John Maccoll a dram, and told him, if he would fetch him the red fox's skin, he would give him what was much better; . . . Depones, that the deponent gave no great notice to these expressions, at the time; but, after he heard of Glenure's murder, believed he meant Glenure, as he was commonly called Colin Roy, which means Red Colin, in the country (*T/A*, 23–24).[16]

In this introductory chapter to the background of the murder, Stevenson has Alan vividly describe his desire either to kill the factor or see him dead, thus deepening the hatred for Glenure disclosed in the *Trial*: "Red Fox, if ever I hold you at a gun's end, the Lord have pity upon ye!"; "Him beaten? No: nor will be till his blood's on the hillside!" (*K*, 12:105, 106). Thus the historical metonymy ("if he would fetch him the red fox's skin") is transformed into the fictional synecdoche: "Will ye bring me his brush?" (*K*, 12:104). Allan reiterates his desire to see Glenure dead and affirms his willingness to personally kill him: "And depones, That he said twenty times over he would be fit-sides with Glenure, where-ever he met him; and wanted nothing more than to meet him at a convenient place" (*T/A*, 21).[17]

The hatred of both James and Allan for the King's factor was driven home by Simon Fraser in his trial presentation:

> In the midst of their most cunning contrivances, they could not refrain from uttering such strong and particular threats against Glenure, as immediately pointed them out for the objects of general suspicion. Both of them have many times threatened him with death, and both of them have even gone beyond general terms (*T*, 85).

It is significant that Stevenson dissociates James Stewart from the hatred toward Glenure in the novel. Although the trial makes no distinction between the two in their hostility toward the factor, Stevenson deliberately attributes the enmity solely to Alan. The objective is quite clear: in order to highlight the innocence of James Stewart and by extension the tragedy of his conviction and the pain of his execution, the reader must not be allowed to believe that there is any justification for his indictment. Nowhere in the text does the novelist represent James Stewart's hatred for Glenure, nor does he indicate any animosity on James's part toward the government in general. Alan is the only Highlander (in the fictional world of *Kidnapped*) who has both motive and opportunity for the crime, and Stevenson prefers it that way. Rather than cloud the waters for the reader regarding the possible guilt of James and the presumptive guilt of Alan, he focuses instead on the legal injustice to James and raises the question of the problematic nature of Alan's conviction. This simplifies the narrative in terms of both plot and characterization. It enables the reader to witness the events from the point of view of an innocent, although not disinterested, bystander—David Balfour. And it brings to the fore the legal questions raised by the trial itself, quite apart from the fact of the defendants' guilt or innocence. Without question, the effect is to present James Stewart as the Highlanders saw him: a man accused, convicted and executed by a legal system that was politically and hereditarily opposed to everything he represented.

David's simple question ("And who is the Red Fox?") gives Alan the opportunity to provide a lengthy narrative history of the years following the Jacobite rebellion for his young friend's benefit. David functions as a surrogate reader. He asks the questions we would ask and serves as our dramatic auditor. By means of Alan's responses, and making due allowance for his characteristic rhetoric and swagger, Stevenson systematically introduces the historical details that form the scaffolding of the Appin murder. From pages 102 through 107, David is virtually a device in an extended Socratic dialogue, delivering a series of short interrogatives or exclamations: "What? Two rents?" "Is that him you call the Red Fox?" "I call it noble, Alan." The questions are all simple and leading, designed to reduce a very long and complicated history of events into a brief chronicle of the time, to tease Alan into giving David a story ("Tell me your tale plainly out") rather than a dry commentary, one that presumably has a beginning and an end. (David keeps asking, "what followed?" and "What did he next?") That such a complex history as is revealed in the *Trial* could be compressed into such a simple, plainly told tale is paradoxically an astonishing achievement and a great deception. For it requires, on the one hand, the heightened imagination of a master storyteller, and on the other, it requires a tacit recognition that no story *as* story can adequately reproduce history's complexities. Stevenson is keenly aware of the ambiguity in the relations among the parties in the entire Appin affair—Glenure and James Stewart, the exiled chief and the tenant farmers, and the barons of exchequer—who effectively controlled the forfeited estates and appointed the factors. But his first concern is with the story itself, with defining its outlines for the reader. Thus David the interrogator encourages Alan the storyteller to deliver the tale, and the more Alan whets the appetite of his young listener, the more the listener prods him on to greater detail and more elaborate explanations. In the process we, as readers, are given a brief insight into the practice of fictional art. For in Alan we have a partisan storyteller, in David a rapt listener, and the tale assumes a character of its own. That its details are drawn from historical artifacts no more alters the fictionality of the story than it diminishes the story's authenticity. Stevenson is working a delicate art here: to keep before the reader a narrative line that entices interest or makes for suspense, to call into question the nature of that narrative line, and to remind us of the uncertainty of its authority. Thus he plays the modern Jamesian game, giving us our story and simultaneously taking it away. For a doubtful story is akin to a false one, and a false one may be worse than no story at all.

But let us return to Alan's story. He begins with the collapse of the rebellion ("When the men of the clans were broken at Culloden") and then homes in on his own chief, Ardshiel, who "had to flee like a poor deer upon the mountains—he and his lady and his bairns." And before he was even safe in France, the "English rogues . . . were striking at his rights. They stripped him of his powers; they stripped him of his lands; they plucked the weapons from the hands of his clansmen that had borne arms for thirty centuries; ay, and the very clothes off their back—so that it's now a sin to wear a tartan plaid, and a man may be cast into a jail, if he has but a kilt about his legs. One thing they couldnae kill. That was the love the clansmen bore their chief. These guineas are the proof of it" (K, 12:104). Stevenson captures here the temper and character of Allan Breck Stewart, a man proud of his heritage and quick to take offense at any real or perceived wrongs to his clan. But Ardshiel is the ostensible subject. By focusing on an individual who suffered, Alan elicits sympathy for all the Highlanders who suffered the same consequences of the failed rebellion. Thus Ardshiel is, in part, standing for the whole—for all the Highland chiefs, and their clansmen, who shared the same fate. If Alan is talking only about his chief, the novelist is talking about all the others who stand behind him, just as Alan's description of what Ardshiel and his clan have to endure is Stevenson's allusion to the acts that were imposed on the Highlands after Culloden: the abolition of the heretable jurisdictions, depriving the chiefs of their power to adjudicate criminal behavior on their own estates; the forfeiture of their estates; the disarming of the Highlanders; and the suppression of the Highland dress. By relating all these crucial political acts through the plain, if expressive, language of ordinary people's experience, Stevenson draws political history into the text without ever calling attention to itself as history. In later chapters, when David is travelling through Mull, references to these acts are brought up directly again, as we saw earlier. But here, when we first encounter them, the acts are presented to us through the eyes of a partisan Highlander who experiences them as anybody with Alan's quick temper and propensity toward vengeance might. Of course, it is given the edge of a Highlander's point of view. This is not a Whig interpretation of events: "They *stripped* him of his powers," "They *stripped* him of his lands," "they *plucked* the weapons from the hands" (italics mine). Between the rhetoric and the diction lies the voice, and the voice in this case is that of a deeply angry man who is more apt to use a sword to redress a grievance than file a brief to recover a claim. Alan in *Kidnapped,* via Allan in the *Trial,* is the voice for all that rage directed toward the clan Campbell—and via the Campbells toward the entire political, economic, and social system that led to the defeat and subjugation of all those who followed Prince Charles just six years earlier.

Since the tenants of Appin are scraping to come up with two rents, presumably it would be simple to find others who would pay more for the land since they would be paying only one rent. But, as Alan gloats, one should never underestimate the loyalty of a clansman: "For these same Stewarts and MacColls and McRobs . . . offered him a better price than any Campbell in all broad Scotland" (*K,* 12:105). Here is where Stevenson deftly merges different elements from the *Trial* into the novel—partly to define the character of Alan, to distinguish Alan's position toward Glenure from James Stewart's, and partly to eliminate those elements that clearly contradict the line of the fictional narrative. Thus, in the presentation on the indictment made by Walter Stewart, one of James Stewart's advocates, a different relationship is established between the pannel and Glenure.

> After Glenure was made factor . . . they continued in the greatest friendship: you see the pannel managing the estate of Ardshiel under Glenure. . . . His management of the estate was not taken from him, and he was still allowed to remit parts of the rents to Ardshiel's family. He has no connexion by blood, or otherways, with the tenants warned to remove; there is not so much as one of them of his name. The estate was annexed for ever to the crown, and was in a few months to fall into the hands of commissioners, appointed by his Majesty, who would probably restore the tenants, as they offered more rent than those put in by Glenure (*T,* 39–40).

Stevenson underscored the lines on the remission of the rents to Ardshiel's family, and the entire passage is marked by double lines down the margin. Thus the picture (at least the picture that the defense lawyer presents) is vastly different from Alan's. Glenure is clearly not the bogey man that Alan creates in this chapter, and the fact that he allows the tenants to continue paying rent to their exiled chief is almost astonishing. This is completely absent from Alan's portrait; yet the issue of the tenants offering *more* rent—which Alan does appropriate—is also seen by Stevenson to have genuine importance. Stevenson selects those details that enable him to construct a narrative that suits his interests. On the character of Allan, and the hatred evinced by him for Glenure, there is sufficient evidence in the *Trial*. But the animosity between James Stewart and Glenure is also presented in the *Trial,* albeit not by James Stewart's advocates. Yet Stevenson discards that issue. For the purpose of *his* text there must be injured innocence. In a way, James Stewart becomes a figure who is larger than life, or rather one whose life assumes a larger importance as he is caught in the vortex of political events.

"Tell me your tale plainly out," says David, in response to Alan's increasingly choleric diatribes against Glenure. Of course, there is always the ironic reversal of meaning that underlies David's request, an injunction that runs as a leitmotif through all of Stevenson's fiction, since the tale cannot really be told "plainly out." But Alan complies nonetheless and describes Glenure's response to the move on the part of the Stewarts to raise the rents to retain their tenancy: "Therefore, he sent for lawyers and papers and redcoats to stand at his back" (*K,* 12:106). In this brief statement Stevenson refers to the entire complex of litigation that preceded the eviction notices, litigation that took place in Edinburgh before the barons of exchequer—who had responsibility for overseeing the forfeited estates—and which involved pleas that James Stewart had entered in defense of the tenants. The legal skirmishing was protracted, James Stewart at first gaining a sist, or stay against the evictions, and then finally losing the argument. But Alan's description is interesting for its revelation of character. In his mind, "lawyers, and papers, and redcoats" are all lumped together in a general class of things or goods that are of little value at best or beneath contempt at worst—things that are certainly destructive of those values that he and his kinsmen hold dear. Lawyers and papers are representative of a regulated and measured world, a world whose procedures and forms are essentially mysterious to the Highlander. Ignorant of the law and the English tongue, probably illiterate in his native Gaelic or Irish, the Highlander is caught in a political and legal web that is totally foreign to his experience. The Scottish law located in the Lowland capital of Edinburgh, and the English law even farther in London, are worlds apart from the hills and lochs of the Grampians. Just thinking of it drives Alan into a frenzy: "And the kindly folk of that country must all pack and tramp, every father's son out of his father's house, and out of the place where he was bred and fed, and played when he was a callant" (*K,* 12:106). Stevenson (through Alan) inserts a single sentence that alludes to the complicated legal skirmishing that preceded the assassination of Glenure, keeping Alan's tone, and immediately following he has Alan launch into a melodramatic tirade about the mistreated and displaced tenants. Psychological portraiture is a high priority for the novelist, and his pains at creating a character who is both consistent and complex is demonstrated in even so simple an example as this one. The history—elliptical, allusive, and largely unrecognized—is delivered to us by means of the created character who is himself a part of that history. If Stevenson amplifies the real Allan Breck Stewart, he ensures that his fictional counterpart is never the sole transmitter for the history. So David, who knows nothing of the events, responds to Alan's attacks with a defense of Glenure that is precisely one offered by a trial witness.

> "It's not this Campbell's fault, man—it's his orders. And if ye killed this Colin tomorrow, what better would ye be? There would be another factor in his shoes, as fast as spur can drive" (K, 12:107).

> That John Stewart said, that he did not so much blame Glenure for turning out the possessors of Ardshiel; for that he was but doing the King's service; and that, if he had not the factory, another would, who would do the same thing (T/A, 20).

The argument is irrefutable, for Glenure is nothing more than a pawn in a game controlled by the government. The historical Allan could not contest the logic of the assertion, and so he reacted viscerally ("He rather the meikle devil had it than Glenure" [T/A, 20]). The fictional Alan is more subtle and even a touch poetic: "Ye're a good lad in a fight . . . but man! ye have whig blood in ye!" (K, 12:107). Stevenson insists on investing Alan with a distinctive charm, reflected in a modest, quiet flattery that overlays a fierce militancy. David picks up the tone instantly: "He spoke kindly enough, but there was so much anger under his contempt that I thought it wise to change the conversation" (K, 12:107). Alan's ability to sustain such apparently contradictory qualities makes him kin to Long John Silver, although without the core of evil that defines that earlier creation. This is a feature of Stevenson's fiction that has frequently been remarked upon: the capacity of a figure to suspend two seemingly antithetical qualities, a striving for good and a propensity for evil—in practice, the war within the self. Stevenson's people talk well, felicitously even, but that does not inhibit the impulsive behavior that is often at odds with the talk. In his fiction there is always a tension between the word and the deed, or the act and the thought, a tension that justifiably determined *Jekyll and Hyde* to be a paradigmatic text for understanding Stevenson's imagination.

Three subsequent chapters in *Kidnapped* are built up exclusively from textual material in the *Trial*. "The Death of the Red Fox" (17) recreates (perhaps reconstitutes would be more accurate) the historical murder. As David leaves Morven and crosses over into the land of the Stewarts, the place names—Balachulish, Lettermore, Appin, Aucharn, Duror—assume their role in the fictional text. They are present not just for historical accuracy but for their exoticism, for a certain romance that attaches to euphonious names whose meaning and contextual associations are nonexistent for all but the most ardent Scottish antiquarians and historians. Stevenson's familiarity with each name, derived from his pencilled study of the text, was so deep that its merest citation was sufficient to conjure up for him the past events associated with the site. In chapters 18 and 21 the "wood of Letter-more" and the "heugh of Corrynakiegh" become part or all of the title, just as Mamore and Koalisnacoan are transferred from the historical document to create the linguistic topography of the fictional text.

But Stevenson's fist priority was the representation of the murder. Since Allan Breck Stewart was charged with the crime, and was assumed to have committed the act, Stevenson needed a way to get his Alan into the chapter. He does it first obliquely, through an observation of David's as he crosses the ferry into Appin: "A little after we had started, the sun shone upon a little moving clump of scarlet close in along the waterside to the north. It was much of the same red as soldiers' coats; every now and then, too, there came little sparks and lightnings, as though the sun had struck upon bright steel" (K, 17:145). He asks the ferryman what it might be, and the boatman responds it must be the British soldiers who are coming to remove the tenants from their farms. Although plausible (in fact, the soldiers were not yet called upon to conduct the evictions), it could just as well be Alan Breck, with his red vest and the reflection from his silver buttons. David thinks of his friend, and asks "why I was going to join myself with an outlaw and a would-be murderer like Alan" (K, 17:146), for the historical Allan was indeed a declared "outlaw and fugitive from his Majesty's laws" (T, 29). Stevenson (like David) finds himself in a dilemma. He declared Alan's innocence in the dedication to the novel, but he introduces details from the *Trial* that argue for his guilt. Although nobody reading *Kidnapped* would associate these details with the historical document, by including them Stevenson satisfies his need for a quasi-impartial justice in the treatment of his original material while at the same time constructing a sympathetic fictional portrait. In a sense, he insists upon having it both ways: he wants his reconstituted Alan to be heroic, but he is loath to defy altogether the textual evidence of the *Trial*, which contravenes any idea of nobility, as Stevenson readily admits in the dedication. Thus at the end of the chapter, right after the murder, David comes upon his friend: "Just inside the shelter of the trees, I found Alan Breck standing, with a fishing rod" (K, 17:151). If this strikes readers as odd it is only because it has no reference outside the historical document. Two witnesses at the trial of James Stewart testified that Allan had gone fishing on the day of the murder (T/A, 32), and Stevenson underscored one line of their testimony: "That before mid-day he went up with a fishing-rod to the water side" (T/A, 33). The prosecution used this testimony against Allan, contending that it was "under pretence of going a-fishing" that he set off to lie in wait for Glenure (T, 6). Stevenson is aware of the problematic nature of Allan's guilt or

[35]

to the very fhort fpace of time they behoved to take in
coming to him. For the 2d witnefs (Mackenzie) depones
(*p*. 11. *l*. 11.), " That Glenure was about a mufket-
" fhot before him in the wood of Lettermore; he
" heard a fhot;——when he came up, he faw Mungo
" Campbell wringing his hands, and his mafter lying on
" the ground.—And Donald Kennedy the fheriff-officer,
" was at that time ftanding by him." And the 3d witnefs
(Kennedy) depones (*p*. 15. *l*. 15.), " That he was but
" about two penny-ftone caft before the faid Mungo, (and
he again before Glenure only " about twice the length
of the room in which the court fat where he deponed");
" and alfo within the diftance of hearing the faid Mun-
" go making great noife, as of one weeping."——Now,
as above faid, can any one who confiders thefe circum-
ftances believe, that in the fhort fpace of time taken by
Mackenzie and Kennedy in coming to the place where
Glenure lay murdered, (which was not only near them,
but in the middle betwixt them), it was poffible for Mungo to do what he fays he did? As, *firft*, " After the fhot,
" he heard Glenure feveral times repeat thefe words,
" Oh! I am dead." 2*dly*, " He thereupon returned
" to Glenure." 3*dly*, " He heard him repeat the
" fame words, and add, Take care of yourfelf, for he
" is going to fhoot you." 4*thly*, " He took Glenure
" from off his horfe." 5*thly*, " Glenure being taken
" from his horfe, leaned *a little* upon Mungo's fhoul-
" der, and endeavoured to have opened his breaft, to
" fee where the bullets wherewith he was fhot, came
" out of his body; but was not able." And, 6*thly*,
" He run up the hill from the road (in the wood; which
wood, he afterwards depones, " was there pretty thick;
and, on the fide from which Glenure was fhot, *very*
rugged and ftony, rifing up-hill towards the fouth"), to
" fee who had fhot Glenure; and faw, at fome diftance,
" a man, with a fhort dark-coloured coat, and a gun
" in his hand, going away from him; and, as the de-
" ponent came nearer him, he mended his pace, and
                    E 2   " difappeared,

The murder of Glenure ("Oh I am dead"), with Stevenson's vertical lines in the margin of *The Trial of James Stewart*. Courtesy of the Princeton University Library, Princeton, N.J.

innocence, and his ambivalence is reflected in his attempt, with its occasional awkwardness, to balance two competing interests—to make Alan innocent of the crime, if guilty of the thought, and yet to draw just enough details from the trial testimony to call that innocence into question.

The features that Stevenson focuses on—and I cannot overemphasize how heavily the original document is scored in the margins and underscored in the text —reveal a good deal about his thinking and his habits of composition. He is drawn to character and the specific details that illuminate character. The chapter on the red fox gives us the small, individuating features that isolate and capture intense hatred, features Stevenson appropriated from the trial testimony whenever he was struck by a word or phrase. Later, when Colin Campbell is killed, he keeps before the reader's eye the motion of sudden, violent death. "O, I am dead!" (*K,* 17:148) is lifted directly from the *Trial* ("Oh! I am dead" [*T/A,* 7]), just as the dying factor's solicitous remark to his nephew, "Take care of yourself" (*T/A,* 7), reappears in Stevenson as "Take care of yourselves" (*K,* 17:149). Stevenson would be struck by the language and adapt it to his own purpose. Thus he was intent upon making Mungo Campbell a shrewd man who found himself in the midst of a traumatic experience: "The lawyer said never a word, but his face was as sharp as a pen and as white as the dead man's; the servant broke out into a great noise of crying and weeping, like a child; . . . At last the lawyer laid down the dead man in his blood upon the road, and got to his own feet with a kind of stagger" (*K,* 17:149–50). But in the trial testimony it was "Mungo Campbell wringing his hands" and making "a great noise as of one weeping" (*T/A,* 11, 15), a portrait not nearly as elevated as Stevenson's. In fact, Mungo Campbell emerges as less than reputable in the course of the trial testimony.

Stevenson's underscoring often highlights aspects of profound pain or despair. "[James Stewart] wrung his hands, expres'd great concern at what had happened, as what might bring innocent people to trouble, and pray'd that innocent people might not be brought to trouble" (*T/A,* 13). This becomes: "But I can think of nothing but this dreadful accident, and the trouble it is like to bring upon quite innocent persons" (*K,* 19:165). What we see are a number of sharp images that Stevenson sees—the cries of Glenure after he is shot, the distraught and weeping Mungo Campbell, the blood of the victim, which covers the lawyer as he tends to him. When the scene moves to James Stewart's house ("The House of Fear") we again see Stevenson incorporating dramatically the salient physical and emotional details of the trial testimony. There is the issue of language, as one witness testified "That Allan Breck and the pannel were in use to converse together, sometimes in English, and sometimes in the Irish language" (*T/A,* 82). Thus, James Stewart "cried out to Alan in the Gaelic," and Alan responded: "I will ask ye to speak in Scotch, for here is a young gentleman with me that has nane of the other" (*K,* 19:163). We might ask why Stevenson is at such pains to take these details into his own text. No commentary could adequately reproduce how extensively he appropriates matter from the *Trial.* But all he takes is a feature or trait of Highland life and often a revelation of character. The language of the country is indeed the custom of the country, and it highlights the separation between the Highlanders and the Lowlanders. The common term for the Gaelic, as I have already said, was "Irish," and Stevenson does not use it simply because by the end of the nineteenth century it would have had little or no meaning to his readers. But it is the only term employed in the documents, in Burt's *Letters* as well as in the *Trial,* and

Stevenson was alert to its significance. A great many of the witnesses could speak nothing but Irish, while the language of the court was English. This meant that translators had to be provided, and they were—by Campbell sympathizers, which meant their translations were problematic. In effect, they were biased against the defendants. "Many of the witnesses could not speak English, and a Campbell acted as interpreter. The transmission of the evidence through such a medium gives it a stiff, inanimate character, and there is little doubt that it bore a Campbell tinge."[18] This point was first made by Hugo Arnot in his commentary on the *Trial*. Not only was James Stewart tried by a jury of his enemies, but any testimony in his favor was not necessarily translated to his benefit. Stevenson was aware of this situation, and he is at pains to illustrate the difficulty of trying to survive, let alone manage a life, in a land where the language is an alien element. Whether it is David futilely trying to communicate to the boatmen when he is stranded on the islet, or, years later, Wiltshire on the island of Falesá, ignorant of the native tongue and uncomprehending of all that goes on. For Stevenson, language is at the heart of our ability to penetrate another's world. The penetration of language is akin to the penetration of mystery, and mystery is always at the edge of Stevenson's story, whether it be the identity of an assassin, the meaning of a murder, or the profound mystery of being.

But Stevenson does not get too far from his main objective. In "The House of Fear" he reproduces the frenetic response to the murder on the part of James Stewart's entire household, including family and servants. They know they will be suspected, and they have every reason to fear an investigation. James Stewart was known to have made threats against Glenure; the house possessed arms in violation of the disarming act; and Allan Breck was a recent visitor who left his distinctive French clothes there in exchange for less conspicuous garments borrowed from his kinsman. All these details go to the construction of a chapter that replicates the events as they were narrated by the trial "deponents," with special attention given to the drawing of individual characters, a feature that surpasses the historical document. Stevenson has the servants running every which way, hiding swords and guns (the entire page 71 of the appendix is scored in the margin). He insinuates a touch of sensuousness by having a "lassie" carrying Alan's "ain French clothes" in order to bury them, much to the vain fighter's chagrin ("Bury my French clothes!" [*K*, 19:164]). The lassie was Katharine Macoll, who testified that she was asked by James Stewart's servants "what she had got in the sack? the deponent answered, it was Allan Breck's cloaths; and that she was going to hide them; and that accordingly the said sack, containing the above cloaths, was hid, in the moor" (*T/A*, 28). James, of course, wants to help his kinsman, but he wants to safeguard himself and his family. What is first necessary is money: "As for

[28]

being then in the cellar, called upon the deponent, who then faw the faid Margaret Stewart put a fide blue coat, a red waift-coat, with fomething elfe that the deponent did not obferve, into a fack, and delivered them to the deponent, defiring her to hide them fome way without. Depones, That the faid Margaret Stewart did not tell the deponent to whom the cloaths belonged ; but that the deponent thought the faid coat and waift-coat were Allan Breck's. Depones, That fhe went away with the faid fack, containing the faid cloaths ; and, as fhe was going up the brae, in order to hide them, was overtaken by Dugald and John Beg Maccolls, fervants to the pannel, who had fome guns and fwords; and the faid Dugald Maccoll afked the deponent, what fhe had got in the fack? the deponent anfwered, it was Allan Breck's cloaths ; and that fhe was going to hide them ; and that accordingly the faid fack, containing the above cloaths, was hid, in the moor, above the pannel's houfe, by the faid Dugald Maccoll, in prefence of the deponent. Depones, That, upon Saturday, the 16th of May laft, in the evening, the faid Mrs. Stewart, fpoufe to the pannel, defired the deponent to carry back what fhe had hid, and leave it at the back of the brew-houfe; which the deponent accordingly did ; and has not feen them fince. Depones, That Alexander Bane Stewart was feen by the deponent about the houfe that evening. Depones, That, fome time in Summer laft, after the above period, Solomon Bane Maccoll, fervant to the pannel, told the deponent, that the faid Mrs. Stewart, fpoufe to the pannel, defired her to conceal what fhe knew about the above cloaths, in cafe fhe fhould be afked

On Allan Breck's clothes, with Stevenson's heavy underscoring and lineation of *The Trial of James Stewart*. Courtesy of the Princeton University Library, Princeton, N.J.

James, it appears he had brought himself so low with journeys to Edinburgh and legal expenses on behalf of the tenants, that he could only scrape together three and fivepence halfpenny; the most of it in coppers" (*K, 19:166*). Stevenson takes a detail from the document—giving Allan Breck money to aid his escape from the country—and makes it his own. David's narration is homely and poignant in its evocation of James's uncompensated, uphill battle against the government, against Glenure, and the ignominy of having nothing left to offer his friend but a few coppers. In the *Trial,* the sum was five guineas, and it recurs regularly: "James Stewart . . . to get . . . five pounds *Sterling,* or 5 guineas; . . . that his friend *Allan Breck*

Stewart was going to leave the country; and that it was *incumbent* on him the said *James,* to supply him with money" (*T,* 9).

In "The House of Fear" Stevenson constructs a portrait of James Stewart that is at odds with the depiction in the historical document, or perhaps with what the historical personage came to represent. Where James became a martyr for the Jacobites at the time of his hanging, in this moment, immediately after the murder of Glenure, he is a bathetic figure, a man caught up in an event that threatens to engulf him and everyone around him. Bound to an exiled chief and tied to a man who is both a deserter from the king's army and a rebel in the Jacobite cause, James Stewart is the picture of desperation and fear as he tries to keep his family together, help Alan escape, and hold off the government authorities. It is an untenable position. In fact, James Stewart and his family and servants were picked up almost immediately after the assassination and incarcerated for months before the trial. Stevenson's fidelity to historical details should not detract from the broader issues of the chapter: the helplessness, or defenselessness, of a poor, agrarian family on the wrong side of a war; the power of the state, through the law, to control and determine life; and the unpredictable consequences of an act of violence on a community. James Stewart's plea that "this dreadful accident" (*K,* 19:167) should not "bring innocent people to trouble" (*T/A,* 13) is a sad, if unintended, irony. For the murder was in no way an accident, and it was destined to do nothing less than bring trouble to innocent people, not the least of them the author of the plea himself.

"The Heugh of Corrynakiegh" is the final chapter in *Kidnapped* to draw completely from the *Trial.* Alan and David are in need of money in order to escape from the country of Appin. They are hiding out in the heugh, or cleft, of a mountainside and enjoying themselves immensely. The scenery is spectacular, the fish are tasty and plentiful, and even the lessons in sword fighting, which David must put up with, are mitigated by the companionship that accompanies them. But this idyllic interlude (which has its parallels with Huck Finn and Jim on the Mississippi) cannot last. The British were sure to find them, however isolated the small hamlet of Koalisnacoan—which even in that far country was a "remote or solitary place" (*T,* 10)—and an escape was essential. Alan then proposed to David to call upon his friend John Breck Macoll, "a bouman of Appin's," and to have him get word to James Stewart about their need for money.[19] In *Kidnapped,* Stevenson has Alan prepare a "cross-tarrie, or fiery cross" to get John Breck's attention, but in the historical document Allan simply whistled, a technique that clearly struck the novelist's fancy, for he uses it with relish in this chapter as well as in "The House of Fear." It was also John Breck's testimony that provided Stevenson with what must have seemed one of the more imaginative inventions in the text:

Allan Breck look'd about among the trees, and finding a wood pigeon's quill, made a pen of it, and, having made ink of some powder he took out of a powder-horn that was in his pocket, he wrote a letter, which he told the deponent he must deliver to William Stewart merchant at Maryburgh; (*T/A*, 97).

But he was a man of more resources than I knew; searched the wood until he found a quill of a cushat-dove, which he shaped into a pen; made himself a kind of ink with gunpowder from his horn and water from that running stream; and tearing a corner from his French military commission (which he carried in his pocket, like a talisman to keep him from the gallows) he sat down and wrote as follows: (*K*, 21:187).

There is, of course, no comparison between the testimony presented through the prism of a translator and Stevenson's richer, lyric reformulation. From the simple description in the trial record he fashions the picture of a man engaged in a creative and practical enterprise. Nothing is wasted, and this from someone whose extravagance was a matter of historical as well as fictional record. Even the French commission, which was testified to by different witnesses, is brought in to do service in the portrait. Every piece of language is a tile that fits the mosaic of the art. In most cases, it is assumed to drive the plot, but more often it contributes to portraiture at the same time. Stevenson did not need Henry James to apply the principles of organic structure to fiction, since they were principles he always held to vigorously. And all the elements—plot, setting, characterization, description —were anchored in a diction whose simplicity was never betrayed by the rare or dialectal or even studied word. The side of Alan revealed in this chapter is as different, in its way, as his fierce combativeness in "The Siege of the Round-House" or his anger and vengefulness in the "Red Fox." Although his intelligence was never in question (he is a smart as well as a brave fighter), he exhibits here a dry wit layered over a shrewd cunning. David continues to play the straight man while Alan, "drolling" with him, expounds on the necessity for such an ingenious construction in order to snare John Breck's attention for the required task. The chapter draws on two salient details in the *Trial*—John Breck's illiteracy, and the five guineas that are finally delivered to Allan (*K*, 21:186, 189–90).[20] More importantly, it offers a crucial interpretation of events. John Breck's testimony at trial was the most damaging to Allan Breck and, by extension, to James Stewart. He stipulated that Allan denied having had anything to do with the murder but that he believed he would be suspected of it regardless—and that, as a deserter, he would be dealt with harshly. John Breck did not believe him, but was persuaded to carry a letter to James Stewart anyway. David captures John Breck's animus in his repulsive depiction of him: "He was a ragged, wild, bearded man about forty, grossly disfigured with the smallpox, and looked both dull and savage. . . . I thought he had little good will to serve us, and what he had was the child of terror" (*K,* 21:186).[21] David—as an outside, unhistorical observer—is allowed to express a visceral antagonism to John Breck Maccoll. Alan, on the other hand, as the fictional incarnation of a historical personage, cannot foretell John Breck's future testimony. At the end of the chapter he declares, "I will always give ye the name of a good man" (*K,* 21:191), an irony apparent only to someone familiar with the trial record, since John Breck Maccoll was an instrumental witness in the government's case against Allan Breck Stewart. Stevenson melds a number of historical details here: Alan hiding in the heugh of Corrynakiegh; the bouman; the five guineas; and the "cross-tarrie" from Burt's *Letters,* this last detail offering a touch of Highland custom and a vehicle for Alan's extended drollery.

Four chapters in *Kidnapped* are drawn from the *Trial.* What purpose was served by such laborious combing of an old and obscure document? For the novelist, judging solely by the minute and extensive markings in his copy, the document was anything but obscure. It was as vividly alive as any contemporary newspaper account of a crime, or any current court proceeding. For the stories in the *Trial*— the depositions and arguments and summations—are abundant and dateless, even as the text itself is very much a dated artifact. Put another way, a story can be timeless and true, even though it is locked in time in a document whose truth is fundamentally indeterminable. *The Trial of James Stewart* is the story of a murder— of who was killed, how, why, and by whom. The text was always available to assiduous antiquarians who searched the labyrinths of law libraries. But Stevenson, having found his own copy of the *Trial,* seized the occasion to retrieve the story within and bring it before a wider world. As a practicing novelist, he knew that the only way to do that was through narrative, that it was narrative that created interest. He certainly was not oblivious to novels that were not driven by plot. After all, he considered George Meredith the premier novelist of his time, and he was an enthusiastic admirer, as well as friend, of Henry James. But he knew intuitively, and by experience—consider the dual receptions of *New Arabian Nights* and *Treasure Island,* for example—that narrative fiction was the more powerful vehicle for capturing an audience's attention. This does not mean that thought and reflection were foreclosed from the fictional borders. But Stevenson knew that to tell a serious story one had to first construct a form that could sustain a reader for the duration. Anybody could go to the *State Trials* and get hold of the Stewart trial. But why would anyone? And if she did, how would she maintain the resolve to read through the interminable pages of the relevancy of the indictment, the repetitive testimony, the prosecutor's summing up, or the defense counsel's argument? The only readers interested in this kind of print were legal scholars and historians, and even the historians' interest had its limits. Arnot provided an abridgement of the trial, and Burton offered it in summary form. Readers were thus absolved from reading the document itself. If they insisted on the real thing, they could go to volume nineteen of the *State Trials,* but even there, despite the extensive annotation, portions of the trial were cut from the printed text. In effect, Stevenson was doing the joint work of the historian and the novelist. He trained his eye on the primary source and culled from it precisely those incidents that made the history fresh and alive. It is easy to say this but very hard to do. For the past is gone, and the Red Fox is no more. Yet for a brief moment, and with no special effects, Stevenson breathes life into Colin Roy Campbell, reviving the man, and his words, before consigning him to his tragic death in history.

Chapter 8

THE TRIAL OF JAMES STEWART

> Rather pity them, and pray for them, for they have
> my blood to answer for.
>
> —James Stewart

Although aspects of *The Trial of James Stewart* appear in numerous places in *David Balfour,* the second volume focuses intently on the legal document in two chapters, "The Heather on Fire" (9) and "The Memorial" (17). If there was a hiatus of six years between the composition of *Kidnapped* and its sequel, the continuation of the trial material in the narrative made it appear as if there was no lapse of time at all. But there was a significant difference in Stevenson's treatment of the trial document. In *Kidnapped,* it was used largely for expository and dramatic purposes —to identify the central figures, establish the context, re-present the actual murder, and create the flight to freedom of the principal suspect, Alan Breck Stewart. In *David Balfour,* on the other hand, the matter of the trial is treated juridically and philosophically, for what it means legally and politically rather than for its picturesque qualities. This is not to say that the human drama was abandoned but simply that the emphasis shifted. The second volume of Stevenson's epic is unquestionably more reflective, and readers have understandably been puzzled by it. They looked for Alan and David to continue their adventures in the same spirit as their earlier open-air flight through the heather. But if the characters have not aged, the novelist has; and his treatment of them is equally more nuanced. Just as he deals openly for the first time in this volume with sexuality, his focus is clearly more intellectual. For in *David Balfour* the issue is the law itself, the very nature of that institution at a moment in time that marked a turning point in Scottish political and cultural life. Stevenson himself was of the law, and in this book he paid homage to that august and alternately pompous fraternity. At the same time, he explored the questions addressed in this practice. For if the law was the palace of justice, as it professed, how just was that palace? Perhaps it is unfair to answer that by reference to a single criminal case, one that by Stevenson's time had an ambiguous, if not a problematic, history. Nonetheless, it was the case that fired the novelist's imagination and enabled him not only to recreate an episode in Scottish

THE

TRIAL

OF

JAMES STEWART

in *Aucharn* in *Duror* of *Appin*,

FOR THE

Murder of COLIN CAMPBELL of *Glenure*, Esq; Factor for His Majesty on the forfeited estate of *Ardshiel*;

BEFORE THE

Circuit Court of JUSTICIARY held at *INVERARAY* on *Thursday* the 21st, *Friday* the 22d, *Saturday* the 23d, and *Monday* the 25th of *September* last; by his Grace the Duke of ARGYLL, Lord Justice-General, and the Lords ELCHIES and KILKERRAN, Commissioners of Justiciary.

EDINBURGH:

Printed for G. HAMILTON and J. BALFOUR. 1753.

CONTENTS.

CONTENTS of the APPENDIX.

N. B. Pannel *means* the prisoner upon trial.

Title page of Stevenson's copy of *The Trial of James Stewart*. Courtesy of the Princeton University Library, Princeton, N.J.

Contents page of Stevenson's copy of *The Trial of James Stewart*. Courtesy of the Princeton University Library, Princeton, N.J.

history with extraordinary veracity, but to reflect upon the more lasting and profound issues concerning the application of justice and the meaning of law.

The primary legal issue that Stevenson introduces from the *Trial* concerns the charges brought against both defendants. In *Kidnapped,* Alan openly declares his innocence to David shortly after the assassination of Glenure: "I swear upon the Holy Iron I had neither art nor part, act nor thought in it" (*K,* 18:155). "Art and part" is a Scots legal phrase that "signifies accession to a crime; and many may thus be involved in the guilt of murder by presence at the spot, besides the one who strikes the fatal blow."[1] One problem presented by the trial was that James Stewart was charged with the murder, although it was clear he was nowhere near the scene of the crime. Allan Breck Stewart, who was believed to have fired the shots, meanwhile eluded capture and could not be brought to court. The legal question was simple: how could James be tried as an accessory when Allan, the principal, was not in custody? Or, as Charles Stewart forcefully said to David: "They cannae bring in James as art and part until they've brought in Alan first as principal; that's sound law" (*DB*, 9:105). But perhaps the law was not quite sound enough, for the prosecution did not accept this distinction: "Allan Breck is not charged in this libel with being the principal, and this pannel as only accessary to the murder of the deceas'd Glenure; they are both charged in the same words with being guilty, actors, or art and part of the said heinous crime" (*T*, 121). In other words, both James and Allan were jointly charged with having conspired to murder Glenure. If James had been ignorant of the assassination, and aided Allan in his escape out of compassion or loyalty, then he could not be charged with complicity in the crime. For "Scotch law . . . recognises no accession *after* the fact, except by such conduct as infers, by legal evidence, previous knowledge, counsel, or co-operation" (Alison, 68). Therefore, the prosecution had to demonstrate that James was either involved in the planning of the murder or that he knew about it prior to its occurrence. Alison commented briefly on this specific issue:

> But it turned out upon the proof that these circumstances . . . showed *previous* knowledge and communication on the part of the pannel; in particular, he was the person who had felt the real enmity against the deceased, and he had expressed his ill-will towards him; and before intelligence of the slaughter could have reached him, he had procured money for the actual perpetrator, and had sent clothes to him, which were returned after the murder by a mutual friend. These circumstances, as indicating a fore-knowledge of the act, were justly held sufficient to implicate the pannel in the murder (Alison, 68–69).

An earlier legal writer was of the same opinion as Alison, that James Stewart was properly charged, art and part, since the circumstances "shewed a previous knowledge of the intended murder, and even a concert and connivance in the commission of it. . . . They went to infer a foreknowledge of the act, and a concert with the murderer in its execution, [and] were therefore justly held, both by the Court and Jury, as amounting to art and part in the crime."[2]

Stevenson, however, does not let the later writers determine the contemporary view of Charles Stewart, James's defender and champion of sound law. For him, it is not simply whether James can be tried in the absence of Alan; he also raises serious questions about the abrogation of the rights and civil liberties of the defendant by the government. "The Heather on Fire" is a long list of abuses suffered by James Stewart and his family, abuses that were specifically prohibited by Scottish law:

> It comes to my ears that James and the witnesses—the witnesses, Mr. Balfour!—lay in close dungeons, and shackled forbye, in the military prison at Fort William; none allowed in to them, nor they to write. The witnesses,

Mr. Balfour; heard ye ever the match of that? I assure ye, no old, crooked
Stewart of the gang ever outfaced the law more impudently. It's clean in the
two eyes of the Act of Parliament of 1700, anent wrongous imprisonment.
No sooner did I get the news than I petitioned the Lord Justice Clerk. I have
his word to-day. There's law for ye! here's justice! (*DB*, 9:107).

These six pages (106–11) put into dramatic form the intricate legal wrangling
documented in the *Supplement* regarding the arrest and incarceration of James
Stewart and his witnesses and were heavily scored and underlined by the novelist.

> That not only the pannel himself was kept in *illegal close confinement,* but that
> likewise his two sons, his two servants the Maccolls, and others in the list of
> witnesses against him, were all confined in the same illegal way in the prison
> of Fort-William; and particularly, that the said two Maccolls had been kept
> there in *shackles,* or *handcuffs,* for the space of three months, and a third Mac-
> coll (the bouman) *shackled* in the same way some shorter time*; he, the
> agent, judged it proper to ask an order from the Lord Justice-Clerk to the
> keepers of the prison where these witnesses were detained, to give access
> to the agent, to see, and inform these prisoners . . . not to be terrified by
> the cruel and illegal treatment they had met with, and to swear nothing but
> what was true.
>
> *Does not this new and unprecedented way of using witnesses deserve the name of
> *torture*? Scandalous and horrid in a free country![3]

Scots lawyers prided themselves on the superiority of their law with respect to
habeas corpus. "The *Habeas Corpus* is the well-known protection of the people of
England against arbitrary imprisonment. But the security which it affords, is, in
many particulars, inferior to that which the Scotch enjoy under the act 1701."[4]
Or: "The Habeas Corpus Act of Scotland, the act 1701, c. 6, a statute which provides a more effectual remedy against undue imprisonment, than is afforded by
that justly celebrated part of English jurisprudence."[5] Charles Stewart delivers
ringing pronouncements to David about the illegality of the government's behavior: "They have the right to hold James in prison, yet they cannot deny me to visit
him. They have no right to hold the witnesses; but am I to get a sight of them, that
should be as free as the Lord Justice Clerk himself? . . . And I am not to see them
until Inverary, when the court is set!" (*DB*, 9:108–9). Although the prosecution
denied any wrongdoing ("the laws of every well governed realm certainly allow
the confinement of persons charged with capital offences, in such manner as they
may be secured, till they can be brought to trial" [*T,* 100]), even they were quick
to defend their practice as being consistent with the act against wrongous imprisonment.[6] The extraordinary complexity of the legal skirmishing with respect to

James Stewart's imprisonment, the confinement of witnesses, and the denial of access to counsel are detailed in nine closely-printed columns of footnotes in Howell's edition in the *State Trials,* all taken verbatim from the *Supplement* (8–18; *H,* 61–69). David Balfour refers to the same document with undisguised Whiggish disdain, since it was, after all, a passionate defense of the Stewart position. "[Charles Stewart] put a paper in my hand, that same mealy-mouthed, false-faced paper that was printed since in the pamphlet 'by a bystander,' for behoof (as the title says) of James's 'poor widow and five children'" (*DB,* 9:107).[7]

Stevenson draws heavily on the partisan pamphlet throughout this chapter: in the long paragraph (*DB,* 9:105–6) describing where and how Alan Breck Stewart can be "summoned," exactly according to Scottish law;[8] through his use of italics, which are virtually intact quotations from the original text; in the narrative of Charles Stewart meeting the defendant for the first time on the Tynedroum road; and for the anecdote of the providential stranger in "Fleming's printing house" (*DB,* 9:109–10) who picked up a proof of the libel from the floor and passed it on to James Stewart's counsel. The mass of detail is so complex and compact that one wonders what Stevenson had in mind by its reproduction. In one sense, "The Heather on Fire" in *David Balfour* is a parallel to "I Hear of the Red Fox" in *Kidnapped.* Stevenson needed a vehicle to provide the information essential to understanding the issues. Charles Stewart plays the same role here vis-à-vis David Balfour that Alan Breck Stewart played in the earlier chapter: he informs and comments, or waxes bilious, and is full of outrage. But here the issues are predominantly legal, rather than social and political. What are the defendant's rights? How has his case been handled procedurally? How has the law been applied? Or abused? To understand the nature of the defense that was mounted for James Stewart, Charles Stewart has to provide information regarding aspects of Scottish law. That so much of this chapter derives from the *Supplement* as opposed to the *Trial* should not be surprising, since the *Supplement* was a passionate and partisan defense of James Stewart and an attack on the legality and legitimacy of the prosecution. What Stevenson highlights are the government's most egregious abuses, which were acknowledged by all later writers, although it is clear that not all those writers believed that an injustice was committed in the verdict. As Burnett said, assuming the credibility and integrity of the witnesses' testimony, the circumstantial evidence provided by the government was sufficient to implicate James Stewart in the murder—despite the absence of the principal suspect.

In *Kidnapped,* Alan anticipated a number of legal maneuvers that were designed to assure a conviction of the defendant: "Well, it'll be tried in Inverara, the Campbell's head place; with fifteen Campbells in the jury box and the biggest Campbell of all (and that's the Duke) sitting cocking on the bench. Justice, David? The same justice, by all the world, as Glenure found a while ago at the roadside" (*K,* 18:157).

As David pointed out, Alan's predictions of a kangaroo court were prescient, except for the fact that eleven rather than fifteen Campbells were sworn on the jury. Nonetheless, despite the overwhelming strength of the government's case, and their successful effort to prevent James from conferring with his lawyers until shortly before the trial, the defendant had a strong group of persuasive advocates. In "The Memorial," which signifies a law case that contains both the facts and arguments in writing, Stevenson introduces James Stewart's lawyers and invents a meeting where they are constructing a legal strategy for their client's defense. To begin with, although David is elated at having reached Inverary in time to deliver his eyewitness testimony to Alan's innocence, and by extension to James's, he is taken aback to discover that his evidence is as likely to work against the defendant as for him.

> "To sum up," said Colstoun, "you prove that Alan was on the spot; you have heard him proffer menaces against Glenure; and though you assure us he was not the man who fired, you leave a strong impression that he was in league with him, and consenting, perhaps immediately assisting, in the act. You show him besides, at the risk of his own liberty, actively furthering the criminal's escape. And the rest of your testimony (so far as the least material) depends on the bare word of Alan or of James, the two accused. In short, you do not at all break, but only lengthen by one personage, the chain that binds our client to the murderer; and I need scarcely say that the introduction of a third accomplice rather aggravates that appearance of a conspiracy which has been our stumbling block from the beginning" (DB, 17:208).

David suddenly recognizes that the reconstruction of events as they are presented in a courtroom may differ markedly from an individual's perception or remembrance of those events. For Colstoun, David's testimony tightens the noose of circumstantial evidence offered as proof of James's complicity in the murder. And as Simon Fraser argued before the court, it was only circumstantial evidence that could be advanced as proof for such a crime. "Indeed, when that is conclusive, it is of all others the most convincing. Witnesses may be partial, they may be perjured, but a closely connected chain of circumstances is liable to none of those objections" (T, 90). Stevenson raises the issue of the problematic nature of evidence itself. One of James Stewart's strongest defenders was George Brown, who forcibly attacked the credibility of those government witnesses that provided the most damaging testimony, particularly John Breck Maccoll.

> But as the whole of this argument is founded upon the oath of the bouman deposing to a long romantic story, in which he is altogether unsupported, I am intitled in law to plead, that his oath is not to be held as legal evidence against the pannel; more especially as it appears, from what has been already

said, that his evidence is disproved in one very material article, in which he deposes to a very strong expression, as applied by the pannel against Glenure, at a time when it is proved they were in perfect friendship together (*T,* 270).

The nature of evidence is a major issue in Scottish law, and a significant distinction is made between written and oral, or parole, evidence. As a lawyer and writer, perhaps even as a philosopher, Stevenson never accepted a statement as true merely because it was written in ink, printed in a book, or deposed in a court-room. He was mainly concerned with uncovering the meaning behind the state-ments; the assertions themselves were never his central consideration. The endless testimony regarding Allan's clothes in the *Trial* is a case in point. Why does the novelist underscore the multitudinous descriptions of the "forfeited" rebel's dress? He does not dispute the reports, or even doubt that Allan wore what he was attested to have worn. But the repetition comes to assume an interest all its own. For in the midst of a drab and colorless world, Allan's "French" dress affirms life and turns its back on despair. It says, "'Bury my French clothes!' and you may as well bury me." The meaning galvanizes the novelist's imagination and enables him to transform a rough and careless outlaw into Alan Breck Stewart, a man who cap-tures the hearts of readers everywhere. There is nothing in the *Trial* that would generate this interest or feeling for Allan Breck Stewart. There is nothing in the history of the actual man, so far as it can be determined, that would make him out to be anything but a disreputable turncoat. Yet from this small motif of dress, the novelist creates a major trait of character. The pride and vanity symbolized by the French dress is but a side of the hope and joy that is equally its symbol. Evidence, for Stevenson, is material for interpretation, and interpretation is far more inter-esting and infinitely more significant. For the imaginative writer, the hermeneu-tics of the case is what the *Trial* is about. He stitches together a string of facts from historical documents and, in the process, re-chronicles history. Yet the facts, when reconstituted, create a wholly original narrative, one whose reality exists inde-pendently of its originating documents. Stevenson has constructed what might be called a paradoxical text, one composed wholly of other texts—a pastiche of pla-giarisms that is, at the same time, a text without precedent.

Although Stevenson was meticulous in recording minute, technical aspects of Scottish law ("James had now no hope but in the King's mercy" [*DB,* 17:213]), he always kept his eye on the central themes, one of which focused on clan rivalry.[9] The government attributed the assassination of Colin Roy to the Stewarts' ani-mosity toward all the Campbells: "Their attachment to their chief was made use of for that purpose. The preservation of his family, the welfare of their country, and even the very being of the clan, were represented as inconsistent with allow-ing Glenure to live" (*T,* 107). The Stewarts, for their part, saw the mirror image of that view in the state's prosecution of one of their own: "This is a scene, gentlemen, of clan animosity. The hatred of the name which I have the honor to bear, rages in high quarters. There is nothing here to be viewed but naked Campbell spite and scurvy Campbell intrigue" (*DB,* 17:209). David, listening to the Stewart lawyers argue among themselves, suddenly recognized the true nature of the conflict: "And it was forced home upon my mind how this, that had the externals of a sober process of law, was in its essence a clan battle between savage clans" (*DB,* 17:207). The joint hatred of the Campbells and Stewarts is treated with equal contempt in David's simple statement. He also saw that the law was more a cover for deep emotions and instinctual behavior than a process designed to adjudicate or resolve conflict. Indeed, David realized that the process of law is the means by which a society presents the face of civility to the world and controls the passions that would otherwise wreak havoc in the social order. Since the murder of Glenure had no other motive than "that spirit of revenge, which was the characteristic of the barbarous highlanders in former times" (*T,* 156), it was incumbent upon the government to prosecute that violent act to the fullest extent possible. And it is here that the fundamental explanation for the trial emerges. The government was primarily interested in bringing the Highlands under control, which meant bringing the Highlanders under the rule of law, particularly the law that emanated from Westminster. The abolition of the heretable jurisdictions eliminated the authority of the Highland lairds in the administration of justice on their lands. The court of justiciary, the criminal court, which was centered in Edinburgh, was even bypassed in the Stewart trial in favor of a circuit court in Inverary, the home of the Campbell clan and the seat of the Campbell laird. Since the murder of Glenure was in essence the murder of the king's representative, the government determined to make an example of the case, to show the Highlanders that there would be no tolerance whatever for any assault on the king's authority. After the failed rebellion, the government was prepared to employ any force necessary to bring the Highlands under absolute control. This is precisely the point that Prestongrange makes to David, and this is why he insists that James Stewart be brought to trial: "Blood has been barbarously shed. It has been shed in direct opposition to his Majesty and our whole frame of laws, by those who are their known and public oppugnants. I take a very high sense of this. I will not deny that I consider the crime as directly personal to his Majesty" (*DB,* 4:42). Prestongrange tries to make clear to David the importance of the trial, which is only nominally criminal.

> "This is a political case—ah, yes, Mr. Balfour! whether we like it or no, the case is political—and I tremble when I think what issues may depend from it. To a political case, I need scarce tell a young man of your education, we approach with very different thoughts from one which is criminal only. *Salus*

populi suprema lex is a maxim susceptible of great abuse, but it has that force which we find elsewhere only in the laws of nature: I mean it has the force of necessity" (*DB,* 4:47–48).

The historical Prestongrange was one of the people responsible for passing the recent law on the forfeited estates, whose declared purpose was to bring the Highlands under control, or to "civilize" them. This theme is invoked repeatedly by the government prosecutors, not least by the historical Lord Advocate:

> This murder was committed on the 14th day of May last, just seven weeks after his Majesty had given his royal assent, and passed into a law, the bill for annexing this and other forfeited estates to the Crown unalienably, and for applying the rents and profits therof for the better civilizing and improving the highlands of Scotland (*T,* 153).

Prestongrange determined to prosecute the case himself in a circuit court, "and to do all that in me lay, consistently with law and justice, to convince the disaffected part of the highlands of Scotland, that they must *submit* to this government, which they have several times in vain endeavoured to *subvert*" (*T,* 116). Stevenson's portrait of the Lord Advocate has been justly admired, but part of its brilliance derives from the historical context that gives the dramatic character an added dimension. Prestongrange enjoyed a reputation as a good and decent Lord Advocate. His role in the Stewart trial, however, was the one blot on his record. It is clear that throughout the proceedings he was a participant in the strategy to make James Stewart an example to all Highlanders who might entertain any notions of rebellion or even subversion. Thus Allan Breck Stewart played a secondary role in the case, and the question of his guilt or innocence was not a primary concern to the Lord Advocate. If anything, it would only complicate the case against James ("Once admitted, it would destroy the whole presumptions of our case against another and a very different criminal; a man grown old in treason, already twice in arms against his king" [*DB,* 4:48]). Charles Stewart recognized the government's main motive when he suggested to David that they were not actively searching for Alan: "They think perhaps he might set up a fair defence, upon the back of which James, the man they're really after, might climb out. This is not a case, ye see, it's a conspiracy" (*DB,* 9:106–7). That James was the central figure was clear to Charles Stewart from early on, and he said as much to David: "'Ye muckle ass!' cried Stewart, 'it's James they want; James has got to hang—Alan too, if they could catch him—but James whatever! Go near the Advocate with any such business, and you'll see! he'll find a way to muzzle ye'" (*DB,* 2:20). When David does not pay sufficient attention to Charles Stewart and brings his argument before the Lord Advocate, he is indeed finally removed from the scene and sequestered on the Bass Rock in order to keep him from testifying at the trial.

One of the central legal issues, as I have noted, was the necessity to prove James guilty as part of a conspiracy. If Allan were innocent, it would destroy the government's case against James. Hence the necessity to try Allan in absentia, to find him guilty, and then to proceed with the case against James. Hence the necessity for Stevenson to prevent David from testifying on behalf of Alan. But at the base of the Lord Advocate's argument rested the essential problem of how to bring the Highlanders into the second half of the eighteenth century.

> The Duke and I are Highlanders. But we are Highlanders civilised, and it is not so with the great mass of our clans and families. They have still savage virtues and defects. They are still barbarians, like these Stewarts; only the Campbells were barbarians on the right side, and the Stewarts were barbarians on the wrong (*DB,* 4:50–51).

Prestongrange is remarkably frank with David in his admission that the prosecution of James Stewart is political; in his acknowledgment that his political duty comes before his judicial duty; and in his recognition of the overriding interest in bringing the Highlands—and by extension the country—of Scotland into the legal and political orbit of the Union. In his fictional portrait of the Lord Advocate, Stevenson draws on the breadth of his experience in reconstructing historical personages. He highlights the strengths of the man, the power and command that comes from the office and is reflected both in his physical presence and in his study: "It was a long room, of a good proportion, wholly lined with books. That small spark of light in a corner struck out the man's handsome person and strong face" (*DB,* 4:39). Stevenson is quite prepared to acknowledge the gifts of intelligence and ambition that spur men to succeed. He is not, however, blind to the problematic nature of those gifts. Simon Fraser presents an alternative portrait to that of the Lord Advocate. Here the novelist introduces a figure who highlights the history of the Fraser clan, and in particular the history of the venal and rapacious Lord Lovat, Simon Fraser's father, who was executed after the rebellion and another famous trial (a record of which Stevenson also owned and scored).[10] Stevenson's reaction to the Master of Lovat comes in the very opening of the chapter.

> There was a man waiting us in Prestongrange's study, whom I distasted at the first look, as we distaste a ferret or an earwig. He was bitter ugly, but seemed very much of a gentleman; had still manners, but capable of sudden leaps and violences; and a small voice, which could ring out shrill and dangerous when he so desired (*DB,* 6:65).

The dichotomies of the man constitute an image of danger and duplicity. That he was able to revive his fortunes and recover the family estate is a testament to his single-minded pursuit of restitution, and his willingness to turn his coat and assist in the prosecution of the Appin murder. But as Prestongrange remarked, Simon was "ambitious" (DB, 6:70), and principles were not his strong suit. He could not escape the taint of his family's history, however, and Stevenson draws on the Frasers' notoriety for abduction in the kidnapping motif foregrounded in "The Memorial," with its references to the abduction of Lady Grange and her sequestration on St. Kilda.

In "The Tee'd Ball," the chapter immediately following "The Memorial," Stevenson brings the whole episode of the *Trial* to a conclusion with the verdict and the scathing speech delivered by the Duke of Argyll to James Stewart.

> The Duke's words I am quite sure I have correctly; and since that famous passage has been made a subject of dispute, I may as well commemorate my version. Having referred to the year '45, the chief of the Campbells, sitting as Justice-General upon the bench, thus addressed the unfortunate Stewart before him: "If you had been successful in that rebellion, you might have been giving the law where you have now received the judgment of it; we, who are this day your judges, might have been tried before one of your mock courts of judicature; and then you might have been satiated with the blood of any name or clan to which you had an aversion" (DB, 18:224).

Because notes were not taken on the last day of the trial, and the Duke's words were recorded subsequently from memory, Stevenson raises a question about the accuracy of the speech.[11] Of course, since he is quoting verbatim from a printed text, his observation that he has the words "correctly" is a bit sly. From the point of view of the narrator, however, since the printed text presumably does not exist, David's measured remarks about the version he is offering are entirely correct. Even in so small a sentence as this, introductory to the substance of the paragraph, Stevenson never loses control of the complex textual design, specifically of the interconnectedness between the fictional narrator, David Balfour, and the authorial presence, Robert Louis Stevenson. Both are omnipresent in the book. Each name is on the title-page, and the division between them is unseen or unclear. It is a textual strategy that brilliantly reinforces the writer's simultaneous commitment to historical reality and fictional art. The writer of the *Supplement* goes so far as to say, "The L——J——G——spoke to the condemned pannel, in an angry style, as many of us by-standers then thought: and we affirm, that the speech spoke was much more acute and bitter than the speech printed" (68). What is interesting about the passage, apart from Stevenson's introduction of doubt, is its reflection upon power and how power dictates social and political behavior. The historical speech was significantly longer than the extract quoted by Stevenson, who refers to the rebellion of 1745, while the Duke goes back to the late sixteenth and early seventeenth centuries.

> To trace your crime from its true original source, I will use the words of our Statute-book, *Those barbarous cruelties and lawless oppressions* practised in the Highlands during several centuries. . . . That obstinate and almost incureable disaffection and aversion to the government in several Highland clans, and in particular your own, ever since the happy Revolution, and the establishment of the crown in the Protestant line (*T,* 286).

The crime for the Duke is very nearly epic in its origin, nothing if not an inevitable consequence of centuries of rebellion and resistance to authority, both the authority of the crown and the authority of the Protestant religion. The Stewarts, by their name and their behavior, were seen as unremitting antagonists to everything that the Campbells' chief, and the Campbell clan, represented: law, loyalty to the British King, and adherence to the Protestant church. By then turning to the recent rebellion, the Duke identifies the immediate origins of the assassination of Glenure: "Yet I may say, with great force of truth, that this murder has been visibly the effect and consequence of the late rebellion" (*T,* 287–88). John Hill Burton found in the Duke's speech, which he also reprinted, "the hereditary enmity of race and party bursting forth through all control of judicial decorum."[12] But Argyll's argument was unpersuasive to the opposition. If the government's aim was to undermine and destroy the spirit of clanship, then the trial had exactly the opposite effect. For the Duke, in his role as Justice-General, exerted the "spirit of clanship" by sitting as judge in a circuit court in his own country where the juries were inevitably composed of Campbells. As it appears in the *Supplement:* "Every hint from the judge will be received by the jury as the commands of the chieftain" (69). Although the Duke and the government were ostensibly committed to extirpating the clan system, in effect it was the clan system that tried and convicted James Stewart. Stevenson repeats this point indirectly when David comments, shortly after the printed speech: "James was as fairly murdered as though the Duke had got a fowling-piece and stalked him" (*DB,* 18:225). In a sense, James is killed in precisely the same way as Glenure, a detail that makes the legal proceedings precisely the same as the Duke claims they would be if the Stewarts had won the rebellion. The Stewarts would be "giving the law," the trial would have been a mock court, and the blood of a Campbell would be exacted in revenge for the murder of a Stewart. Thus Stevenson uses the Duke's own words against James Stewart to turn the argument against him, to make us aware of how arbitrary the system of law is, of how the trial is nothing more than a veil that covers the will to exert power over one's enemy, and the exercise of that power by

[69]

weak men are nature; but the foibles of men diſtinguiſh-
ed by their abilities, as they can hardly be concealed,
nay are ſometimes revealed even by themſelves; ſo they
can never be forgiven.

And here let me leave it to the reader to conſider,
whether this ſpeech, together with the whole tenor of theſe
proceedings, does not furniſh ground to apprehend, that
the late acts of parliament, for aboliſhing the ſpirit of
clanſhip, may contribute in a great degree to confirm the
evil they meant to deſtroy. For, by appointing circuit-
courts to be held at Inverary in the country of Argyle,
and under the very walls of the caſtle, where the majo-
rities at leaſt of juries muſt be compoſed of Campbells,
his Grace, who, by his office of Juſtice-General, is inti-
tled to preſide at theſe courts, has thereby an opportunity of exerting that ſpirit of clanſhip in ſo much a
ſtronger manner than before, as the authority of *judge* is
added to the influence of *chief*. Every hint from the
judge will be received by the jury as the commands of
the chieftain. And if any caſe ever can happen
where the judge can be biaſſed, whether a rival clan or
private reſentment is in queſtion, (and no highlanders are
without the one, and few men without the other), it will
be vain to expect the jury impartial. In this caſe, of
the jury eleven were Campbells; and what effects the
hints from the bench had upon them, may be gathered
from the obſervations of the judicious pannel, who knew
too much of the nature of clanſhip, not to be certain of
his fate, from the firſt check that was given his Advocates. If it ſhall be ſaid, the loyalty of the clan
Campbell is a ſufficient ſecurity againſt ſuch apprehen-
ſions, I ſhall beg leave to aſſert, that it was clanſhip in
general that the legiſlature meant to deſtroy; for every
degree of ſovereign power in a ſubject is inconſiſtent with
the good of the ſtate, as it may be exerted to its ſubver-
ſion. Nor has this very clan always had their hands
free from the *ſtain* of *rebellion* againſt eſtabliſhed government. That indeed was the government of another
family.

"It was clanship in general that the legislature meant to destroy." From *A Supplement to the Trial of James Stewart,* which was bound together with Stevenson's copy of *The Trial of James Stewart.* Courtesy of the Princeton University Library, Princeton, N.J.

force. Undoubtedly, if the Stewarts were in power then the Campbells would be in the dock. Thus the Duke's words are actually true, although for the wrong reasons. He believes they are absolutely true, since right is on the side of the government and the clan Campbell. But as the opposition writer of the *Supplement* reminds us, the Campbells have their own checkered history: "Nor has this very clan always had their hands free from the *stain of rebellion* against established government" (69).

It remained only for Stevenson to hang James—which he did later on, in an aside, while David was moving in good society—and all thoughts of internecine clan warfare, distant trials, and indistinct defendants were long gone.

There was never the least word heard of the memorial, or none by me. Prestongrange and his grace the Lord President may have heard of it (for what I know) on the deafest sides of their heads; they kept it to themselves, at least; the public was none the wiser; and in course of time, on November 8th, and in the midst of a prodigious storm of wind and rain, poor James of the Glens was duly hanged at Lettermore by Balachulish (*DB*, 20:262–63).

Stevenson condensed a dramatically profound execution that had been vividly recounted in the *Edinburgh Courant* of November 21 and reprinted in November 1752 in *The Scots Magazine:*

> The storm was so great all this time, that it was with the utmost difficulty one could stand upon the hill, and it was near five before the body was hung in chains. There were a great number of the country people present; and sixteen men of the command in Appin are stationed at Ballachelish to prevent the gibbet's being cut down (556).

The hanging concluded the Glenure affair, but it only began the legend that became the Appin murder. To be hanged in chains was a particularly cruel punishment, reserved for the most heinous capital crimes. That it was applied to James Stewart, who was deliberately hanged on the spot where the original murder was committed, highlighted the government's resolve to make an example of anyone who dared oppose the state. What they made instead was a martyr of a late rebel, and added yet another name to the long "catalogue of Jacobite martyrs" who died in the good cause.[13]

The Stewart trial quickly became a cause célèbre in Scottish legal history. The *Supplement,* the first extended critique of the proceedings, was published separately as a pamphlet shortly after the printed *Trial.* It was also sold bound up with the longer document, the edition that Stevenson owned. David Mackay provides a bibliography of books and articles that comment on the case, down through 1907, the year of his edition for the Notable British Trials series.[14] Of these commentaries, Arnot and Burton, the authorities Stevenson requested from his father, are among the most important. Howell provides the most extensive annotated edition of the trial, and Omond writes from a perspective that is virtually contemporaneous with Stevenson's. What is interesting about all these commentaries is how partisan they appear despite the intervening years. One would expect the *Supplement* to reflect its pro-Jacobite and anti-government bias, coming as it does at the moment of the events—and Arnot, writing thirty years after the trial, might be excused the passion of his principles. But the tone of partisanship enters into Burton's narrative, a full century later, while Omond feels compelled to establish the political context for his position. In a sense, Stevenson is actually the most detached and subtle of the interpreters of the Appin tragedy. For while each of the writers establishes a position, if not by explicit declaration then by descriptive commentary, it is only Stevenson's text that retains the ambiguity, or mystery, that surrounded the incident in the first place, and that was never satisfactorily resolved. Every one of the commentators believed he could summarize and fix the event for historical understanding. But Stevenson, in the process of composition, engaged in a form of historical interpretation that was ultimately more sophisticated than that proffered by the authorities, for it assumed a complexity that was invariably discarded in the seemingly straightforward historical accounts. Perhaps, in Aristotelian terms, it was the artistic as opposed to the merely historical truth. The historians proper all retain the passion of their convictions, which ring clear in their defense of the defendant, but none conveys the doubt and uncertainty that complicate the issues in the fictional treatment and hence provide a fairer representation of the truth. This is noticeable in the treatment of Prestongrange, who is chastised for his role in the trial, but whom Stevenson sees as someone caught between the devil and the deep sea, forced to do the government's work, which he was determined upon, yet conscious of the injustice that was inevitably administered in pursuit of that work. There is no evidence that the historical Prestongrange doubted the justification for the trial, or even the guilt of the accused. Indeed, it was apparently his own decision to prosecute the case in Inverary, an unprecedented act that was universally condemned by the commentators. For fictional purposes, Stevenson gives him a depth that is not immediately apparent in the historical record. His portrait as mentor (not to mention surrogate father) to the aspiring law student, David Balfour, is constructed without regard to the historical evidence (Prestongrange had three daughters, but none were named Barbara). In a sense, the issue has to do with the distinction between art and history. Stevenson drew on the extensive speeches of the Lord Advocate from the *Trial,* combined them with his knowledge of political psychology and the legal mind, and created a portrait of a man that may well be truer than the one history itself could provide, were it at all able.

There were a number of issues raised by the trial that virtually all writers agreed upon. It was without precedent for the Justice-General, in practice an honorary office, to preside at a criminal trial. In this case, the officer was the Duke of Argyle, who, as Burton said, was "resolved to preside at the trial of a Stewart and a Jacobite for the murder of a Campbell and a Hanoverian" (91). Further, the trial was held at Inverary, Argyle's seat and the territory of the clan Campbell, where the jurors selected were bound to be predominantly of that clan. If it was a procedure that was not deliberately designed to secure a conviction, there is little doubt that it was the next best thing to it, and Arnot, Burton, and Omond all declared that the trial should have been held at the high court in Edinburgh. They remarked on the uniqueness of the Lord Advocate personally conducting the prosecution, although there was no prohibition against it. What these technical details all added up to—Argyle sitting on the court, the trial in the seat of the murdered man's clan, the Lord Advocate assuming responsibility for the prosecution, and a jury of fifteen composed of eleven Campbells—was a trial without the slightest pretense of fairness toward the defendant.[15] Further, the historians viewed both the venue and the jury as simply another part of the clan nature of the conflict, which included the assassination of Glenure as well as the trial of James Stewart, a form of retribution by the murdered man's kin. There is nothing that any of the historians disagreed about with respect to the legal and technical issues of the trial. On another level, the writers commented extensively on the incarceration of James Stewart and the sequestration of his family and witnesses. As we have seen, this was a significant matter in the *Supplement,* drawn upon heavily by Stevenson and commented upon extensively by Arnot, Howell, and Burton. Clearly the abuse or dismissal of habeas corpus—the act anent wrongous imprisonment—was not taken lightly by subsequent writers. Then there was the matter of evidence, an issue that was viewed differently by various commentators. Since virtually the entire case against both defendants was based on circumstantial evidence, the question turned on the validity and the legitimacy of such evidence. For Burnett, circumstantial evidence is often the most reliable, not subject to the distortions of memory that can characterize parole testimony, and it is perfectly appropriate to base a case upon it. For Burton and Omond, the weight of the circumstantial evidence argued for Allan Breck Stewart as the assassin of Glenure. On the other hand, it was insufficient to justify a case against James Stewart. Both Arnot and Burton also questioned the role of translators in the trial, arguing that they were Campbells who were, in effect, providing a biased edge to the translation of witnesses' testimony, thus further tipping the case against James Stewart.

But in the end it was Burton and Omond, both of whom had strong loyalties to the government (and neither of whom was disposed to see any virtue in the Jacobite cause), who attempted to put the Stewart trial in perspective. Both viewed the proceedings as a judicial tragedy, although Burton had less sympathy with James Stewart than Omond. Burton focused on the murder as a "solitary crime" which was the final "expiring flame" in the failed Jacobite cause.[16] Although the proceedings against James Stewart were clearly illegal, and the trial a perversion of justice, the very fact that it was known and commented upon was a testament to the success of free British institutions. The trial thus served as an example of how the institutions are greater than the figures who at any one time may be responsible for subverting those institutions. Omond, on the other hand, saw the crime and the trial in the context of the overall effort to suppress the Jacobites and bring the Highlands under the influence of the king's government. The act for annexing the forfeited estates (introduced by Prestongrange in parliament) was a major instrument in pursuing this objective, and it was the forfeited estate of Appin that occasioned the murder of Glenure. Thus the government had no choice but to pursue a prosecution in order to establish its credibility, to convince the Highlanders they had no alternative but to submit to the authority of the crown, and to insure that no similar crimes would occur in the future. The trial was nothing if not political, and Omond, the historian of Scotland's lord advocates, had little doubt that James Stewart "was sacrificed to political considerations" (2:57).

The law is the avenue to power and success in the world, and it is hardly surprising that David is determined to join the profession. The legal personnel in *David Balfour*—Prestongrange, the Duke of Argyle, Simon Fraser, Charles Stewart, and the lawyers in "The Memorial"—represent a fraternity comfortable with the machinery of power. They are not all equal, of course, nor do they all win their cases, but in the world at large it is the lawyers who legislate and adjudicate, who compose and dispose. Yet the view of lawyers is nothing if not ambiguous. When David declares to Prestongrange that "It is my design to be called to the bar" (*DB*, 17:221), the Lord Advocate "bitterly" responds: "You should certainly be called; the bar is the true scene for your talents" (*DB*, 17:221). For he recognizes how adept David is at negotiation and manipulation—even verbal casuistry—and he knows better than anyone how much that constitutes the work of the legal profession. It is hardly coincidental that one of Stevenson's most brilliant creations was based upon the profound and intimidating Lord Braxfield, the hanging judge, transformed into Weir of Hermiston in the novelist's unfinished masterpiece. The law as subject enabled Stevenson to reflect upon fundamental philosophical principles: the nature of civil society; the relationship between justice and mercy; the primacy of logic over feeling; and, at bottom, the problematic nature of the judicial enterprise itself. For the law, apart from its technical components, is nothing more than a tapestry of the world that becomes our design for living. The lawyers and judges create the design and weave the tapestry, but in the end it is an arbitrary construction, capable of being discarded or unravelled when it no longer accommodates our needs or our vision. This is why the Stewart and Macgregor trials are such significant texts. They illustrate the problematic nature of evidence; or, rather, they demonstrate how evidence can be perceived differently depending upon your viewpoint or your political interest. The law then becomes a subject for writers who put their own construction on the story, retelling it without regard to the lawyers and judges who presented and tried the case, in effect creating their own stories out of those woven by the legal technicians. Thus in "The Memorial" the Stewart advocates comment repeatedly on David's story, on the truth that presumably inheres in his narrative and will therefore serve as the basis for future histories of the legal case. "Sheriff Miller tells us historical writers are to date from it, and I would not wonder. It is only my fear they would date from it as a period of calamity and public reproach" (*DB,* 17:213). There is a wry, self-reflexive note about this comment, as Stevenson clearly has before him the later narratives of the Stewart trial that are predicted in the chapter, set as it is before they were composed, yet written by the novelist after their publication. Stevenson is playing with intertextuality here, with the trial as documentary text, its subsequent commentaries (Arnot, Burton, et al.), its final fictional reconstruction (which is an extended grace note on the trial and its interpreters), and its full circle return to the period just prior to the original trial text. Stevenson uses primary and secondary historical texts to create an intricate collage, one that depends upon those texts and at the same time anticipates them. *David Balfour* is, in part, a discourse on history, on the reconstruction of history, and on its own creation as historical fiction.

Chapter 9

THE BASS ROCK

"It's an unco place, the Bass"
—Andie Dale

Stevenson was known as a gifted descriptive writer. From his depiction of the sand swept Scottish coast of "The Pavilion on the Links" in the late seventies through the breaking of a Pacific dawn in "The Beach of Falesá" in the early nineties, his work evokes an atmosphere from the physical setting while investing that setting with symbolic meaning. Stevenson's insistence upon a map to accompany *Kidnapped* was hardly an afterthought for a novel that David Daiches later described as topographical. But so too was its sequel. Andrew Lang, reviewing *Catriona* at the time of its publication, half-comically pleaded for help: "Obviously, we need a map of old Edinburgh, as it was in 1750, and we need topographical notes and illustrative anecdotes."[1] Both books focus on particular places and give to them a full measure of their historical significance. So many of the chapter titles in *Kidnapped* and *David Balfour* are place-names, entities whose meaning derives largely from their history. In *David Balfour,* chapters 14 and 15 are situated on the Bass Rock and offer a striking illustration of Stevenson's use of place as a way to represent Scottish history.

Abducted by the Highlanders on the Gillane Sands and carried away before being ferried to the Bass, David "could see the three huge towers and broken battlements of Tantallon, that old chief place of the Red Douglases" (*DB,* 13:163). With this imposing structure in his field of vision, David can situate himself and serve as the conduit to reiterate and develop a number of familiar themes. For one, there is the panoramic sweep of Scottish history embedded both in the physical monument of Tantallon Castle and in the house of Douglas, whose "memorable emblem of the Bloody Heart" was still in evidence above the entrance to the castle.

> For centuries, Tantallan was the great and principal strength and defence in the east of this proud and powerful family. It was so admirably situated and so skilfully constructed, that it mocked every military enterprise for its

The Bass Rock, by John Slezer. From *Theatrum Scotiae* (London, 1693). Courtesy of the National Library of Scotland, Edinburgh.

conquest. Its destruction was regarded as impossible; hence the popular conviction, "Ding down Tantallan?—mak a brig to the Bass,"—accomplishments viewed as equally hopeless.[2]

Yet at the time of David's capture, the castle was nothing but a ruin, having passed out of the hands of the Red Douglases (Stevenson's metonymy for the family's well-known emblem of the bloody heart, sculpted in stone above the entrance) into the family of Dalrymple, who dismantled the castle and allowed it to decay. Thus from the moment of his capture, David—ever observant and invariably informed—calls attention to the problematical nature of power, its cyclical rise and fall. Certainly, he recognizes that the seemingly unassailable might of the Tantallon fortalice is now merely a shell, a mass of stone immense in its proportions but utterly empty and useless, or to use the favorite word of the gazetteers employed in the subsequent chapter by Stevenson, a "ruin." The novelist does not have to proceed through a litany of events describing the history (or more likely the genealogy) of the Douglas family and Tantallon Castle. Rather, the "broken battlements" and the oblique allusion to the armorial shield are sufficient for his purpose. The castle and family both represent the transformation of powerful entities, the decay of an impregnable fortress ("the venerable and classic ruins of Tantallan Castle"), and the waning power of a notable family.[3] Time alters all, and even the mighty are brought to naught in the end. This theme, which runs through Stevenson's work, becomes pronounced in the last years and is most visible in *David Balfour.* We might adapt the writer's earlier translation (as essayist) of

François Villon's famous line, "Autant en emporte ly vent," and apply it to David's small observe with respect to Tantallon Castle and the house of Douglas: "So much carry the winds away."

David Balfour, Stevenson's unerring eye, offers an initial view of that "wounderful crag," the Bass Rock.[4] "It is just the one crag of rock, as everybody knows, but great enough to carve a city from" (*DB,* 14:165). Contrast this first with the *New Statistical Account:*

> Facing Tantallan Castle on the north, in the mouth of the Frith, about a mile and a-half from the shore, stands the immense rugged circular rock called the Bass. It is fully a mile in circumference. It rises 420 feet above the surface of the sea, and from the fathomed depth of the waters around, it may be estimated about 600 feet in total height. On the north, it is peculiarly lofty and precipitous, and stupendously overawing (2:330).

And next with the Bass Rock: "But an abrupt rock tower, rising out of the sea to the height of four hundred and twenty feet, must be always an imposing object."[5] Although the primary purpose of these nineteenth-century reports is descriptive, the writers are nonetheless intent upon conveying a sense of the power that inheres in the physical majesty of the natural structure. While Stevenson's objective is less formal and more subtle, it might even be said to be poetic in its impulse. The evocativeness of his sentence comes from its understated simplicity ("It is just the one crag of rock") crossed with the immense sweep of the image ("but great enough to carve a city from"). This is enough to give a sense of the raw size of this free standing rock offshore in the mouth of the Forth. The terms "rock," "crag," and "Bass" are repeated with such regularity that they reinforce the visual image of the strength and solidity of the Bass. David continues:

> With the growing of the dawn I could see it clearer and clearer; the straight crags painted with sea-birds' droppings like a morning frost, the sloping top of it green with grass, the clan of white geese that cried about the sides, and the black, broken buildings of the prison sitting close on the sea's edge (*DB,* 14:165).

Stevenson, like his cousin Bob, had an impressionist's brush and an artist's eye for color, and in the darkest places he sought the light and the contrast. In these lines he brings the colors of the Bass to the fore, colors that highlight the majesty of the rock in the dawning light, the ubiquitous birds who made the island a virtual sanctuary, the solan geese who made it an aviary, the touch of green that identified a pasturage, and the dark ruins of the buildings that housed the state prisoners who had been held on the island.

During his long disquisition on the legal perfidy awaiting James of the Glens, Charles Stewart, Writer, turns his attention from the defendant's to David Balfour's fate: "Ye're not to be tried then, and ye're not to be murdered; but I'm in bitter error if ye're not to be kidnapped and carried away like the Lady Grange" (*DB*, 9:111). And then he adds for David's benefit: "It was old Lovat that managed the Lady Grange affair; if young Lovat is to handle yours, it'll be all in the family. What's James More in prison for? The same offence: abduction. His men have had practice in the business" (*DB*, 9:111). The abduction of Lady Grange from Edinburgh in 1732, her transport across the Highland line and her confinement on St. Kilda, the remotest of the western islands, is one of the more sensational incidents in Scottish history. Lady Grange (whose father shot President Lockhart in the middle of an Edinburgh street) was known for her "fierce, proud, vindictive, and jealous temper."[6] Her behavior encouraged the public belief that she was disturbed in her mind and that her husband, the Justice-Clerk of the Court of Session, was the model of patient suffering. Thus there was more relief than regret at the funeral conducted shortly after her disappearance. Nine years later, however, word reached Edinburgh that Lady Grange, far from dead, was in fact held prisoner on a distant and isolated western island. What deepened the fascination of the story was the rumor that her husband, under cover of the most pious Presbyterian demeanor, had been responsible for his wife's kidnapping and imprisonment in order to prevent her from disclosing his subterranean life as a Jacobite intriguer. But it was not until the publication of Lord Grange's letters one hundred years later that what had been unsubstantiated gossip in the 1730s was confirmed. John Buchanan, writing in the last decade of the eighteenth century, could only repeat the gossip.

> This affair happened about the year 1733, owing to some private misunderstanding between her ladyship and Lord Grange, whom she unfortunately married. But the real cause continues a secret, since her ladyship never returned. . . . Some people imagined, that she knew something of the rebellion that broke out in 1745, at that time, and meant to have divulged the secret, which is not very probable.[7]

The story was extremely curious, and it was recorded by Robert Wodrow in his *Analecta* and Boswell in the *Journal of a Tour to the Western Hebrides.* Buchanan (whom as we saw earlier Stevenson had read very closely) introduced it as part of the history of St. Kilda.

> This island will continue to be famous, from its being the place of imprisonment of the Hon. Lady Grange, who was, by private intrigue, carried out of her own house, and violently put on board a vessel at Leith, unknown to

any of her friends, and left her great personal estate in the possession of that very man who entered into this horrid conspiracy against her; he sent her to this wild isle, where she was barbarously used, and at last finished her miserable life, among those ignorant people, who could not speak her language.

A poor old woman told me, that when she served her there, her whole time was devoted to weeping; and wrapping up letters round pieces of cork, bound up with yarn, and throwing them into the sea, to try if any favourable wave would waft them to some Christian, to inform some humane person where she resided, in expectation of carrying tidings to her dear friends in Edinburgh.[8]

In the nineteenth century, Lord Grange's letters were printed in *The Miscellany of the Spalding Club,* volume 3 (1846), which *Blackwood's Edinburgh Magazine* drew upon for an extensive review of the case (September 1849). John Hill Burton devoted seven pages to Lord Grange in his history.

Stevenson actually listed Lady Grange as one of the topics in the letter to his father outlining his prospective Highland history. On the face of it, he does nothing more in *David Balfour* than refer to the affair on three separate occasions. First, in "The Heather on Fire," cited above, and next, in "Gillane Sands," when Alan is getting ready to escape to France and wonders why David, who is clearly being stalked, will stay behind and court danger: "Are ye to be speerited away like Lady Grange? . . . Would ye stick your head in the mouth of Sim Fraser and the ither Whigs?" (*DB,* 13:157) Just after Alan gets into the boat, David is indeed overcome by a trio of Highlanders and taken to the Bass Rock, where he is held captive in order to prevent his appearance and testimony at the trial of James Stewart. Alan's reference to Lady Grange tightens the image of kidnapping, recalling the original trepanning of David on board the *Covenant,* as well as the forcible abduction of Jean Key alluded to in "In Balquidder." Simple as it is, with little or no adornment, the allusion draws on a major theme in both novels, the open use of force to attain one's ends. In the cases of Lady Grange and David Balfour (in *David Balfour*), the motives were primarily political; in that of Jean Key, they were conjugal, sexual, and financial, and not necessarily in that order. And behind all these stark assertions of power lay the spectacular case of Simon Fraser, Lord Lovat, whose shadow hovers over his shrewd and opportunistic son in *David Balfour.* The father's forcible marriage and rape of Amelia Murray in her own house, Castle Dounie, and her subsequent imprisonment on the isle of Aigas, in order to secure his claims to the Lovat estate, was unquestionably the most notorious case in Highland history. Lovat and his clansmen were tried, in absence, by the high court of justiciary for rape (among other charges). As Charles Stewart told David Balfour, it was "old

Lovat" who was behind the kidnapping of Lady Grange, and thus it was fitting that Sim Fraser (to use Alan's easy colloquialism) should be responsible for the imminent abduction of David Balfour.[9] Here again Stevenson merges the historical characters and events with the fictional, thereby historicizing the fiction and dramatizing the history. The real personages and events are so intertwined with the invented that the constructed text dissolves the distinction between fiction and history. David, as a fictional actor in a historical drama, becomes a surrogate for innocents abused by power and privilege. As he is forcibly carried to the Bass, his first thoughts are of the dead child Ransome and his warning of "the *twenty-pounders*," the children abducted and sold into slavery in the plantations.[10] David finds himself back in the position he was in on the *Covenant,* only this time there will be no Alan, no shipwreck, and no escape: "I saw myself hoe tobacco under the whip's lash" (*DB,* 14:164). The image of slavery, or enforced servitude, is carried over from *Kidnapped,* and it augments the theme of naked and arbitrary power exercised over the innocent and powerless, over women and children. Ransome was nothing more than a throwaway child, someone who survived longer than he probably had a right to. Jean Key was a young woman whose small inheritance was all the temptation necessary for the aggressive, acquisitive instincts of James More. As for Lady Grange, nobody in Edinburgh would miss the alcoholic daughter of a murderer, and all would feel gratitude for the good fortune of her liberated husband. David Balfour, as the fictional hero in a historical drama, serves as witness and voice for all these lost innocents, long gone but now recovered through his master's art.

On the simplest level, the Bass serves as a dramatic setting for David's sequestration, the Scots legal term ordinarily applied to the confiscation of an estate or the diversion of its income and here used for the forced removal and concealment of a person.[11] It does not require an imaginative leap to find in the term the buried image of people as property, an image that continues the slavery motif begun with the kidnapping of David in the first volume. It is worth noting that Scotland in the eighteenth century had no law against kidnapping, which shows up as a slang term in Francis Grose's dictionary.[12] Someone prosecuted for the act would be indicted under the charge of plagium, which was, in reality, a criminal charge of stealing a human being, rather than a material object.

> The first instance of a trial for this offence . . . 1752 . . . the indictment bore not only murder but "the stealing or away-taking of a living child". . . . Again, in the case of Margaret Irvine, Aberdeen, September 1784, a libel for *plagium* or man-stealing was found relevant after a full debate on the relevancy of the charge, and the prisoner, upon conviction, sentenced to death.[13]

In effect, David was stolen in much the same way his estate was stolen earlier by his uncle; and as his property was recovered, so too will he be recovered. But Stevenson's sharper point is never far below the surface. The whole scheme of kidnapping or trepanning boys like Ransome—or young men like David, recent widows like Jean Key, or contentious wives like Lady Grange—was deeply rooted in Scottish life and culture, and it affected both the sparse Highland country and the dense Lowland cities. The words that indicate the practice show up throughout the period in criminal trials, most notably the famous trial of Peter Williamson against the magistrates of Aberdeen, which Stevenson would have read about in Burton's *History* or in *Blackwood's* magazine. There was also the notorious Annesley trial, which served as the background for Scott's *Guy Mannering,* and which some have suggested was a source, as well, for *Kidnapped:*

> An attempt was made, I say, to kidnap the lessor of the plaintiff; . . . but the third attempt was more successful; and in about four months after the death of the late lord Altham, the lessor of the plaintiff was sent into America, and there sold for a common slave.[14]

Kidnapping was a practice, Stevenson reminds us, so habitual that David thinks nothing of using the term "sequestration" just as the lawyers use the legal phrase "in durance" to describe Lady Grange's imprisonment, as if she had been formally charged and convicted of a crime rather than lifted off the streets of Edinburgh and hustled away to St. Kilda (*DB,* 17:209).

Safely hidden away, sequestered on the Bass, David has little to do but observe his habitat, including his jailer with the "swarthy countenance":

> Andie Dale was the Prefect (as I would jocularly call him) of the Bass, being at once the shepherd and the gamekeeper of that small and rich estate. He had to mind the dozen or so of sheep that fed and fattened on the grass of the sloping part of it, like beasts grazing the roof of a cathedral. He had charge besides of the solan geese that roosted in the crags; and from these an extraordinary income is derived. The young are dainty eating, as much as two shillings a-piece being a common price, and paid willingly by epicures; even the grown birds are valuable for their oil and feathers; and a part of the minister's stipend of North Berwick is paid to this day in solan geese, which makes it (in some folks' eyes) a parish to be coveted (*DB,* 14:166).

Apart from the wry twist of the sobriquet, the description is a compressed narrative of Bass fact. The island (after it passed to the Dalrymples) was indeed "let on lease to a keeper,"[15] and the old garden, just under the summit and the largest of the three terraces that formed the "sloping acclivity" of the Bass,[16] was a natural pasturage, its soil rich from the droppings of the sea birds as well as the composition of the native grass.[17] David Balfour said they could not eat the island sheep because they were "specially fed to market" (*DB,* 14:169), a detail borne out by the *New Statistical Account,* although David and the *New Statistical Account* differ as to the number of sheep grazed (attributable either to the nearly one hundred years that separate the two accounts or to the different source that Stevenson used for his information).

The solan geese, or gannets, were without doubt the most distinctive creatures of the Bass, and their natural history was the subject of numerous commentaries by travelers and scientists. The birds are native as well to St. Kilda, and Stevenson read about them in Martin ("The solan geese are daily making up their nests from March till September; they make in the shelves of high rocks.")[18] and Buchanan ("The fulmar furnishes oil for the lamp, down for the bed, the most salubrious food, and the most efficacious ointment for healing of wounds; in a word, says the poor St. Kildians, deprive us of the fulmar, and St. Kilda is no more.")[19] A considerably fuller description is offered in the *New Statistical Account.*

> The solan goose is a bird of annual migration. They come to the rock early in February in successive increasing flocks. It is about the beginning of August that the young are taken, after which the old begin to depart. They prepare to migrate as soon as their young are taken from them. They linger till October, and by December they were wont to be almost entirely gone. . . . Only the young birds are taken and sold. . . . The feathers are valuable, and skilfully prepared for use: the grease is carefully secured, and sold for a variety of purposes. The flesh is of a fishy peculiar flavour, an epicurean *bonne-bouche;* not, however, adapted to universal taste or enjoyment. . . . It has long ceased to be 2s. 6d. The keeper tells us, twenty years ago it was only 1s. (2:321–22).

John Fleming, in "Zoology of the Bass," provides a detailed historical and current account of the solan geese, and asserts that "the process of incubation lasts throughout a period of nearly seven months, or from March to September" (396). David, carried to the island on the 30th of August and held there until the 23rd of September, noted that "the geese were unfortunately out of season, and we let them be" (*DB,* 14:169). Finally, regarding David's observation with respect to the gannets as an item of currency, "It is a curious remnant of olden ecclesiastical privilege, that twelve solan geese, *entire, with the feathers on,* are annually paid to the minister of North Berwick,—the vicar of the Bass" (*NSA,* 2:333).

A narrative of Bass fact, or a variation on a major chord. Although it appears effortless in the reading, the density if not complexity of the material ought to be remarked upon. The cited passage contains just four sentences. The first introduces the keeper of the island, the official term that Stevenson alters satirically

("Prefect") and then broadens and modernizes ("gamekeeper"); the second refers to the sheep's pasturage, makes oblique reference to the size and loftiness of the rock, comparing it to a cathedral, which has profound implications given the history of the island as a Bastille for religious prisoners; and the third and fourth sentences are devoted to the solan geese, identifying their variety of uses in terms of the human population. It was the geese that made the parish worth having, and it was the geese that made the island worth letting, details worth remembering because they establish the background for Black Andie's story in the subsequent chapter.

Stevenson's focus on the island serves a number of purposes: it dramatizes the practice of kidnapping and enforced concealment that constitutes a motif in the novel; it highlights the history of a geologic structure which has passed from an impregnable fortress to a virtual ruin, the rock still intact, but its utility and meaning in human terms long since gone, with nothing but the vestiges of the past to be found in the "black, broken buildings" of the prison and the relics on the grounds. The Bass has quite literally gone back to being the province of the birds, with a remnant of sheep "grazing the roof of the cathedral." Facing Tantallon across the bay, it is as if one ruin is looking at another, and Andie, who as a smuggler stores his "merchandise" in the "ruins of Tantallon," becomes a connection between the two once indomitable fortresses—and now all but empty monuments to human ambition and pride.

With nothing but time on his hands, David reflects on the "strange nature" of his place of confinement. He has already commented on the geology and zoology of the island; now he continues with the botany: "The old garden of the prison was still to be observed, with flowers and pot-herbs running wild, and some ripe cherries on a bush" (*DB*, 14:170). These details were first noticed by one of the Covenanters imprisoned there in the late sixteen-seventies: "The Bass is a very high rock in the sea . . . covered it is with grass on the uppermost parts thereof, where is a garden where herbs grow, with some cherry trees, of the fruit of which I several times tasted."[20] A later botanist noted that "In the garden . . . flowers seem to have been cultivated, and there are still one or two garden flowers growing wild."[21] But the impulse behind David's most profound thoughts is the history of the Bass itself.

A little lower stood a chapel or a hermit's cell; who built or dwelt in it, none may know, and the thought of its age made a ground of many meditations. The prison too, where I now bivouacked with Highland cattle thieves, was a place full of history, both human and divine. I thought it strange so many saints and martyrs should have gone by there so recently, and left not so much as a leaf out of their Bibles, or a name carved upon the wall, while the rough soldier lads that mounted guard upon the battlements had filled the neighbourhood with their mementoes—broken tobacco-pipes for the most part, and that in a surprising plenty, but also metal buttons from their coats (*DB,* 14:170).

David is now going beyond the surface of the Bass rock, beyond its size and its inaccessibility, beyond the sheep and the solans that color the rock and fertilize the soil, beyond the great crag in nature to the Bass in human history, a history that is past but (in David's mind) still present. For the history of the island is recorded in a variety of ways, including the record of the legal transmission of the land, which is the history of the families who controlled it, of the defenders of the island as a last Jacobite redoubt, of its transfer to the Dalrymples, and finally as a place where Highland cattle thieves can secure their hostage in complete freedom and an enterprising smuggler uses his position as keeper to engage in the "free trade."

David wonders about all this history. Why is there no visible record? Why has no one made his mark and identified his presence, left some reminder that would tell future generations, "I am the man, I suffered, I was there"? He is perplexed at the complete absence on the part of the "saints" or "martyrs" (terms that have themselves become part of the history of the prisoners of conscience) in leaving their names, or any record of their presence, for later generations. And that absence is contrasted with the unmistakable presence of the long dead soldiers through their broken tobacco pipes. Indeed, there were so many pipes on the Bass that one later commentator satirically described it as a kind of archeological layer, "the *Tobacco-pipe* Deposit. It abounds in the decapitated stalks and broken bowls of tobacco-pipes," continuing for nearly three pages as if he had uncovered the ruins of an ancient city.[22] Is it an irony of history that men of the spirit should disappear without a trace while those of the flesh leave behind an abundance of relics that trace, if not immortalize, their lives? Although he is not fully aware of the implications of his question, David tries to understand the disparity between the two worlds, the spiritual and the profane, and in his own imagination he gives shape to both: "I thought I could have heard the pious sound of psalms out of the martyrs' dungeons, and seen the soldiers tramp the ramparts with their glinting pipes, and the dawn rising behind them out of the North Sea" (*DB,* 14:170). These fancies, as David calls them, are a way of imagining history and ensuring that a record survives even when no record appears at all. But there are records, although they are unknown to David. There are more, in fact, than one could want or care about. The Wodrow Society, not to mention Robert Wodrow himself, author of the four volume *History of the Sufferings of the Church of Scotland,* collected and recorded voluminous accounts of the trials of the prisoners of the Bass.

Indeed, the martyrology of the Covenanters is a kind of passion play unto itself. In other words, it is not as if history has been silent regarding these matters. But it is also fair to say that nobody, short of a compulsion, would actually read that history. That Stevenson read it, at times even with a strange fascination, is a curious matter pertaining to his own history and psychology. But that he wrote about it without seeming to reflects his supreme art. Stevenson's fiction was written for a generation that did not grow up with the martyrs of the church—and even more for generations to come. As the real history receded further into the distance, the writer's sentences were all that remained to conjure up those best and worst of times.

Although David personally lacked the information for the construction of these fancies of the Bass, all his knowledge derived from the tales told by the keeper, Andie Dale:

> He was extraordinary well acquainted with the story of the rock in all particulars, down to the names of private soldiers, his father having served there in that same capacity. He was gifted besides with a natural genius for narration, so that the people seemed to speak and the things to be done before your face. This gift of his and my assiduity to listen brought us the more close together (*DB,* 14:170–71).

At this point, Stevenson introduces the gamekeeper as more than a jailer and smuggler. He is a gifted storyteller who can pass along the island's history that has come down to him from his father, thus continuing an oral tradition of tale telling that translates the history of the Bass into the story of the rock. Stevenson calls attention to the tale as a vehicle for conveying factual information in a spellbinding manner. The picture of Andie holding David in thrall is a vivid illustration of the connection between artist and audience, between artifact and receptor. Andie is simultaneously creator and teller of tales, in that he constructs the stories in the process of recounting them. For David, he is both the keeper of the Bass and the keeper of the story of the Bass. As such, he presides over a dominion both material and imaginative, limited on the one hand by the island and the sea, and on the other by his remembrance and reconstitution of the stories told him by his father. It goes without saying that Andie's history is only as good as his father's information and his own memory.

But in presenting Andie as storyteller of the Bass (the third storyteller in *David Balfour,* after Robert Louis Stevenson and David Balfour) Stevenson deepens and complicates the plot and structure of the text. For David Balfour, quite apart from Stevenson, has his own important tale to relate, and it is one that must be told in court in Inverary. He offers it first to Andie, hoping that the keeper will free him in time to testify on behalf of an innocent man. But the prefect is unmoved by the story ("It's a queer tale, and no vary creditable, the way you tell it" [*DB*, 14:175]), although he allows that David may have convinced himself of its veracity. For Andie, the tale that David narrates is merely one part of a larger story, and he, older and wiser, sees farther and deeper into the implications of that story. What Stevenson is suggesting here is that all our stories are true for us, who construct them and repeat them with a sure sense of their veracity. But we do so without regard to their existence in the larger world outside ourselves. David speaks plainly to Andie and tells him only what he believes necessary. He assumes that Andie will accept his point of view—and his presentation of the evidence, so to speak—and admit his argument. Yet even David recognizes the tentative or problematic nature of all our narratives. He is afraid that if he does not get to Inverary in time to testify, it will have a negative effect on the testimony itself—it "would cast the more discredit on my tale, if I were minded to tell one" (*DB*, 14:173). In other words, there is no automatic assumption regarding the truth of our stories; rather, there is a propensity for recognizing their subjective origins and, by extension, their self-interested impulses. Although Stevenson's use of first-person narrators might argue for his desire for a narration that was close to objective, given the personality of the protagonist, in actuality his fiction consistently experiments with questions of point of view and epistemology. On the syntactical level, David worries about his tale of the events surrounding the Appin murder being discredited; on the structural level, the reader wonders about David's larger tale and how to understand its significance. But Andie turns around and augments David's story with another, adding the experience of years and knowledge of the world. In the process, he complicates and deepens David's story's meaning, all the while echoing David ironically by making the "maitter clear and plain" to him. He points out that no harm will come to David by holding him on the island while a good deal of harm might come to Andie Dale if he sets him free. As for James Stewart, the worst that could happen is one more Highlander would be hanged, and the country would only be the better for it. At David's remonstrance that James Stewart is innocent, Andie ends the chapter with a remark of utter simplicity and profundity, in a sentence whose perfect pitch underscores its poignancy: "'Ay, it's a peety about that,' said he. 'But ye see in this warld, the way God made it, we cannae just get a'thing that we want'" (*DB*, 14:175).

What immediately follows "The Bass" is one of Stevenson's most celebrated set pieces, "The Tale of Todd Lapraik," an interpolated story that is regularly compared with Scott's "Wandering Willie's Tale" in *Redgauntlet*. The chapter exhibits Stevenson's linguistic and imaginative skill in handling dialect and the supernatural, although in actuality he had done both in the early 1880s in "The Merry Men" and "Thrawn Janet." That "The Tale of Tod Lapraik" is often excerpted from the complete chapter ("Black Andie's Tale of Tod Lapraik") and printed separately as an intact short story says nothing of its integral role in the section on the Bass and in Stevenson's larger scheme for incorporating historical materials in all aspects of the novel's structure.

Stevenson prepares the reader for "The Tale of Tod Lapraik" by establishing, in the opening frame, an eerie and chilling atmosphere for the inserted story of possession and exorcism. There are the strange sounds of the sea and the seabirds, the noises that seemed to reverberate in the very porches of the rock, the terrifying stories told by Neil, the redheaded Highlander who functions as an alternate and competing storyteller, and the superstitious fear felt by his companion clansmen. Andie tells David that it is all in the nature of the Bass and so affirms the island's queer strangeness. If ever a place were designed for the accommodation of different forms of experience, alternating between graphic realism and supernatural vision, between sheer terror and absolute fantasy, then it is the Bass rock. It is "an unco place," says Andie, an unco place by night, unco by day, and with its own unco sounds. One night while the Bass residents are sitting around a fire, and David unconsciously starts whistling a tune he remembers as Alan's, he is taken aback when Neil tells him to stop, that the song was not "canny musics," that "it will be made by a bogle and her wanting ta heid upon his body" (*DB*, 15:178). David is perplexed: how can a song that he associates with his good friend be a bogle's song? More precisely, how can the real be confused with the supernatural, since bogles are not exactly of this world? At this point, Stevenson intrudes with a note at the foot of the page:

> A learned folklorist of my acquaintance hereby identifies Alan's air. It has been printed (it seems) in Campbell's *Tales of the West Highlands*, Vol. II, p. 91. Upon examination it would really seem as if Miss Grant's unrhymed doggrel (see chapter 5) would fit with a little humoring to the notes in question (*DB*, 15:178).

Stevenson's footnote is authentic and accurate: J. F. Campbell's multi-volume collection of Gaelic folktales was an invaluable repository of Highland oral popular culture.[23] That Stevenson would find and exploit this national treasure is not surprising. That he would cite it directly, however, is unusual. In a way, he is engaging in a form of postmodernist textual play, unexceptional for an audience raised on Jorge Luis Borges and John Barth, but quite uncommon for readers in the eighteen-nineties. In the manuscript, for example, he inserted the parenthetical phrase "(why should I conceal the name of Dr. Bumkopf?)" after "A learned folklorist of my acquaintance," satirizing broadly the kind of plodding Germanic scholarship that he often joked about with his cousin Bob. The phrase never made it into the printed text, possibly because the humor was so obvious that it detracted

John Francis Campbell, 1843–48, by David Octavius Hill and Robert Adamson. The folklorist was commonly known as Campbell of Islay. Courtesy of The J. Paul Getty Museum, Los Angeles, Calif.

from the slyer tone of the note. Also, the parenthetical doubt "(it seems)" as to whether "Alan's air" has really been printed is deliberately provocative if not playful. Since the notes are in the volume on the page cited, Stevenson can only be questioning whether the music is truly Alan's air. This is an absurd supposition since Alan is nothing more than the author's puppet, however real his historical being. But there is a subtler reason for this badinage. With the insertion of the qualifier, Stevenson places the entire footnote in doubt, inclining readers to dismiss it as bogus and, in effect, consigning Campbell and his *Tales of the West Highlands* to a world of complete fancy.

But there is nothing fanciful about the original source. On the cited page in Campbell's second volume, a series of musical notes is printed following the narrative of a variant of tale number 30 ("The Two Shepherds").[24] Campbell introduces this fifth version of the story: "The supernatural being described as Bauchan, is probably BOCAN, a little buck, a hobgoblin, a ghost, a sprite, spectre . . . and he seems but a half-tamed specimen of the same genus as the terrible being before described." This Bauchan is called "COLUINN GUN CHEANN, The Headless Trunk" (*PT,* 2:89), which in Stevenson's translation becomes Neil's bogle "wanting ta heid upon his body." The song is not "canny musics." In the course of the tale, Coluinn Gun Cheann, who terrorized a small neighborhood, was finally beaten by a local hero and driven away from his favorite haunts, singing a "doleful" lament: "Far from me is the hill of Ben Hederin, / Far from me is the pass of murmuring" (*PT,* 2:90). This song's "words are still sung by women in that country to their children, to the following notes, which tradition says was the very air"—hence the musical notes printed in Campbell and the reference to it as "Alan's air" at the foot of the page in *David Balfour.* This is all by way of prologue to the main tale of Tod Lapraik. The reference to Campbell gives validity to the oral tale, and to folklore, as a form of history adhered to by people who transmit these tales from generation to generation—and by those who hear and commit them to memory, as the women do who are still singing the words to the headless bogle's song in the example cited by Stevenson.[25]

That folktales are a form of history is a theme repeatedly invoked by Campbell, as he speculates on the possible meanings of the tales after they are presented:

> If stories be distorted history of real events, seen through a haze of centuries, then the giants in this tale may be the same people as the Gruagach and his brother in the last (*PT,* 1:61);
>
> If this be history, it is the story of a wife taken from an inferior but civilized race. . . . If it be mythology, the hoodie may be the raven again, and a transformed divinity (*PT,* 1:69);
>
> I am inclined to think that it is a very old tale, a mixture of mythology, history, and everyday life, which may once have been intended to convey the

moral lesson, that small causes may produce great effects; that men may learn from brutes, Courage from the lion and the wolf, Craft from the fox, Activity from the falcon, and that the most despised object often becomes the greatest (*PT,* 1:102).

Campbell constantly tries to assess the historical and mythological elements of the tales, alternating between the realistic and the supernatural, between the historical and the allegorical. For example, he remarks in introducing yet a sixth version of the "The Two Shepherds":

> The next makes the supernatural beings robbers, and is a further argument in favour of the theory that all these traditions are fictions founded on fact; recollections of wild savages living in mountain fastnesses, whose power, and strength, and cavern dwellings were enlarged and distorted into magic arts, gigantic stature and the under-ground world (*PT,* 2:93).

Campbell's belief that folk stories have their origins in actual human experience is a motif that runs through the volumes. Although it is nowhere evident that Stevenson shares that conviction, the constant cross-cutting between fiction and fact in Campbell's volumes serves the novelist's own purposes. By honing in on the most important printed body of Gaelic folklore, Stevenson joins his own intellectual fascination with Catriona's "daft-like Highland tales" (*DB,* 23:299) to his broader aim of providing a representative account of rural life in Scotland. The supernatural plays such an essential role in the ordinary life of Scotland that the imaginative writer has only to find a way to integrate the materials near at hand. And those materials are the stories passed from parents to children ("Told by Neill Gillies a fisherman at Inverary . . . he learned it from his parents" [*PT,* 1:135]), from village elders, male and female, who had committed a single story to memory, or who were "practised" narrators with a variety of stories ("In reciting his stories he has all the manner of a practised narrator; people still frequent his house to hear his tales" [*PT,* 1:38]). The range of "reciters" and "informants" was wide. Stories could come from laborers, ferrymen, housewives, stable boys, blind men, or fishermen. Likewise, they could come from the notable storyteller in the village, who continues the tradition until people like Campbell of Islay, with his assistants, go out into the country and collect the tales, write them down as accurately as they can in Gaelic, translate them into English, and print them, often in both languages.

Stevenson thus had a ready resource. He could draw on the rich materials in Campbell's collection and integrate them into his own project. Like the folklorist, he could then transmit the oral tale as an illustrative example of common experience. "The tales represent the actual, every-day life of those who tell them, with great fidelity. They have done the same, in all likelihood, time out of mind, and that which is not true of the present is, in all probability, true of the past; and therefore something may be learned of forgotten ways of life" (*PT*, 1:lxix). The tale is also representative of a kind of literature (popular) and a kind of history (mythical and allegorical). At the same time, it is compelling in its own right as a work of imaginative projection, or perhaps even as a work of the imagination. And the delivery of these stories by narrators as practiced and skilled as Andie Dale made the entire form nothing less than a dramatic art.

"The Tale of Tod Lapraik" begins with Andie's description of his father, Tam Dale, who was then a young soldier stationed on the Bass: "He was fond of a lass and fond of a glass, and fond of a ran-dan; but I could never hear tell that he was muckle use for honest employment" (*DB*, 15:179). The narrative, which constitutes a wonderful long paragraph, sets the picture of a young soldier who lives for nothing but his pleasures, yet who has a spark of conscience and a glimmer of something more in this world than women and liquor. "He had glints of the glory of the kirk; there were whiles when his dander rase to see the Lord's sants misguided, and shame covered him that he should be . . . in so black a business" (*DB*, 15:179). For Tam Dale is guarding the prisoners of conscience, and Stevenson thus deftly moves his whole text back to the late seventeenth century and the persecution of the Covenanters. This was not a new theme; indeed, Stevenson's first publication, a slim pamphlet titled *The Pentland Rising*, was precisely on this subject. But the history of that period is here presented obliquely and with considerable subtlety. In the previous chapter, the Bass was presented as a symbol of exile and punishment, a province of the natural world, of the solans and the wild flowers, of rock and rain and wind, and not the common residence of men. Yet men of faith who were held accountable for a strict adherence to an uncompromising form of Presbyterianism, who were charged with holding conventicles, were imprisoned there in appalling conditions, from a few months to six years, and some either died on the rock or were broken in their bodies. One example can be seen in the field preacher, John Blackadder, who was sent to the Bass in 1681: "In his cage there, bad air, foul water, and want of exercise induced dysentery and rheumatism, which completed the wreck of the once powerful frame of the stalwart Covenanter, now an old man of seventy."[26]

Among the notable prisoners of conscience was Alexander Peden, a minister who occupied one of the "more loathsome living sepulchres . . . in the dungeons of the fortress."[27]

> In thir days, dwalled upon the Bass a man of God, Peden the Prophet was his name. Ye'll have heard tell of Prophet Peden. There was never the wale of him sinsyne, and it's a question wi' mony if there ever was his like afore. He was wild 's a peat-hag, fearsome to look at, fearsome to hear, his face

like the day of judgment. The voice of him was like a solan's and dinnle'd in folks' lugs, and the words of him like coals of fire (*DB*, 15:180).

In the view of a later scholar, "Peden was a subtle, shrewd, and prescient preacher whom the people credited with gifts of second-sight and prophecy, of which traditional illustrations were from his day indelibly fixed in rural memories, and averred to have been amply fulfilled."[28] The popular tradition of Peden as a seer was acknowledged even by Robert Wodrow, who in the main preferred to keep his own history free of "providences," yet who still cited the incident of Peden's disinterment and reburial as a sign of his prophetic gift: "This raising him after he was buried, Mr Peden, before his death, did very positively foretell, before several witnesses, some of whom are yet alive who were present, from whom I have it, else I should not have noticed this here."[29] Peden served Stevenson as a convenient allusion to the entire period of Covenanter history and as a singular example of the depth of spirituality that impelled not just him but all the martyrs of the Bass, as they came to be known. He was a model of moral purity, however eccentric his behavior, and Stevenson used him freely as a reference point. In 1876, reviewing an edition of Christopher North's essays, he said of the author of *Noctes Ambrosianae*, "In things moral, [he occupied] all sorts of intermediate stations between a prize-fighter and Peden the Prophet."[30]

Stevenson drew his portrait of Peden from Patrick Walker, "the quaint biographer of . . . heroes of the Covenant," whom the novelist often credited with having influenced his style, as he said in a letter to J. M. Barrie.[31]

> When I was a child and indeed until I was nearly a man I consistently read Covenanting books. Now that I am a graybeard—or would be if I could raise the beard—I have returned and for weeks back have read little else but Wodrow, Walker, Shields, etc. Of course this is with an idea of a novel; but in the course of it I made a very curious discovery. I have been accustomed to hear refined and intelligent critics—those who know so much better what we are than we do ourselves— . . . trace down my literary descent from all sorts of people, including Addison, of whom I could never read a word. Well, laigh I' your lug sir—the clue was found. My style is from the Covenanting writers (*L*, 8:205).

Stevenson's copy of *Biographia Presbyteriana* (1827), a compilation of Walker's writings, is in the Beinecke Library, heavily marked by him throughout. The two anecdotes relating to Peden in "The Tale of Tod Lapraik" are lifted from Walker's life.[32] Although no portrait of Peden exists, the cameo that Stevenson creates is a projection from Walker's narrative. Peden was a wanderer, homeless and outcast for most of his life. For twenty-three years "the mountains and moors were his haunts."[33] When he was near death he "sent for Mr. Renwick, who hasted to him, who found him lying in very low circumstances, overgrown with hair, and few to take care of him, as he never took much care of his body, seldom he unclothed himself, these years, or went to bed."[34] Peden's wanderings, driven by his need to avoid capture, connect him with David Balfour, who eludes the soldiers in *Kidnapped* but ends up in the same place as the preacher in *David Balfour,* a rapt auditor of Andie's narrative and, by extension, a witness to the voice of Prophet Peden himself.

Stevenson recounts the two anecdotes of the "shaggy prophet" with the caustic, cunning, and uncompromising spirit immediately after the introductory physical description. The initial quote is from Walker.[35]

6. While prisoner in the Bass, one Sabbath morning, being about the public worship of God, a young lass, about the age of thirteen or fourteen years, came to the chamber-door, mocking with loud laughter. He said, "Poor thing, thou mocks and laughs at the worship of God; but ere long, God shall write such a sudden, surprising judgment on thee, that shalt stay thy laughing, and thou shalt not escape it." Very shortly thereafter, she was walking upon the rock, and there came a blast of wind, and sweeped her off the rock into the sea where she was lost.

While prisoner there, one day walking upon the rock, some soldiers passing by him, one of them cried, "The devil take him." He said, "Fy, fy, poor man, thou knowest not what thou 'rt saying, but thou wilt repent that": at which words the soldier stood astonished, and went to the guard distracted, crying aloud for Mr. Peden, saying the devil would immediately take him away. He came and spoke to him, and prayed for him; the next morning he came to him again, and found him in his right mind, under deep convictions of great guilt. The guard being to change, they desired him to go to his arms; he refused, and said he would lift no arms against Jesus Christ his cause, and persecute his people, I've done that too long. The governor threatned him with death to-morrow at ten a clock; he confidently said three times, tho' he should tear all his body in pieces, he should never lift arms that way. About three days after the governor put him out of the garrison, setting him ashore: he having wife and children took a house in East-Lothian, where he became a singular Christian. Mr. Peden told these astonishing passages to the foresaid James Cubison, and others, who informed me (*Six Saints,* 49–50).

Now there was a lass on the rock, and I think she had little to do, for it was nae place far dacent weemen; but it seems she was bonny, and her and Tam Dale were very well agreed. It befell that Peden was in the gairden his

lane at the praying when Tam and the lass cam by; and what should the lassie
do but mock with laughter at the sant's devotions? He rose and lookit at the
twa o' them, and Tam's knees knoitered thegether at the look of him. But
whan he spak, it was mair in sorrow than in anger. "Poor thing, poor thing!"
says he, and it was the lass he lookit at, "I hear you skirl and laugh," he says,
"but the Lord has a deid shot prepared for you, and at that surprising judgment ye shall skirl but the ae time!" Shortly thereafter she was daundering
on the craigs wi' twa-three sodgers, and it was a blawy day. There cam a
gowst of wind, claught her by the coats, and awa' wi' her bag and baggage.
And it was remarked by the sodgers that she gied but the ae skirl.

Nae doubt this judgment had some weicht upon Tam Dale; but it passed
again and him none the better. Ae day he was flyting wi' anither sodger-lad.
"Deil hae me!" quo' Tam, for he was a profane swearer. And there was
Peden glowering at him, gash an' waefu'; Peden wi' his lang chafts an'
luntin' een, the maud happed about his kist, and the hand of him held out
wi' the black nails upon the finger-nebs—for he had nae care of the body.
"Fy, fy, poor man!" cries he, "the poor fool man! *Deil hae me,* quo' he; an' I
see the deil at his oxter." The conviction of guilt and grace cam in on Tam
like the deep sea; he flang doun the pike that was in his hands—"I will nae
mair lift arms against the cause o' Christ!" says he, and was as gude's word.
There was a sair fyke in the beginning, but the governor, seeing him resolved, gied him his dischairge, and he went and dwallt and married in
North Berwick, and had aye a gude name with honest folk frae that day on
(*DB,* 15:180–81).

On the face of it, Stevenson simply lifted these two anecdotes from Walker and
incorporated them into Andie's narrative. But a closer reading reveals more than
the casual appropriation of another author's material. In the case of the first example, Stevenson expanded it to almost twice its length; in the second, he compressed the material and reduced Walker's paragraph by a fifth. In the end, the
novelist's two paragraphs are just a bit longer than Walker's, but the style, tone,
and dramatic effect have been substantially altered. Stevenson drew all the inci-
dental narrative details and much of the diction from Walker. He admired the
Covenanting writer's plainness of speech, his occasional piquancy of language, and
the immediacy and unadorned quality of his narrative. He admired, as well,
Walker's effort to convey the incidents as they were reported to him and to stand
by themselves as examples of Peden's remarkable gift for prophecy. But Stevenson could not leave it to Walker to pictorialize the figure of Peden, to create a picture so vivid that both auditor (David Balfour) and reader would be riveted by the
scene before them, galvanized by the image of the preacher with the "luntin' een"
and drawn to the possibility that his prophetic powers were indeed real.

Stevenson transforms Walker's text into another that highlights the beauties of the Scots language and brings the glamour of poetry to its prose. He had done this earlier in "Thrawn Janet," and he did it as well in the Scots poetry in *Underwoods*. Now he repeated the task in a popular tale (presented as an interpolated story) told by an accomplished storyteller on a desolate rock off the Lothian coast in the Firth of Forth. Scots was not the language of the Highland tales collected by J. F. Campbell and his team. The language they encountered was, of course, Gaelic or "Irish." Stevenson has taken a small (or large) liberty here, in that he has transferred a Gaelic Highland tale to a Lowland setting, converted the teller to a Lowlander, inserted the reputed experience of a historical Lowlander (Alexander Peden) in the narrative, and delivered the entire story in the best Scots that anyone could manage. In the process, he demonstrates how seemingly unadorned material can be made even more homely and still be transformed into poetic prose.

If we compare Walker's first paragraph with its reworking in Andie's tale, we can see how Stevenson aimed for a variety of effects and how he managed to achieve them. Walker begins with the focus on Peden ("While prisoner in the Bass") while Stevenson starts with the young girl ("Now there was a lass on the rock"), employing an instinct for suspense as well as a colloquial manner that goes beyond his original's directness of speech. Stevenson fastens on the diction and phrasing he finds particularly compelling and then enforces and expands it beyond Walker's capacity or interest. It is clear that Stevenson is attracted to the directness of Walker's narrative, the seemingly unselfconscious way of recording the incidents of Peden's life, while he himself deliberately and meticulously revises those plain elements in his own text. Stevenson constructs a canvas that includes not just a portrait of Peden but also of the young girl and the young soldier who are a part of the scene. He develops a small picture that has a psychological and social dimension to it in place of Walker's bare sketch, the sole purpose of which is to awe us with the uncanny prophetic ability of Peden. Thus Stevenson takes the terms "lass" and "lassie" and reiterates them four times. (Walker used the term "lass" just once.) The young girl becomes more familiar, and as she is also bonny, she becomes even more appealing. And what is a young girl to do in such a desolate and forlorn place? She naturally takes up with Tam Dale, and when she passes Peden "at the praying" she does what any young girl might do in those circumstances—she mocks him. Stevenson later adds and repeats the Scottish "skirl" to give vividness and bite to her laughter and mockery. The overall objective is to provide a fuller picture of the lass, to give her body, so to speak, and not just make her an object upon which to pin another example of the saint's prophetic abilities. In the process, he also offers a fuller, more concrete portrait of Peden, alone in the garden and devoted to prayer, rather than the somewhat abstract figure engaged in the public worship of God. Stevenson even adds a note of compassion to the fierce prophet by having him repeat the phrase from Walker: "'Poor thing, poor thing!' says he, and it was the lass he lookit at." With this small revision, repeating the phrase from Walker, and then having Peden look at the young girl, Stevenson gives him a touch of pity, which is not the image of Peden that most stands out in Walker's life, a life in which the prophet was known more for pronouncements of wrath than expressions of sorrow or pity: "'Your death shall be both sudden and surprising'; which was verified shortly thereafter: that man, standing before a fire smoking his pipe, dropt down dead, and that without speaking more" (*Six Saints,* 1:56); "God shall punish that blasphemous mouth and cursed tongue of yours, in such manner as shall be astonishing and affrighting to all that shall see you" (*Six Saints,* 1:58). This was the man who prophesied that Scotland would be preached to with a "bloody sword," an image that was subsequently identified with Peden. Yet Stevenson allows for a note of pity, even a bit of kindness, as Peden looks at the lass and tells her, "But the Lord has a deid shot prepared for you, and at that surprising judgment ye shall skirl but the ae time!" Stevenson lifted the phrase "deid shot" from another part of Walker's life, where Peden was reputed to have foreseen the death of Charles II: "'What's this I hear?' and hearkned again a little time, and clapt his hands, and said, 'I hear a dead shot at the throne of Britain; let him go yonder, he has been a black sight to these lands, especially to poor Scotland; we're well quit of him; there has been many a wasted prayer waired on him.' And it was concluded by all, the same hour, in the same night, that unhappy man Charles II. died" (*Six Saints,* 1:64–65). For the rest of the paragraph, Stevenson takes Walker's last, matter of fact line and expands it into two vivid and unforgettable sentences that constitute a snapshot of the lass's final moments. He converts Walker's English into a graphic and idiomatic Scots to finish the story, with her last pitiful cry fulfilling Peden's prophecy.

Stevenson's revision of Walker is not just an exercise in stylistics, although that is the most obvious way to look at it. The anecdote and even the significant details are Walker's, but the vignette is the novelist's. The shape Stevenson gives to the material, what he adds that is absent from the original, gives us an insight into his interests and his imagination. For one thing, he eliminates the "thirteen or fourteen years" of Walker's girl, effectively raising her age and featuring her sexuality. This is no longer simply a pubescent girl taunting a saint of the church but a young woman attracted to men, a young woman who spends her time flirting with them both because of her attraction and out of boredom. There is the suggestion that the lass is not altogether respectable—perhaps she is a cutty sark—but, in any case, she is someone familiar enough with physical pleasure to taunt the pale and ghastly figure of a man, wrapped in a cover, who represents the antithesis of sexuality. Indeed, Peden was identified in his life for having foresworn sex and embraced chastity, a consequence of having been accused by a servant of impregnating her in a house where he stayed. Peden declared his innocence: "'Give me meat and drink; for I have got what I was seeking and I will be vindicate, and that poor unhappy lass will pay dear for it in her life, and will make a dismal end; and for this surfeit of grief that she has given me, there shall never none of her sex come in my bosom'; accordingly he never married" (*Six Saints,* 1:46). He was harsh towards women, and he prophesied disaster upon a number for their infidelity. But Stevenson softened this aspect of the man and made him speak to the young lass "mair in sorrow than in anger." This attitude reflected the novelist's take on the scene more than the Covenanter's. Stevenson drew upon psychology to create a realistic portrait of the girl, providing the setting and background for her behavior and implying her inability to refrain from her mockery. In the process, he creates a link between Peden and the girl so that, even though her death was inevitable, the caustic saint was still touched with sadness at the destiny he had no power to alter. If the anecdote was just a single incident in a large catalogue of Peden's prophecies (it is the only one in Walker's *Life* that takes place during Peden's period on the Bass), for Stevenson it touched on issues that were always central to his imagination. It addressed issues of desire, of adventure, and of the ineluctable grip of fate on people's lives, from the humblest and least privileged, like the lass, to the highest and most gifted, like Prophet Peden, each singled out by destiny, or rather each fulfilling destiny's assigned role.

In the second paragraph, Stevenson not only reduces the length of the original, but he connects it to the preceding anecdote, bringing Tam Dale (the source for Andie's tale in the first place) into the forefront of the narrative, thereby making the two anecdotes one continuous story. Walker's second paragraph is essentially detached from the first, the only tie being Peden as the subject. In Stevenson's version, Tam Dale is the link between the two, since the example of the lass in the first paragraph has its effect ("Nae doubt this judgment had some weicht upon Tam Dale"). The episode in Walker is transferred wholesale into Andie's tale, but again Stevenson deepens and dramatizes the experience. He uses the devil both as a term for objurgation and as a literal-symbolic figure of damnation. This idea is present in Walker, but it is dramatized more vividly in Stevenson, both through Peden's sarcasm ("*Deil hae me*") and through his prophetic vision: "I see the deil at his oxter." Stevenson revises the rhetorical phrasing ("he would lift no arms against Jesus Christ his cause") to a more active and modern form of expression ("I will nae mair lift arms against the cause o' Christ!"). The threatening with death becomes a "sair fyke," the putting out of the garrison becomes "gied him his dischairge," and the singular Christian becomes "aye a gude name with honest folk." Of course, what we see here is completely consonant with Stevenson's habit and practice as a writer of fiction. He draws on the skeleton of Walker's story—Peden at his daily worship; the mockery of a casual and careless young woman, more innocent than malicious; the telling phrases; the dramatic predictions; the sudden reversals leading to death and conversion. Then—rather than leave them as anecdotes suspended in time, serving as moral apothogems or "remarkable passages" in the life of one exceptional Covenanting minister—he fashions that skeleton into a full-bodied figure, complete with language and movement and expressiveness that reveal not just the prophecies but place those prophecies in a human context. Those prophecies are made to seem more comprehensible because they are made a part of ordinary human experience; they cannot be as easily dismissed as they might be if they remained solely the province of the "faithful" or of the recorders of the lives of the saints. In the context of rural superstition, Peden's foretelling the lass's being carried away bag and baggage—a providential sign striking at her faithlessness and her abuse of God's ministers—seems not as far fetched as it might if read only in the context of Walker's text, which signals the reader before beginning that he is in the presence of stories of faith and providence. By deepening the portrait of Peden, Stevenson aids in creating the context. In the second paragraph he provides a striking picture of the grim man whose long cheeks, burning eyes, and black fingernails only add to our sense of his being an outcast, of his having some connection with worlds beyond our grasp. Thus his forecast of hell for the young soldier seems so plausible that it is enough to turn around his life: "The conviction of guilt and grace cam in on Tam like the deep sea." Although Walker's phrase—"deep convictions of great guilt"—is striking enough to have attracted notice. This sentence, with its clarity of expression and sweetness of sound, is an augur of the poetic minimalism that Stevenson brought to modernist fiction.

Immediately following the two paragraphs focused on Prophet Peden, Andie Dale proceeds to recount the story proper, the quiet contest between Tam Dale and Tod Lapraik for the charge of the Bass. Here is the description of the solan goose that attempts to attack Tam while he is catching the solans, the mystery of "Thon Thing" twisting and dancing alone on the Bass, and the shooting of the devil or warlock. Here is the subsequent discovery that Tod Lapraik was dead at his loom at the moment the Thon was fired at with a rifle loaded with lead shot and a "siller tester," or silver halfpence—the latter of which was recovered from Tod's "bluidy corp"—while the "leid draps" had absolutely no effect on his body. The story, as story, is both a wonderful illustration of a supernatural folktale and a model of Scots prose. The latter aspect largely accounts for the high regard in which the piece has always been held. But Stevenson was ever the architect as well as the craftsman, and he clearly framed the story of Tod Lapraik within the chapter. Thus, as soon as Andie finishes his narrative, we are released from our trance (much as if we had just watched a movie) and returned to where we were at the start of the chapter—with David and the Highlanders seated quietly "beside the fire" (*DB,* 15:177). Even in this seemingly inconsequential detail there is authority from Campbell: "This story was told to me at Inverary, April 25, 1859, by Gillies. It was told with the air of a man telling a serious story, and anxious to tell it correctly. . . . Those who sat about the fire argued points in the story" (*PT,* 1:142). If Campbell attested to the fire at the recitation of this narrative, in another instance he might speculate on its actual presence: "A child would not easily forget a story learned amongst a lot of rough farmers, seated at night round a blazing fire, listening to an old crone with palsied head and hands" (*PT,* 1:218). It is not that the fire around which Andie tells his story comes from Campbell—indeed, that assertion might almost sound foolish, but rather that a detail that could plausibly be imagined by the author of the fictional text assumes authenticity as a result of its notation by the scholar in the source text. Stevenson even leaves a break on the page between Andie's tale and the return to David's narration, following Campbell's practice of separating the oral tale from his own commentary on where and when it was recorded, by whom it was told, on its possible origins, and, most importantly, on its similarities with other tales. Campbell repeatedly attempts to identify the different versions of every story, a tactic that has the effect of reminding the reader that virtually every tale has siblings and cousins with uncanny resemblances. And it is this idea—that popular tales share common elements—which provides the impetus for Stevenson to bring his chapter to a dramatic end. For no sooner does Andie conclude his tale than a quarrel erupts with Neil, who "knew all the stories in the Highlands" and was reminded by this one of another he heard just like it.

> "She would ken that story afore," he said. "She was the story of Uistean More M'Gillie Phadrig and the Gavore Vore."
>
> "It is no sic a thing," cried Andie. "It is the story of my faither (now wi' God) and Tod Lapraik. And the same in your beard," says he; "and keep the tongue of ye inside your Hielant chafts" (*DB,* 15:190).

These words lead to a brief struggle that ends peacefully only because David intervenes to prevent Neil from stabbing Andie. Neil, in turn, orders his fellow Highlanders to refrain from coming to his defense. The chapter ends abruptly, with David concluding to himself that the Highlanders had orders not to harm him and that Andie, who remained paralyzed during the episode, was a coward.

But the speed and violence of the conclusion only deflect readers from the incident that triggered it. Neil's remark that the story of Tod Lapraik was not original is an assertion that implicitly questions its authenticity as a unique story of Andie's father. This is tantamount, from the son's point of view, to hearing his father called a liar. Yet Neil is correct. The story of Tod Lapraik *is* a version of a popular tale, one recorded by Campbell in chapter 30 (the same chapter identified at the beginning of chapter 15 in *David Balfour,* with its reference to the headless trunk and the footnote cited earlier regarding Alan's air). Stevenson continues the practice (or game) he began at the start of this chapter of incorporating elements of Campbell's tales into his own text. In this instance, though, he goes further in that the substance of "The Tale of Tod Lapraik" is largely outlined on the last three pages of Campbell's chapter (*PT,* 2:99–101). The first mention of "Uisdean Mor MacIlle Phadraig, a local hero, famous for slaying 'Fuahthan' (bogles)," appears in a variant form following "The Tale of Connal" in the first volume of *Popular Tales* (1:152). But it is in the second volume, after "The Two Shepherds" and the tale of the headless trunk that Neil had cautioned David about, that he appears in full force.

> 8. At some time of the world the lord of Gearloch TIGHEARNA GHEAR-LOCH had a CEATHEARNACH, who used to be slaying FUATHAN bogles, and routing out the spoilers. The name of this stalwart man was UIS-TEAN MOR MAC GHILLE PHADRIG (*PT,* 2:97).

This opening serves as prologue to a narrative of two closely printed pages and it lists, among other things, the hero's possession of a gun and a sword, important details given Campbell's repeated reminders that in popular tales "iron is invested with magic power," that frequently "a gun is the weapon which breaks the spells," and that "the gun and the sword, are alike magical" (*PT,* 1:lxxv–lxxvi).

The following story (number 9), which is significantly shorter, has connections with a tradition of French folktales concerned with werewolves, except that the wolf in France "is a goat in the Highlands" (*PT,* 2:99). Uistean has learned about a Fuath who was killing people on "the yellow knoll of Gairloch."

> Uistean came, and on the way at the foot of the knoll Uistean went into the house of a yellow-footed weaver that was living there. Said the weaver to Uistean, "Thou hadst best stop the night."
>
> "Well, I will do that," said Uistean; "I am going to kill the Fuath of Tombuidh to-night."
>
> "Perhaps that is not so easy," said the weaver; "with what wilt thou kill Gaohair Mhoil-Bhui, the goat of Maol-buidh?"
>
> "With the gun," said Uistean.
>
> "What," said the weaver, "if the gun will not suit?"
>
> "If it will not suit," said he, "I will try the sword on her."
>
> "What," said the weaver, "if the sword will not come out of the sheath?"
>
> "Well," said Uistean, "I will try my mother's sister on her."
>
> And on every arm that Uistean named, the weaver laid ROSAD, a spell, but on the dirk which he called his mother's sister the weaver could not lay

a spell. Then Uistean went up to the top of the knoll, and on the top of the knoll was a pit in which the goat used to dwell (*PT,* 2:99–100).

Uistean tries the gun and then the sword with no success. The goat taunts him:

"Where now is thy mother's sister?" said the goat.

When Uistean heard this he sprang on the goat, and the first thrust he gave her with the BIODAG dirk, she let out a roar. . . .

And he did not see the goat any more. Uistean turned back to the weaver's house, and when he kindled a light, he found the weaver under the loom, pouring blood.

"If it was thou who madest so much loss on the yellow knoll, thou shalt not get off any farther," said Uistean.

Then he killed the weaver under the loom, and no man was slain on the yellow knoll since then, by goat or bogle (*PT,* 2:100).

Campbell then cites one final version of this story (Number 10), but he declines to print it because it is in Gaelic, would require translation, and is essentially identical to the preceding one. He does, however, note the following:

The goat is called GABHAR MHOR RHI BEAGACH F HEUSAGACH, a great hairy-bearded goat; and the dirk is called CATRIONA PUITHAR MO SHEANA MHATHAIR, Catherine, my grandmother's sister. He finds the BREABADAIR weaver in bed, with a wound in his thigh, and gives him his death thrust there (*PT,* 100–101).

Neil's calling the goat "Gavar Vore"—as opposed to Campbell's "Gabhar Mhor"—is simply Stevenson's acknowledgment that the "v" in Gaelic is often pronounced or spelled with an "m," a detail he called attention to in *Kidnapped* when David says he was "set on shore at last under the wood of Lettermore (or Lettervore, for I have heard it both ways) in Alan's country of Appin" (*K,* 17:146).

What is most interesting in the "Tale of Tod Lapraik" is the way Stevenson converted a skeletal folktale into a vivid and compelling short story that blended realism with supernaturalism. He took (by way of Campbell) a French peasant's simple tale of lycanthropy and transformed it into a story with a human focus, thus giving life to Tam Dale, who changed from a hedonist in his early days as a soldier on duty on the Bass to a hardworking keeper of the rock and supporter of a family. Stevenson lifted the soldier from Walker, the one who married and moved to East Lothian after his experience with Prophet Peden, but Stevenson actually created him after the lifting, giving him a name and a family and an occupation at which he was remarkably proficient. Stevenson's description of Tam's taking the solans accords well with the procedure narrated in the *Statistical Account* and adds to the accuracy of the narrative.

They are taken from the rock by the keeper, who descends with a rope fastened around his waist, and held above by his assistant; another rope is fastened to the rock above, which he holds around his hand, to facilitate his movements. He lays hold of the bird with a hook, draws it toward him, and kills it with a stroke on the head; then with great force throws it from him over the projections of the rock to the sea below, where the men in the boat are prepared to pick it up. The act of throwing, the keeper tells us, is the most difficult and perilous effort in the process (*NSA*, 321–22).

At last the time came for Tam Dale to take young solans. This was a business he was weel used wi', he had been a cragsman frae a laddie, and trustit nane but himsel'. So there was he hingin' by a line an' speldering on the craig face, whaur it's hieest and steighest. Fower tenty lads were on the tap, hauldin' the line and mindin' for his signals. But whaur Tam hung there was naething but the craig, and the sea belaw, and the solans skirling and flying. It was a braw spring morn, and Tam whustled as he claught in the young geese (*DB*, 15:183–84).

Of course, the *Statistical Account* cannot begin to convey the sense of danger and the heightened emotion evoked by the visual scene of the rock and the sea and the sky, with Tam swaying back and forth like a fly on a long fishing line. But Tam is not the only figure in Stevenson's story. There is his father, and Sandie Fletcher, the fisherman who is also a marksman, and, of course, the narrator as a young boy. Stevenson gives life to a broadly known supernatural tale by superimposing a realistic structure over the folkloric elements. Thus if the Highlands substituted a hairy goat for the French werewolf, Stevenson turned the goat into a solan goose, since it made sense to have as an animal of choice one that was native to the island. If the tale embodied the belief that iron contained magical powers and was the "principal safeguard against evil spirits" (*PT*, 2:89), Stevenson gave even that superstition a twist of modern humor when Tam brandished his knife at the lycanthrope and forced it to retreat ("It seemed the solan understood about knives" [*DB*, 15:185]). The novelist can only have enjoyed a private pleasure in knowing that Uistean's knife was called Catriona. But the most profound merging of the real with the supernatural comes in an extended paragraph in which Andie describes Thon Thing leaping and spinning and capering all by itself on the Bass rock. In trying to understand what he is seeing, he draws a comparison, as well as a sharp contrast, with the behavior of young women: "I hae seen lassies, the daft queans, that would lowp and dance a winter's nicht, and still be lowping and dancing when the winter's day cam in. But there would be folk there to hauld them company, and the lads to egg them on; and this thing was its lee-lane" (*DB*, 15: 188). The apparition, dancing alone on the rock, forces Andie to think about what drives people to dance in the first place, or more broadly, what compels them to express their physicality. The answer is sexual desire: "And the lassies were bits o' young things wi' the reid life dinnling and stending in their members; and this was a muckle, fat, crieshy man, and him fa'n in the vale o' years." Youth and sex are not simply an expression of life but are life itself. In the early part of Andie's story, the lassie paid dearly for wanting nothing more than to enjoy a bit of that life, which to her mind meant flirting with soldiers and laughing at weird looking old men. She paid, in effect, for being natural, for being herself, for not being old enough and smart enough to know the limitations of naturalness in the world at large. The brilliance of this prose paragraph is a function of its joining the spectral image of the apparition with the vivid picture of the lassies and of the way its positive idea is embedded in its very negation. The idea of paradise comes to us through the image of hell: "Say what ye like, I maun say what I believe. It was joy was in the creature's heart; the joy o' hell, I daursay: joy whatever." The pleasure in the moment that the warlock derived from his solitary dancing was worth all the future pain that he was sure to pay. Stevenson turns the interpolated story of Tod Lapraik into a characteristic short story of his own, one with a moral at its center—where good and evil are obverse and reverse, and where even the werewolf, so to speak, has its point of view. In the popular tale there is no explanation for the gavar vore's killing of people on the yellow knoll; in the novelist's story it is clearly Tod Lapraik's revenge for having lost the post of keeper of the Bass to Tam Dale. Stevenson's version of Campell's recorded tale ends predictably enough, and it is close enough for Neil to identify it as Uistean's. In reality, the story of Tod Lapraik is on another plane altogether, for it has been converted into a Stevensonian fable of the apparent helplessness of good before the power of evil, and of the arbitrariness of victory in the battle. Thus the folkloric elements of Andie's story (drawn from Campbell)—as well as those elements of religious history (drawn from Walker)—are united by Stevenson's insight into psychology and his construction of personality. This construction makes Prophet Peden and Tod Lapraik (each of them outcasts in his own way, the one for moral purity, the other for diabolic possession) nonetheless parts of a larger common experience. And it is an experience of compassion as well as revenge, of sacrifice as well as venality, of pride and courage as well as meanness and cowardice. For Stevenson, a story that draws on diablerie, folklore, or the supernatural always rests upon the human response to those inexplicable and even unbelievable events. It is not the mysterious nature of the incidents that engages his interest but, rather, how those incidents might serve as uncanny illuminations of the human mind and of ordinary human experience. Drawn as they are from popular superstitions and beliefs, they become in turn windows to the creative imagination, the means by which the common fears and anxieties of everyday life are transmogrified into bogles of the mind. What makes a Stevenson story disturbing, however, is that the bogles are as lifelike as they are unnatural, as real as they are make-believe. They are characteristic of both his art, practiced with unceasing rigor, and his imagination, predicated on scepticism and endowed with faith.

EPILOGUE

What, finally, are we to make of *Kidnapped* and *David Balfour*? Or put another way, what are we to make of its magus, Robert Louis Stevenson? If we remember Scott Fitzgerald's remark that a novelist writes for his own generation, the critics of the next, and the schoolmasters ever after, then we must admit while his own generation was attentive, the schoolmasters were largely absent. It took years, nearly a century, before Stevenson began to attract the kind of critics who commonly paid court to Henry James and James Joyce. Serious analysis had been reserved almost exclusively for *Jekyll and Hyde,* a text that was barely remarked upon at the time of Stevenson's death, but that subsequently never ceased to fascinate critics who found in it the dark side of Victorian culture, human nature, and possibly even Stevenson himself. Yet he was certainly deeply admired long before an odd amnesia set in about his work. Just how was he seen when the news went out from Samoa that he had collapsed from a brain hemorrhage in the early afternoon on December 13, 1894, exactly one month after his forty-fourth birthday? At first, the reports were tentative, but quickly the rumored death gave way to confirmation—years later Walter de la Mare recalled the "gigantic black letters" on the "newspaper placards" announcing the "Death of R. L. S."—and the obituaries appeared immediately.[1] The coverage ranged from the large metropolitan dailies in England, Scotland, and the United States, to weekly, monthly, and quarterly magazines. Stevenson's death coincided, fortuitously, with the publication of the first volumes of the Edinburgh Edition, so there was a prime opportunity for critics to prepare sweeping reviews of his career. But the newspaper obituaries—certainly the big ones in cities like New York and Glasgow and San Francisco—were themselves retrospectives that provided their audience with an extensive summary and evaluation of the writer's work. From the vantage point of a present day reader, they offer a glimpse into the cultural and intellectual world of the late nineteenth century, and into the mind of its readers. For while it is true that the heart of a writer's work often discloses itself years later to fresh readers unmoved by an earlier generation's time-bound interests, it is equally the case that later readers, in thrall to their own ideas, are often blind to the very qualities that made the writer compelling in his own time. Nowhere is this cultural misreading —of one generation's understanding blurred or transformed by another's—more dramatically illustrated than in the reception of Stevenson's work. Few writers in modern memory enjoyed such encomiums while alive, and none could have survived them long. But it is instructive to see precisely what his readers saw, or thought they saw, when they opened a new book.

To begin with, Stevenson's versatility and inventiveness were admired. It was as if every new book was a surprise—"We have here a fresh and striking example of Mr. Stevenson's remarkable intellectual versatility and flexibility"—and the reviewers were at a loss how to explain it.[2] Although the range of Stevenson's work across genres and periods was clearly impressive, what is striking is how many recognized certain fundamental qualities that were not obvious in a writer whose popular reputation rested on adventure and sensationalism. What seems remarkable are the number of critics who insisted upon viewing Stevenson primarily as a psychologist—that is, as a writer whose principal aim was the creation of "character as the chief spring of action."[3] Reviews of The Merry Men brought this out, as did virtually all the commentary in the Balfour novels on David and Alan and Catriona and Barbara Grant. Allied with this idea that Stevenson's central concern was "human nature and human issues," was the persistent focus on the reality and verisimilitude of his work.[4] For some, verisimilitude explained the grip with which he held his readers, while others resorted to analogies with painting.[5] His "picture" was "like one of Meissonier's," an allusion more recognizable then than now, but one that draws a complimentary analogy with a French historical painter known for his truth of detail.[6] The observations regarding the veracity in Stevenson's work naturally carried over to the commentary on his historical fiction. As the New York Times pointedly said in its review of Kidnapped, Stevenson had "the true Defoe manner . . . which makes the whole thing, though you know it to be fiction, to read as if it were fact."[7] Whether it was the Nation singling out the "acutely descriptive" language in The Merry Men, or the Athenaeum praising the "dialect" in the same volume, there was a consistent perception that Stevenson was someone who wrote about the world as it was, even when he was writing about the past.[8] And this view shored up the conviction that his historical fiction was unexcelled and one could only go back to Scott and Thackeray for measurable comparisons. Further, although it choked some to admit it, Stevenson may even have surpassed Scott. "In the line of the Scottish historical novel [Kidnapped is] the best thing after Scott. It is questionable indeed whether Scott himself has left anything to match the figure of Alan as a representation of the Highland characteristics of courage and vanity combined."[9] For a later literary historian, Stevenson's Scottish novels were "much more modern . . . and technically conscious" than Scott's, and they were "much more sparing in their method."[10] Additionally, there was not a critic who failed to recognize that it was Stevenson's profound knowledge of his country and its language that contributed to the reality with which he reproduced and preserved a period that had been reduced either to an historical memory or an embroidered mythology.

There was one aspect of Stevenson's work, a quality not easily separated from biography, that deeply impressed his contemporaries but was noticed only minimally, if at all, in subsequent years. It pertained to the physical and intellectual effort he put into his writing, an effort ordinarily apparent only to other writers. Harold Frederick, for example, reviewing with plaudits the posthumous *Weir of Hermiston,* noted the writer's artisanship in explaining why Stevenson's reputation developed slowly at first and then emerged full-grown as if in a sudden instant. "He had taken such perfect and tireless pains from the beginning to maintain the highest level of workmanship that finally the superb, lofty average of it simply compelled attention."[11] Astute readers glimpsed the learning that lay behind the stories that moved with such effortless ease: "With all his creative faculty, he had the critical faculty and he put it at the service of the creative. Few can do that."[12] These critics saw that Stevenson's literary culture was broad and deep, and that he absorbed all the Scottish, English, French, and American authors not to plagiarize them—a deliberate misconstruction of his famous remark about playing "the sedulous ape"—but to incorporate them into his own original and fluid creations. The range of his reading was impressive, but not any more than the "fastidiousness" with which he constructed his texts, "wrought out, with infinite pains . . . altering and re-altering, until there was given to the public that delightfully easy reading which . . . is invariably the outcome of very hard writing."[13] This admiration for the "studious and experimental" artist—one newspaper said he had "the genuine literary touch of the scholar"—is perhaps one of the more unfortunate losses in the picture later readers had of Stevenson.[14] His contemporaries, on the other hand, were never in doubt as to his role as a model for writers and his work as a model of writing. They chronicled his "long and painful apprenticeship to his art," charted its evolution, and summed up his final achievement.[15] According to *The Scotsman,* Stevenson "has a right to a first place among the craftsmen of letters of his age and language."[16]

Finally, there was the matter of style. If any single quality marked Stevenson as a supremely gifted writer it was his "mastery of words . . . not surpassed in distinction and music by that of any English story-teller."[17] For present day readers, who believe that style in writing is purely subjective, it may be difficult to comprehend the passion with which Stevenson's critics were at pains to describe the experience of his language, which was really the experience of reading him. "For ease there has been nothing like Stevenson's style since Lamb, while for vivacity and vividness there is nothing like it elsewhere in English prose."[18] Some attempted to explain the workings of the style—"to be clear and to be expressive and always to be brief"—while others saw it as the very aim of his art: "his real object was to write English."[19] Whatever the tributes, and to recite them would be supererogatory, Stevenson's contemporaries recognized, as few have done since, that the tactile and sensuous qualities of his style—grace, polish, lucidity, allusive-ness, delicacy—were bound up with all else they said about him as an artist. They recognized that he was a man who read in order to write and one who was inde-fatigable in revising every sentence that passed over his page. On occasion, a note of disbelief slips in, as if to ask, who today would spend so much time on revision? At the same time, there was respect for the tenacity of the writer in his quest to achieve some perfection in the prose that was impossible in the life. Yet nobody suggested that Stevenson was rolling on the floor after Flaubert—the bon mot was not really the objective. Rather, it was a prose that was a natural glove for the narrative, one that would never call attention to itself, so tightly did it fit the skin. Indeed it *was* the skin. Stevenson's style could plausibly be seen as the counterpart to Eastern calligraphy, whose perfection was the sole aim of the culture's most revered figure, the scholar-artist. Stevenson had a high admiration for all things Japanese. Of all Stevenson's many and varied works, the critical consensus, virtu-ally by acclamation, was that *Kidnapped* and *David Balfour* exhibited all his best qualities in their finest form. The books represented "the topmost reach" of his art, "the high water-mark of [his] powers as a novelist," and were his "most sub-stantial claim to fame."[20] None thought *Kidnapped* a boy's book, and not a few were shrewd enough to see a "more compact and highly-wrought style" in *David Balfour,* attributed to Stevenson's last years in the Pacific and his maturity as a writer.[21]

In the eyes of Stevenson's readers, these two books constituted a masterwork of fiction, and they were eager to slot it into the recognizable form of the histor-ical novel, hence the repeated invocation of the name of Scott. Yet, over time, these books lost their status as historical fictions. *Kidnapped* was transformed into a popular classic for boys, and *David Balfour* disappeared into semi-oblivion. The historical character of the novels was virtually relegated to Stevenson's own com-ment in his dedication and to the occasional scholar, like David Daiches, who called our attention to the world that stood behind the story. But in a sense Stevenson's own contemporaries were in the dark as to his larger objectives—to create a historical fiction within the context of the nineteenth-century realistic novel and to base that fiction so completely on fact that it would be impossible to distinguish between the two genres. He succeeded by refining down the realistic-historical novel, which was almost a contradiction in terms, into an art where the style became a poetic instrument yet the realistic base was never lost. Time was reduced to a brevity worthy of an Aristotelian, and the history embedded in the elegance and simplicity of the plot concealed itself so as not to turn the book into just another Victorian triple-decker. Stevenson created a social and political chronicle without ever giving the impression of having done so. It was at bottom an anticolonialist document, both a proclamation and an elegy for a vanished culture, a statement on the power of art to reclaim the past and reconstitute its victims and its villains, in the process giving them all a place in the endless stream of years that we call history, but that is really nothing more, nor less, than life itself. It was, in the end, one of the most daringly inventive achievements in English prose fiction, and one that was virtually sui generis. To duplicate it required both scholarship and artistry of a high order, and it was not until the late twentieth century, with the collapse of the genres of fact and fiction, or perhaps their merger, that the originality of his experiment could be appreciated. Both in the impulse that intuited a major subject in an old crime, and in the technique that brought that idea to life, Stevenson paved the way for later writers like Truman Capote, Norman Mailer, and W. G. Sebald.

Kidnapped and *David Balfour* formed the arc of Stevenson's career. When he was writing the first book, he was a midlist author, still making a name for himself, familiar to the Grub Street fraternity as exceptional but not above publishing in a disposable pulp weekly. By the time of *David Balfour* he was R. L. S., known throughout the English-speaking world simply by his initials. Yet, in a fundamental way, Stevenson never really changed, even though his style and his manner matured in the course of those seven years. The painstakingness with which he ground out the last chapters of *Kidnapped,* or the handwritten composition of two complete versions of *David Balfour,* is more than an emblem of his art. For he always wrote with such intense exactitude—one has only to look at a manuscript page to see the meticulous care of his hand—as if he were writing against physical illness itself, even against mortality, as if to write were to live, to endure, and in the end endurance, like ripeness, was all. Stevenson did not really have to compose *David Balfour.* Certainly, the wish to finish the story was strong, the blandishments from McClure for syndication were enticing, and the need to support that complex agrarian enterprise known as Vailima was compelling. But he had numerous other projects pending and in various stages of production. It was the art that made him do it. The desire to complete the work—the compulsion to do the work—drives the work. *David Balfour* was written for Stevenson himself, and he occasionally experienced private pleasures in the composition. When David, who had been given the task of copying documents in Prestongrange's office, remarked that "The copying was a weary business," the manuscript shows that Stevenson was suffering from writer's cramp and that he was literally writing with his other hand. Who would know this? But it did not matter, anymore than it mattered whether anybody knew that Mr. Henderson had been imported into *Kidnapped* from a real-life missionary author. Stevenson felt no need to supply notes to his fiction because his fiction was not fiction but life, an artist's gift to the country of his birth and the language of his people. *David Balfour* completed the story that had begun seven years earlier. It was not a pretty story, made up as it was of blood and exile and death, much like the history of Scotland that Stevenson delivered to a rapt audience of Scotsmen in Honolulu the year before he died. But in a strange way it was Stevenson's own story. Like David, he had been a young man in search of adventure, and like David he washed up on some "ultimate islands," although he was no longer looking to find his way home. Like David, he too told his story looking back, in full knowledge that his words, like David's words, would provide a coda to his life. For Stevenson's destiny was really the destiny of the artist, and his great legacy was to leave us with a portrait of the artist, not quite young, yet wise enough and charitable enough to forgive even the worst of us, and to remind us, through his art, that balm for suffering is a gift of the gods.

NOTES

Prologue

1. Captain Charles Johnson, *The History of the Lives and Actions of the Most Famous Highwaymen, Murderers, Street-Robbers* . . . (Edinburgh: John Thomson Jr. and Co., 1814). For a full discussion and bibliography of this text's role in the composition of *Treasure Island* see Roger G. Swearingen, *The Prose Writings of Robert Louis Stevenson: A Guide* (Hamden, Conn.: Archon Books, 1980), 68–69.

Chapter 1—A Scots Historian

1. Stevenson's letters have been edited and superbly annotated by Ernest Mehew and published in eight volumes by Yale University Press. There are occasional small differences between the holographs and the printed form, mainly in the introduction of italics and quotation marks for published works, and in the normalization of capitals—Stevenson was notoriously indifferent to these matters. My practice is to quote from the original holograph when Stevenson's deliberate italics stand out on the page, or when his casualness with respect to accidentals conveys a bit of the speed and flavor of the epistolary voice. In any case, all letters cited in the text from archival sources will be followed immediately by reference to the Yale edition. B: Beinecke Rare Book and Manuscript Library, Yale University, New Haven, Conn.; P: Firestone Library, Princeton University Library, Princeton, N.J.; HL: Huntington Library, San Marino, Calif.; *L: The Letters of Robert Louis Stevenson,* 8 vols., ed. Bradford Booth and Ernest Mehew (New Haven: Yale University Press, 1994–95).

2. See also Swearingen, *The Prose Writings of Robert Louis Stevenson,* 120. On December 28, Scribner's received another note from Stevenson: "The books have come. But how about Dr Eggleston? Small manners are what I am especially after" (*L,* 6:91). Charles Scribner replied on December 31: "I send you to-day the articles by Dr. Eggleston which have appeared in the Century Magazine. None of Dr. Eggleston's work on American history has yet been published in book form, and all that he has done is I think contained in these articles. The earlier ones will probably be of no special service, but the later ones on social life in the colonies will interest you. I also send you to-day two numbers of the New York Nation which give an account of the Memoir of Queen Katherine, a copy of which you want and which I hope to secure for you" (P; see also Roger Burlingame, *Of Making Books: A Hundred Years of Reading, Writing, and Publishing* [New York: Charles Scribner's Sons, 1946], 19).

3. B, 2962–65; *L,* 8:176, 179; see also Swearingen, *The Prose Writings of Robert Louis Stevenson,* 182.

4. P, c. 20 May 1889; *L,* 6:300.

5. P, late August 1890; *L,* 6:410–11. Burlingame's letter to Stevenson, June 20, 1890.

6. Stevenson was also quick to recognize their use by other writers. Thus he remarked on the playwright Thomas Heywood's *A Woman Killed with Kindness:* "The death of the two pirates in *Fortune by Sea and Land*—is a document. He had obviously been present, and heard Purser and Clinton take death by the beard with similar braggadocios" (*L,* 3:322).

7. Lord Guthrie, *Robert Louis Stevenson: Some Personal Recollections* (Edinburgh: W. Green and Sons, 1924), 36 (hereafter referred to as LG). Guthrie's book, published posthumously, first appeared as a series of articles in 1919 and 1920 in the *Juridical Review,* an Edinburgh journal directed broadly at the legal community.

8. *Edinburgh University Calendar, 1875–76* (Edinburgh: James Thin, 1875), 86–87 (hereafter referred to as *EUC*).

9. Robert Bell, *A Dictionary of the Law of Scotland,* 3rd ed., revised and greatly enlarged by William Bell (Edinburgh: J. Anderson and Co., 1826), 169, 172.

10. J. Irvine Smith, "The Rise of Modern Scots Law," in *An Introduction to Scottish Legal History* (Edinburgh: Robert Cunningham and Sons, 1958), 44–45. Viscount Stair "presented Scots Law as a complete and coherent system, Scots law as we have since known it" (45).

11. "It is clear, therefore, that although English sources were not neglected, the main sources of authority for the pleader and the judge were to be found in the Roman Law and the commentators . . . in all cases where native law and custom did not provide precedent or guidance" (A. C. Black, "The Institutional Writers," in *An Introductory Survey of the Sources and Literature of Scots Law* [Edinburgh: Robert Macklehose, 1936], 61).

12. "*Act of Sederunt* . . . in *Scotch Law,* an ordinance for regulating the forms of procedure before the Court of Sessions, passed by the judges in virtue of a power conferred by an Act of the Scotch Parliament," *Oxford English Dictionary,* 2nd ed. (Oxford: Clarendon Press, 1989).

13. William Bell, *A Dictionary and Digest of the Law of Scotland* (Edinburgh: J. Anderson, 1838).

14. John Maclaurin, preface to *Arguments and Decisions in Remarkable Cases before the High Court of Justiciary* (Edinburgh: n.p., 1774), v.

15. Notebook on candidates examined in "General Scholarship," Faculty Records 65, Advocates' Library.

16. Faculty Records 65, Advocates' Library.

17. *Register of the Private Examinators (Law),* 3 June 1857–10 July 1908, Faculty Records 67, Advocates' Library.

18. *Faculty of Advocates # 14, Account of the Treasures Intromissions from 31 December 1874 to 31 December 1875,* 1–2, Faculty Records 46, Advocates MS, Advocates'

Library. Two months after passing the bar Stevenson made use of the library. On September 30, 1875, he borrowed Chambers' four volume edition of Robert Burns, and
on October 21 he checked out Lockhart's *Life of Burns,* both of which served as
sources for his article on the poet for the *Encyclopedia Britannica.*

19. In Edinburgh, using the collection of the Advocates' Library, he also drew
upon the English edition of Jean Cavalier's *Memoirs of the Wars of the Cevennes,* 2nd ed.,
(London: J. Clarke, 1727); *A Cry from the Desart; or, Testimonials of the Miraculous Things
Come to Pass in the Cevennes,* 2nd ed., trans. with a preface by John Lacy (1707); a
translation of Francois M. Misson's *Le Théatre Sacré des Cevennes* (1707); Antoine
Court's *Histoire des Troubles des Cevennes* (1760); and de Bruyes' *Histoire du Fanatisme*
(1692). No doubt he consulted other books in the Advocates' Library (Swearingen,
The Prose Writings of Robert Louis Stevenson, 36).

20. "Mr. R. L. Stevenson 17 Heriot Row," Faculty Records 278, Advocates MS,
p. 617, Advocates' Library.

21. "Mr. Robert Louis Stevenson 17 Heriot Row," Faculty Records 277, Advocates MS, p. 908; "Mr. R. L. Stevenson 17 Heriot Row," Faculty Records 278, Advocates MS, p. 617, Advocaes' Library.

22. R. L. S. to Bob Stevenson, September 13, 1880. HL, 2489; *L,* 3:100–101.

23. "But Stevenson never, with all his reliance on his memory, hesitated to ask
help—he seemed to take for granted his right, as an author, to demand help from
live authorities, as he would go for help to the printed page" (Rosaline Masson,
introduction to *Kidnapped* by Robert Louis Stevenson [London: Collins, n.d.], vii).

24. R. L. S. to Thomas Stevenson, December 12, 1880. B, 3458; *L,* 3:140.

25. Graham Balfour, *The Life of Robert Louis Stevenson* (London: Metheun, 1901),
1:187.

26. John Steuart commented on Stevenson's long fascination with the Highlands: "For years . . . he had been an ardent student of Clan lore and Highland character, had . . . ransacked Celtic archives in search of a Highland ancestry for himself.
Moreover, in various trips as an embryo engineer, he had been deeply impressed by
the grandeur and gloom of the mountains and glens, islands and skerries, of the
west" (*Robert Louis Stevenson* [Boston: Little, Brown, and Company, 1924], 1:344).

27. LG, 2, 43. See also Joseph Furnas, *Voyage to Windward* (New York: Sloan,
1951), 199; Jenni Calder, *Robert Louis Stevenson: A Life Study* (New York: Oxford University Press, 1980), 170.

28. "Wednesday 21 [actually 22] June 1881" (*L,* 3:194).

29. R. L. S. to Aeneas Mackay, *L,* 3:201.

30. R. L. S. to Sidney Colvin, *L,* 3:197.

31. *Testimonials in Favour of Robert Louis Stevenson, Advocate* (Edinburgh, 1881).

32. Rosaline Masson, *The Life of Robert Louis Stevenson* (Edinburgh: W. & R.
Chambers, 1923), 202.

33. Balfour, *The Life of Robert Louis Stevenson,* 1:190.

34. Edmund Gosse later acknowledged this central point made by the contrib-
utors: "These letters show, at least, how widely Stevenson's knowledge of Scotch

history had been recognised already by an inner circle of experts." Introduction to *The Works of Robert Louis Stevenson,* vol. 10, *Kidnapped* (London: Cassell and Company, 1906), 4.

35. Gordon Donaldson and Robert S. Morpeth, *Who's Who in Scottish History* (New York: Barnes and Noble, 1973), 230.

CHAPTER 2——COUNTRY OF THE POOR: THE HIGHLANDS

1. Balfour, *The Life of Robert Louis Stevenson,* 1:194.

2. A second edition appeared in 1759 and a new edition in 1815. Stevenson was asking for the fifth edition (1818), which had an extensive introduction and notes by R. Jamieson. The disappearance of the second volume of this edition, containing Marshal Wade's reports on the Highlands following the 1715 rebellion, was a noticeable irritant, as he wrote to his father on November 28: "It is most vexatious about Burt, as I was just going to use him at once" (*L,* 3:124). And again in early December: "If the second volume of Burt is not at home, then it has fallen out in the custom house. I must have another" (B, 3459; *L,* 3:130).

3. "I bought you two books today [including] Colonel Stewart's sketches of the character & manners of the Highlander of Scotland. . . . The latter is rich in matter as to the Highlander in the British Wars & will I feel sure furnish you with valuable matter as to the fidelity of the Highlander" (B, 5769).

4. R. L. S. to Thomas Stevenson (B, 3460; *L,* 3:127).

5. The pages of Stevenson's notebook were scrupulously preserved, in a manner of speaking. Along with the end covers of a nondescript tablet, they were cut, pasted, and bound in a red morocco case, with "Highlands" Original Manuscript by Robert Louis Stevenson embossed in gilt on the binding.

6. *Gentlemen's Magazine,* vol. 24, 1754, 342; *Monthly Review,* November 1754, 342.

7. Edmund Burt, *Letters from a Gentleman in the North of Scotland* (London: S. Birt, 1754), 1:11 (hereafter referred to as EB).

8. David Stewart, *Sketches of the Character, Manners, and Present State of the Highlanders of Scotland,* 3rd ed. (Edinburgh: Archibald Constable and Co., 1825), 1:v–vi (hereafter referred to as ST).

9. "Colonel David Stewart's Sketches of the Highland Regiments," *Blackwood's Edinburgh Magazine* 63 (April 1822): 3.

10. *Remarks on Col. Stewart's Sketches of the Highlanders: chiefly reflecting the Jacobitism of the Highlanders, etc.* (Edinburgh, 1823), 1.

11. John Buchanan, *Travels in the Western Hebrides: From 1782 to 1790* (London: G. G. J. and J. Robinson, 1793) (hereafter referred to as *TH*).

12. John Knox, *A Tour through the Highlands of Scotland, and the Hebride Isles, in 1786* (London: J. Walter, 1787).

13. *Robert Louis Stevenson's "Kidnapped; or, The Lad with the Silver Button": The Original Text,* ed. with an introduction by Barry Menikoff (San Marino, Calif.: Huntington Library Press, 1999), 15:129 (hereafter referred to as *K*).

14. Buchanan, *Travels in the Western Hebrides,* 50–51.

15. "Highlands" notebook, page 5, Huntington Library, HM 35317 (hereafter referred to as HN). The Roman numeral and the page number following the citation are Stevenson's reference to the Jamieson edition (see note 17). Although I have Jamieson's introduction, my access to Burt's *Letters* was to the 1754 edition, which is the source for my quotations.

16. Buchanan, *Travels in the Western Hebrides,* 87.

17. Edmund Burt, *Letters from a Gentleman in the North of Scotland,* 5th ed. (London: Ogle, Duncan, and Co., 1822), 1:xxxvi (hereafter referred to as RJ).

18. ST, 1:141–42n.

19. Stevenson records an anecdote (which he transcribed under the heading "Highland Hospitality" [HN, 16]) of a poor man with a large family who left the West Lothians: "I expressed my surprise how he would leave so fine and fertile a country, and come to these wild glens. 'In that fine country,' answered the man, 'they give me the cheek of the door, and hound the constables after me; in this poor country, as you, Sir, call it, they give me and my little ones the fire-side, with a share of what they have'" (ST, 1:142n).

20. HN, 10.

21. David Daiches and John Flower, *Literary Landscapes of the British Isles: A Narrative Atlas* (London: Bell & Hyman, 1979), 205.

22. ST, 1:119–20; *Statutes,* 19, George 2, c. 39.

23. A modern writer disputes the role of "concealment" in the colors of the dress: "The surviving fragment of the Culloden coat . . . shows both the high degree of sophistication that the weaver's art could achieve, and how small a part the notion of camouflage played in the dress of the clans" (Christian Hesketh, *Tartans* [London: Octopus Books, 1972], 45).

24. T. B. Howell, comp., *A Complete Collection of State Trials,* vol. 19, *The Trial of James Stewart* (London, 1813), 4. Since the Stewart trial is accessible for most readers in Howell's great collection, I have elected to use it as an initial reference. On occasion, however, I will cite the original 1753 edition that Stevenson owned and marked throughout.

25. Stevenson, *David Balfour* (New York: Charles Scribner's Sons, 1893), 25:326 (hereafter referred to as *DB*).

26. See Nathaniel Lloyd, *A History of the English House from Primitive Times to the Modern Period* (London: Architectural Press, 1931).

27. "Till within these two or three years, the principal fuel of the common people was turf . . . 1795 Statistical Account" (*Scottish National Dictionary,* 9:447). "For I had not been half an hour at the inn (standing in the door most of the time, to ease my eyes from the peat smoke)" [*K,* 16:139].

28. Review of *Travels in the Western Hebrides, from 1782 to 1790, London Review and Literary Journal,* June 1793, 440. The reviewer continued: "Men, women, and children, cattle, sheep, and hogs, dogs, cats, and poultry, live together around a central fire, and not unfrequently take their food out of the same dish."

29. "The trouble I am having over the last chapters of *Kidnapped* is incredible. I have written one chapter seven times, and it is no great shakes now it is done; while all the earlier part is only a first and second writing" (*L,* 5:249).

30. See Barry Menikoff, "*New Arabian Nights:* Stevenson's Experiment in Form," *Nineteenth-Century Literature* 45, no. 3 (December 1990): 339–62.

CHAPTER 3—COUNTRY OF THE BRAVE: THE HIGHLANDS

1. *State of the Society in Scotland, for Propagating Christian Knowledge; Giving a brief Account of the Condition of the Highlands and Islands of Scotland [etc]* (Edinburgh: R. Fleming, 1741), 3.

2. General Wade, "Report, &c., Relating to the Highlands, 1724," in *Historical Papers Relating to the Jacobite Period, 1699–1750,* ed. James Allardyce, 1:133–34 (Aberdeen: New Spalding Club, 1895).

3. *The Trials of James, Duncan, and Robert M'Gregor, Three Sons of the Celebrated Rob Roy in the Years 1752, 1753, and 1754* (Edinburgh: J. Hay and Co., 1818), xiii (hereafter referred to as *Sons*).

4. Wade, "Report, &c., Relating to the Highlands," 132.

5. "Memoriall Anent the True State of the Highlands . . . before the Late Rebellion," in *Historical Papers Relating to the Jacobite Period, 1699–1750,* ed. James Allardyce, 167.

6. *The Highlands of Scotland in 1750* (Edinburgh: W. Blackwood & Sons, 1898), ix. Includes an introduction by Andrew Lang.

7. Wade, "Report, &c., Relating to the Highlands," 146.

8. "Memoriall," 174, 173.

9. Or as the Memorialist puts it, "that torrent of Lawless power, which lay always as thorns in our Sides, to disturb our peace at their pleasure" ("Memoriall," 176).

10. See Anne Grant, *Essays on the Superstitions of the Highlanders of Scotland* (London: Longman, Hurst, Rees, Orme, and Brown, 1811), 1:138–39.

11. Stewart offers the barest citation for the quote—"Westminster Journal."

12. Mehew cites this source in his footnote to the letter.

13. Buchanan, *Travels in the Western Hebrides,* 244.

14. Donald Gregory, *The History of the Western Highlands and Isles of Scotland,* 2nd ed. (London: Hamilton Adams and Co., 1881), 72–74.

15. Ibid., 69; see also W. F. Skene, "Clan Gille-eon," in *The Highlanders of Scotland* (1837; repr., Stirling: E. McKay, 1902), 306–12.

16. John Jamieson, *An Etymological Dictionary of the Scottish Language* (Paisley: Alexander Gardner, 1880), 3:593.

17. Andrew Lang sketched this figure—calling him "Blind Pew"—in a letter to R. L. S. after reading the early chapters in *Young Folks Paper.*

18. *State of the Society,* "List of the Members of the Society . . . alive the 1st of January, 1741," 40–55.

19. Robert Wodrow, *Analecta* (1731; repr., Edinburgh: Maitland Club, 1843), 4:235–36.

20. *State of the Society,* 23.

21. Ibid., 27–28.

22. Wodrow, *Analecta,* 236.

23. Review of *Travels in the Western Hebrides, London Review and Literary Journal,* June 1793, 441.

24. Knox, *A Tour through the Highlands of Scotland, and the Hebride Isles, in 1786.*

25. Ibid., lxxxix.

26. Review of *Letters from a Gentleman in the North of Scotland, to His Friend in London, Monthly Review,* November 1754, 342.

27. "Stewart's Sketches of the Highlands of Scotland, and Military History of the Highland Regiments," *Edinburgh Magazine* (March 1822): 330.

28. "Colonel David Stewart's Sketches of the Highlands Regiments," *Blackwood's Edinburgh Magazine* 11 (April 1822): 396.

CHAPTER 4—BROKEN SEPT: CRIMINAL LAW AND THE CLAN GREGOR

1. James Dalrymple (1619–95) systematized Scots law in the *Institutions* (1684), commonly known as "Stair's Institutes"; George Mackenzie (1636–91), Lord Advocate and founder of the Advocates' Library; John Maclaurin (1734–96) took the title Lord Dreghorn when he was appointed to the bench; David Hume (1757–1838), professor and author of *Commentaries* on Scottish criminal law (1797); and John Erskine (1695–1768), professor and author of *Principles of the Law of Scotland* (1754) and *Institutes of the Law of Scotland* (1773).

2. The church represents the other major tradition for history and record-collection. It constitutes a parallel effort to record the event both for its own sake and to demonstrate God's purposes in this world and/or His glory as manifested in men's lives. Robert Wodrow is the most conspicuous example of the church, and churchman, as historian.

3. William Kennedy, *Annals of Aberdeen,* vol. 1 (London: A. Brown and Co., 1818).

4. John MacLaurin, *Arguments and Decisions* (Edinburgh: J. Bell, 1774), iii.

5. *A Biographical Dictionary of Eminent Scotsmen,* ed. Robert Chambers (Glasgow: Blackie and Son, 1855), 1:80.

6. Hugo Arnot, *A Collection and Abridgement of Celebrated Criminal Trials in Scotland. From A.D. 1586 to 1784.* (Glasgow: A. Napier, 1812), iii.

7. Chambers, *A Biographical Dictionary of Eminent Scotsmen,* 80.

8. Hugo Arnot, *The History of Edinburgh: From the Earliest Accounts to the Year 1780* (Edinburgh: T. Turnbull, 1816).

9. "Baron Hume," *Gentlemen's Magazine,* November 1838, 555.

10. David Hume, *Commentaries on the Law of Scotland, Respecting Crimes* (Edinburgh: Bell and Bradfute, 1844), 1:1.

11. Arnot, *History of Edinburgh,* 374.

12. *Scots Magazine* 60 (July 1798): 465.

13. Hume, *Commentaries on the Law of Scotland,* 1:2.

14. Ibid., 1:3.

15. Ibid., 1:15.

16. Stair A. Gillon, "Criminal Law," in *An Introductory Survey of the Sources and Literature of Scots Law,* 371.

17. Arnot also had complained that "indictments are sometimes laid upon the statute law, sometimes on the civil, sometimes on the Levitical [and] the Scots statute-book is full of unrepealed laws, absurd, tyrannical, and oppressive" (*History of Edinburgh,* 374).

18. Gillon, "Criminal Law," 373.

19. Robert Pitcairn, comp., *Ancient Criminal Trials in Scotland: From the Original Records and MSS* (Edinburgh: Bannatyne Club, 1833), 1:xiii.

20. Quoted in Gillon, "Criminal Law," 372.

21. One of the subscribers to Pitcairn's edition was the father of Charles Baxter, Stevenson's closest Edinburgh friend and to whom he dedicated both *Kidnapped* and *David Balfour.*

22. Pitcairn is an important source for citations in both the *OED* and the *Scottish National Dictionary.*

23 This correspondence dates from December 12, 1880. *L,* 3:139.

24. This correspondence is dated *"Early November 1881." L,* 3:246.

25. John Hill Burton was barely diplomatic when he suggested that were it not for "fictitious literature" Rob Roy would "have been just now no more distinguishable in a list of the half-freebooter, half-drover scamps with whom he was associated" (*Narratives from Criminal Trials in Scotland* [London: Chapman and Hall, 1852], 1:54).

26. For our purpose, we can focus on six crucial texts that Stevenson utilized for his composition. I list them in the chronological order of their first publication; an asterisk indicates Stevenson's possession of an individual text. *BW:* "Memoir of Rob Roy Macgregor, and Some Branches of His Family," *Blackwood's Edinburgh Magazine* 2 (October 1817); RR: Walter Scott, introduction to *Rob Roy,* in *The Waverley Novels* (Philadelphia, 1856). (The novel was originally published in 1818, with Scott's Introduction and Notes first appended to the Waverley edition published by Robert Cadell of Edinburgh in January 1830.); WFS: W. F. Skene, *The Highlanders of Scotland.*

All these volumes examine the sept of the Macgregors within the context of Scottish and English history—and from the vantage point of the first half of the nineteenth century, when the issues posed by the Highland clan system were more abstract and intellectual than concrete and immediate.

27. Within the space of three years there were a rash of publications that focused on the Macgregors and the Highlands. The *Culloden Papers,* a comprehensive collection

of letters and papers from the estate of Duncan Forbes of Culloden, appeared in 1815, and Walter Scott's extensive review was published a year later in the *Quarterly; Blackwood's* came out with the memoir of Rob Roy in 1817; and *Rob Roy* and the *Trials* of Rob Roy's sons saw print the following year. As Scott himself remarked, "Every thing belonging to the Highlands of Scotland has of late become peculiarly interesting" (review of *Culloden Papers, Quarterly Review,* January 1816, 283).

28. Acts of the Parliaments of Scotland, 50 James 6, c. 26.

29. Ibid., 8 Charles 1, c. 30.

30. Ibid., 4 W. & M., c. 62.

31. Allardyce, "Memoriall," 170.

32. *Sons,* ii, xxi.

33. Wade, "Report, &c., Relating to the Highlands, 1724," 134.

34. Acts of the Parliaments of Scotland, 4 W. & M., c. 62.

35. "The chief . . . was patriarchal head of the whole sept" (Scott, review of *Culloden Papers,* 294).

36. Scott, review of *Culloden Papers,* 292.

37. John Bartholomew, "The Highland Clans in the Law of Scotland," *Juridical Review* 13 (1901).

38. Bartholomew, "The Highland Clans in the Law of Scotland," 210.

39. Ibid., 211.

40. The association in Stevenson's mind between Loch Katrine as the Macgregors' fastness and his heroine Catriona as a Macgregor can be seen in his orthography. Stevenson's original spelling for David's Highland girl friend was "Katriona." In the autograph manuscript of *David Balfour,* after he decides on the "C," he goes back through the manuscript, puts a line through the "K" and inserts a "C" above it.

41. See chap. 4, note 25.

42. "He blended in his own character the capacity of a police-officer and of a free-booter—that is to say, he ensured against depredation the cattle of those lowlanders who paid him black-mail, and recovered them if stolen; and, on the other hand, he laid waste and pillaged the property of those who refused their tribute" (*Culloden Papers,* 324).

43. *Blackwood's Edinburgh Magazine* 2 (October 1817): 76.

44. Burton, *Narratives from Criminal Trials in Scotland,* 1:68–69.

CHAPTER 5—REBEL WITH A GRACE NOTE: ROBERT MACGREGOR

1. Pitcairn, *Ancient Criminal Trials in Scotland,* 2:70.

2. Burton, *Narratives from Criminal Trials in Scotland,* 1:14–15. "There were still greater numbers of these outlaws and BROKEN-MEN out in 1715" (RJ, xl). "Several clans which, by the encroachment of their neighbours, or the miscarriage of their own schemes of ambition, had been driven out of their lands, were in no condition to find the security required by law, and were, therefore, denounced as outlaws and broken men" (Scott, review of *Culloden Papers,* 306).

3. Scott, review of *Culloden Papers,* 294.

4. "The first Laird of Appin was a natural son of Lord Lorn, the last of the name of Stewart who possessed that title and estate. . . . The son, seeing his hopes destroyed, seized on a portion of his father's estate, and, as disputes were not in those times often referred to legal decisions, he resorted to the law of the sword, and being supported by some of his father's tenants, sent for assistance to his mother's friends. She was of the Maclarens, a tribe at that time numerous in Balquhidder, in Perthshire. They joined Stewart their kinsman in Argyleshire, and in a pitched battle beat off the forces of his brothers-in-law, and thus established his right by the sword to the lands he claimed, and settled them on his posterity, who kept possession of them till sold by the last Laird of Appin, in the year 1765" (ST, 2:441).

5. *Sons,* 157.

6. Stevenson collapses the two charges into one, directing the reader to the act of violence and the issue of compulsion.

7. See chap. 6, note 13.

8. *Sons,* lxiv; "The (enclosed, planted, and partly embellished) park or demesne land lying around a country seat or gentleman's house. [Quot.] 1775 JOHNSON A small plantation, which in Scotch is called a policy" (*OED*).

9. Jamieson, *An Etymological Dictionary of the Scottish Language,* 1:217.

10. "Extract of a sentence of fugitation pronounced in a Circuit Court of Justiciary held at Perth upon the 25th of May 1751, against him the said James, and against Robert and Ronald his brothers, and five others of his accomplices, for his and their failing to appear to stand trial for the foresaid crimes" (*Sons,* 8).

11. It is continued in *David Balfour,* where James More first introduces himself to David: "You have my name, I perceive . . . though it's one I must not use myself" (*DB,* 5:56).

12. Robert Forbes, *Jacobite Memoirs of the Rebellion of 1745,* ed. Robert Chambers (Edinburgh: W. & R. Chambers, 1834), 425.

13. "Alan was little pleased with a route which led us through the country of his blood-foes, the Glenorchy Campbells" (*K,* 14:215).

14. "[Jean Key] had informed her friends that, on the night of her being carried off, Robin Oig, moved by her cries and tears, had partly consented to let her return, when James came up, with a pistol in his hand, and, asking whether he was such a coward as to relinquish an enterprise in which he had risked every thing to procure him a fortune, in a manner compelled his brother to persevere" (Walter Scott, introduction to *Rob Roy* [Philadelphia: Parry and McMillan, 1856], 12).

15. "The evidence taken upon the trial leaves no vestige of doubt as to the guilt of Rob Oig in the murder of M'Laren" (*Sons,* cx).

16. "*P.S.* Robert Macgregor, alias Campbell, was executed in the Grass-market, Edinburgh, Feb. 6. pursuant to his sentence. He acknowledged the violent methods he had used to obtain the lady, behaved decently, and declared himself of the communion of the church of Rome" ("Edinburgh," *Scots Magazine* 16 [January 1754]: 49–50).

CHAPTER 6—PIPES AT DUSK: JAMES MORE MACGREGOR

1. See chap. 4, note 40, for Scott's sketch of Rob Roy in the *Culloden Papers.*

2. Scott is quoted from his correspondence in the *Scottish National Dictionary,* ed. William Grant and David D. Murison (Edniburgh: Scottish National Dictionary Association, 1971), 8:491: "An old follower of Rob Roy who had been at many a spreagh." A modern historian offers another description: "Rob Roy Macgregor, a legendary Jacobite figure of this period, was in fact a bankrupt drover who defaulted on his debts due to the Duke of Montrose. . . . The blackmail he levied on his cattle-owning neighbours was of course a protection racket" (Bruce Lenman, *An Economic History of Modern Scotland 1660–1976* [Hamden, Conn.: Archon Books, 1977], 70).

3. "This was an appellation given to the independent Companies of which the regiment was formed. It arose from the colour of their dress, and was applied to them in contradistinction to the regular troops, who were called Red Soldiers, or *Seidaran Dearag*" (ST, 1:248).

4. Or as Milton's Christ put it: "The first and wisest of them all profess'd / To know this only, that he nothing knew" (*Paradise Regained,* bk. 4, lines 293–94).

5. According to the author of the memoir that prefaces the *Trials,* James's father, Rob Roy, was in "all accounts" represented "as endowed with . . . uncommon strength" (*Sons,* lxiii). "Although *Mor* is great, the word does not always mean great power, or superior talent. It was more frequently given to men of large size, or portly persons" (ST, 1:app., xxxv–xxxvi*n*).

6. "Memoir of Rob Roy Macgregor, and Some Branches of His Family," *Blackwood's Edinburgh Magazine* 2 (December 1817): 288–89, and *Sons,* 117–19. The *Sons* version is quoted directly from "Edinburgh," *Scots Magazine* 14 (November/December 1752): 556–57, 606.

7. The term "befall"—to fall out in the course of events, to happen, occur— appears in the text also in the past tense, "befell," and is used to describe the chronology of events, or what I would call in the context a synonym for "history."

8. I have already mentioned the early story, *The Rajah's Diamond;* see also my introduction to Stevenson's late novella, *The Beach of Falesá* (Stanford, Calif.: Stanford University Press, 1987).

9. "Memoir of Rob Roy Macgregor, and Some Branches of His Family," 288.

10. Francis H. Groome, ed. *Ordnance Gazetteer of Scotland: A Survey of Scottish Topography* (Edinburgh: T. C. Jack, 1882), 1:111, 1:119.

11. James Macgregor's trial was first summarized by John Maclaurin less than twenty-five years after the event in *Arguments and Decisions.* The Macgregor trials were then cited or summarized over the next seventy-five years. See John Burnett, *A Treatise on Various Branches of the Criminal Law of Scotland* (Edinburgh: G. Ramsay, 1811); David Hume, *Commentaries on the Law of Scotland;* Archibald Alison, *Principles of the Criminal Law of Scotland* (Edinburgh: W. Blackwood, 1832); and John Hill Burton, *Narratives from Criminal Trials in Scotland.* In the twentieth century, William

Roughead also reviewed the case in "The Abduction of Jean Key," *Juridical Review* 29 (1917).

12. *Culloden Papers,* 317–18. Stevenson recalls Lovat in precisely this context in *David Balfour:* "It was old Lovat that managed the Lady Grange affair; if young Lovat is to handle yours, it'll be all in the family. What's James More in prison for? The same offence: abduction. His men have had practice in the business" (*DB,* 9:111).

13. Hume, *Commentaries on the Law of Scotland,* 1:310.

14. Alison, *Principles of the Criminal Law of Scotland,* 226–27.

15. Hume comments extensively on the crime of hamesucken: "The injury here is not to be measured by the mere bodily suffering, but by the alarm and terror attending the assault in the whole circumstances of the case, and especially the colour of the ultimate and meditated wrong. This point was argued at large in the case of James Macgregor; and it was decided in that of his brother Robert, who suffered death for invading Jean Key in her own house, and forcibly carrying her from thence, to compel her to a marriage" (*Commentaries on the Law of Scotland,* 1:320).

16. "At the instigation of [Rob Oig's] brother James, he formed the resolution of making his fortune by a second marriage; and as he had but little chance of succeeding by honourable means, branded as he was by a sentence of outlawry for the most odious of crimes, he determined to put in practice all the resources of that rude policy for which his clan had been hitherto distinguished. The progress and result of this fatal interprise, in which James acted the part rather of a principal than a subordinate agent, are fully detailed in the following trials" (*Sons,* cxvi).

17. This historical episode is described at length in the *Blackwood's* article, and it is used extensively by Stevenson in the last chapters, down to and including the loss of James More's "pockmanteau." Dunkirk is in fact the place where James More, as an agent for the British government, sought to capture Alan Breck Stewart.

18. "New Light in the Story of Lady Grange," *Blackwood's Edinburgh Magazine* 66 (September 1849): 349–50.

CHAPTER 7—THE APPIN MURDER

1. Stevenson's faith in fiction as a vehicle for the expression of his deepest ideas strengthened as he matured. Nonetheless, he accepted E. L. Burlingame's offer for a series of essays for *Scribner's Magazine.* He wrote some of his best-known essays for this periodical.

2. Autograph manuscript, "Note to *Kidnapped.*" Enclosed with autograph manuscript of *Kidnapped; or, The Lad with the Silver Button.* Huntington Library, HM 2410.

3. G. W. T. Omond, *The Lord Advocates of Scotland* (Edinburgh: D. Douglas, 1883), 2:47.

4. "Rambles among Books: The State Trials," *Cornhill Magazine,* April 1882, 455.

5. H. L. Stephen, ed., *State Trials Political and Social* (London: Duckworth, 1899), 1:vii, viii: "The charm of State Trials lies largely in matters of detail. . . . And this effect can only be reproduced by considering a mass of detail, picturesque enough in itself" (ix–x).

6. T. B. Howell, *A Complete Collection of State Trials and Proceedings for High Treason and Other Crimes and Misdemeanors* (London: T. C. Hansard, 1816), 1:xxii.

7. In an interesting aside, Hugo Arnot comments on how the translators at the trial of James Stewart, who were aligned with the prosecution, interpreted the Gaelic of the witnesses in a way that prejudiced the defendant and benefitted the government.

8. Augustine Birrell, "Notes about Books," *Atalanta,* September 1888, 714–15.

9. D. L. Cameron, "The Appin Murder: Notes on the Historical Groundwork of *Kidnapped* and *Catriona,*" *Atalanta,* September 1894, 779.

10. Stephen, *State Trials Political and Social,* 1:xii–xiii.

11. Stevenson extensively marked his copy of the Lovat trial, which is now in the Beinecke Library.

12. David Mackay, ed., *Trial of James Stewart: The Appin Murder* (Edinburgh: William Hodge & Company, 1931), vii.

13. William Roughead (1870–1952), Writer to the Signet in Edinburgh, began contributing his compelling summaries of criminal cases to the *Judicial Review* as early as 1901. He was read with avidity by Henry James.

14. *The Trial of James Stewart* (Edinburgh: G. Hamilton, 1753), 81. This extensive volume consists of the proceedings proper, the indictment, the prosecution's argument, presented mainly by the Lord Advocate Prestongrange and Simon Fraser, and the defense attorneys' pleadings. In addition, there is a substantial appendix that includes the depositions of the witnesses. Some texts of the *Trial,* though not all, contain *A Supplement to the Trial of James Stewart* that was bound in with the original volume and is largely a defense of the Highlander. Stevenson's copy contained both the original *Trial* and the *Supplement.* References to the *Trial* will appear within the text as *T,* and the appendix will be cited as *T/A,* since both the trial section and the appendix were separately paginated.

15. Mr. Walter Stewart, one of James Stewart's advocates, made a point of contrasting Allan's extravagance with his defendant's selfless conduct: "This Allan Breck Stewart, my lord, was the son of one Donald Stewart, a particular friend, and distant relation of the pannel's. He died while his children were infants, and, upon his death-bed, committed them to the care of his friend, naming him tutor and curator to them. The pannel faithfully executed this trust, took care of the children's education, and managed their effects to the best advantage. Allan turning extravagant, when he grew up to man's estate, and having spent what was left him by his father, inlisted in his majesty's service, without clearing accounts with the pannel, who used to supply him with money, and pay little debts for him, even after he became a soldier, though he knew he had already given him more than his patrimony" (Howell, *A Complete Collection of State Trials,* 19:20; cf. *T,* 42).

16. The *Trial* provided Stevenson with two additional names for Glenure, not including the sobriquet, and he quickly made use of both of them: "But when it came to Colin Roy, the black Campbell blood in him ran wild" (*K,* 12:105). "Or

why would Red Colin be riding his horse all over my poor country of Appin, and never a pretty lad to put a bullet in him?" (*K*, 12:108).

17. The *OED* cites this sentence for illustrating "fitsides," drawn from the *Scots Magazine,* which published extensive extracts from the Stewart trial from March through December 1753.

18. Burton, *Narratives from Criminal Trials in Scotland,* 92.

19. Stevenson glosses "bouman" succinctly from a longer note in the *Supplement* (see *K*, 315).

20. "*John Breck Maccoll* bouman to Appin in Koalisnacoan, aged forty years, married, sworn, purged and examined. . . . And this is truth, as he shall answer to God; and depones he cannot write" (*T/A*, 103); "and the deponent [John Breck Maccoll] inquiring what he had brought, the said Alexander Stewart informed him, that he had brought five guineas and some cloaths" (*T/A*, 99).

21. Breck of course means "smallpox"; Stevenson minimizes the effect of the disease on Alan's appearance (*K*, 9:73), but he clearly highlights it here.

CHAPTER 8—THE TRIAL OF JAMES STEWART

1. Archibald Alison, *Principles of the Criminal Law of Scotland,* 60.

2. John Burnett, *A Treatise on Various Branches of the Criminal Law of Scotland,* 285.

3. *A Supplement to the Trial of James Stewart. Containing Papers omitted by the Publishers of the Trial; Observations on the Trial; with Anecdotes relating thereto; James Stewart's Dying Speech, and a few Particulars respecting his Behaviour. By a By-Stander.* (London: n.p., 1753), 14. Stevenson inserted double vertical lines by the asterisk, and underlined the word "new" in his copy.

4. Archibald Alison, *Practice of the Criminal Law of Scotland* (Edinburgh: William Blackwood & Sons, 1833), xxxv.

5. Ibid., 151.

6. Although the correct date of the act was 1701, Stevenson took his date from the *Supplement:* "The act of parliament, in the year 1700, anent wrongous imprisonment, prohibits and discharges close confinement of any prisoners after eight days from the time of commitment" (15).

7. The following lines appear below the place and date of publication on the title-page of the *Supplement:* "Printed for the Benefit of a poor Widow, and her five Children. Price One Shilling."

8. Alison, *Practice of the Criminal Law of Scotland,* 335–37.

9. "No appeal is competent from the Court of Justiciary to the House of Lords; and it is only competent to obtain a remission of the sentence by pardon, or remission from the Crown, or reversal in the legislature" (Alison, *Practice of the Criminal Law of Scotland,* 677; cf. Arnot's acid view of the limits of appeal from decisions by the Justiciary Court: "In a country where such anxiety has been shown to guard against oppression from the crown, it surely will not be said, that the liberty of petitioning for royal mercy is a sufficient remedy against iniquity" [*History of Edinburgh,* 375]).

10. *The Trial of Simon Fraser, Lord Lovat;* the salient details are provided by David in a single, summary paragraph (*DB,* 6:64–65).

11. "When the sentence was pronounced against James Stewart at Inverary, the gentlemen who attended the trial the preceding days, having been all tired with it, did not take notes the last day: but, as far as they can recollect, the substance of what the Lord Justice-General then said to the pannel, was as is above set down" (Howell, *A Complete Collection of State Trials,* 250n).

12. Burton, *Narratives from Criminal Trials in Scotland,* 94.

13. Ibid., 92. Stevenson added two paragraphs to his manuscript in which David discoursed on the meaning of the entire affair and, in essence, bade farewell to politics and the public life, which is nothing but a "detestable business." This is an extremely interesting reflection, but it was not a part of the original manuscript. The paragraphs were added in response to Sidney Colvin's review of the galley slips and his request that more information be supplied.

14. Among the references, prior to the publication of *Kidnapped,* are the following: John Burnett, *A Treatise on Various Branches of the Criminal Law in Scotland;* Hugo Arnot, *A Collection and Abridgement of Celebrated Criminal Trials in Scotland;* Howell, *State Trials;* "Memoir of Rob Roy," *Blackwood's Edinburgh Magazine* 2 (December 1817); David Stewart, *Sketches of the Highlanders; Remarks on Col. Stewart's Sketches;* George Borrow, *Celebrated Trials,* vol. 4 (London: Knight and Lacey, 1825); John Hill Burton, *Narratives from Criminal Trials in Scotland;* G. W. T. Omond, *The Lord Advocates of Scotland.*

15. In Alan's speech to David, Stevenson made these points more succinctly than all the commentators.

16. Burton, *Narratives from Criminal Trials in Scotland,* 97.

CHAPTER 9—THE BASS ROCK

1. Andrew Lang, "Mr. Stevenson's New Novel," *Illustrated London News,* September 16, 1893, 350.

2. *The New Statistical Account of Scotland* (Edinburgh: William Blackwood and Sons, 1845), 2:329.

3. Ibid., 319.

4. Thomas M'Crie, "Civil and Ecclesiastic History of the Bass," in *The Bass Rock* (Edinburgh: n.d., ca. 1847), 3. M'Crie is quoting Hector Boece and cites "Bellenden's *Boece,* vol. 1, p. 37."

5. Hugh Miller, "Geology of the Bass," in *The Bass Rock,* 84.

6. John Hill Burton, *History of Scotland: From the Revolution to the Extinction of the Last Jacobite Insurrection* (London: Longman, Brown, Green, and Longmans, 1853), 2:306.

7. Buchanan, *Travels in the Western Hebrides,* 145–46.

8. Ibid., 144.

9. John Hill Burton asserts that "Lord Lovat has been accused of being the main instrument in the celebrated abduction of Mrs. Erskine," but he also states that there

is no evidence beyond the circumstantial, unless Lord Lovat's denial, "which is certainly very much in the tone of the man who denied with an oath the charge of swearing, be considered as evidence against him" (*Lives of Simon Lord Lovat, and Duncan Forbes of Culloden* [London: Chapman and Hall, 1847], 187, 191).

10. See *K,* 5:48, 29:269.

11. The term is used extensively in the trial of James Macgregor, since Jean Key's estate was sequestrated by the Court of Session.

12. Francis Grose first defines the term CRIMP as "a broker or factor . . . who disposes of the cargoes of the Newcastle coal ships," then adds: "also persons employed to trapan or kidnap recruits for the East Indian and African companies" (*A Classical Dictionary of the Vulgar Tongue,* 3rd ed. [London: Hooper and Co., 1796]).

13. Alison, *Principles of the Criminal Law of Scotland,* 281.

14. "The Trial . . . between . . . James Annesley . . . and . . . Richard Earl of Anglesea . . . [1743]," in Howell, *A Complete Collection of State Trials,* 17:1147. The terms "kidnapped" and "slavery" are pervasive throughout this trial record, which Howell called "the longest trial ever known at the bar" (1439).

15. Samuel Lewis, *A Topographical Dictionary of Scotland* (London: S. Lewis, 1846), 1:123.

16. Miller, *The Bass Rock,* 103.

17. "The pasture of the island is said to be peculiarly good for the feeding of sheep, and Bass mutton has long been celebrated. The saline matter scattered by the spray of the ocean may contribute to the nutritious quality of the grass" (John H. Balfour, "Botany of the Bass," in *The Bass Rock,* 417).

18. Martin Martin, *A Description of the Western Islands of Scotland Circa 1695,* ed. Donald J. Macleod (Stirling: E. Mackay, 1934), 307.

19. Buchanan, *Travels in the Western Hebrides,* 127.

20. "Memoirs of the Rev. James Fraser of Brea, Minister of the Gospel at Culross," in *Select Biographies,* vol. 2, ed. W. K. Tweedie (Edinburgh: Printed for the Wodrow Society, 1847), 344.

21. Balfour, "Botany of the Bass," in *The Bass Rock,* 424.

22. Miller, *The Bass Rock,* 89.

23. J. F. Campbell, *Popular Tales of the West Highlands, Orally Collected, with a Translation,* 4 vols. (Edinburgh: Edmonston and Douglas, 1860–62; hereafter referred to as *PT*). The tradition of Gaelic storytelling was strong, and "Campbell of Islay, along with his assistants, spent some years wandering up and down the Highlands and Islands recording the folk-tales from the lips of the uneducated peasantry" (Donald J. Macleod, introduction to Martin, *A Description of the Western Islands,* 36). It was "in the late 1850s when Campbell of Islay and his team began their great work of collection" (D. A. MacDonald, "Gaelic Storytelling, Traditional," in *A Companion to Scottish Culture,* ed. David Daiches [New York: Holmes and Meier Publishers, 1982], 141).

24. In the manuscript, Stevenson left spaces for the volume and page numbers to be added ("Vol. , p. .") thus suggesting that the physical text was not near him when he was writing these lines.

25. "A generation ago, [story-telling circles] were still flourishing vigorously, and there lived Highlanders, men and women, with long memories for what they had heard from their fathers. Book lore for them had no meaning; they were the living books themselves, from whom famous collectors and folklorists, such as J. F. Campbell, Gregorson Campbell, MacInnes, MacDougall, the late Dr. Carmichael and many others, gathered in the most direct and reliable way the very large amount of Highland oral popular literature now available in the original Gaelic, or in translation, to the reading public of every country" (Macleod in Martin, *A Description of the Western Islands,* 36).

26. James King Hewison, *The Covenanters* (Glasgow: J. Smith and Son, 1908), 2:343.

27. "Reoccupying the Bass Rock," *Edinburgh Evening Dispatch,* November 22, 1902; clipping pasted in The Huntington Library copy of *The Bass Rock.*

28. Hewison, *The Covenanters,* 2:501.

29. Robert Wodrow, *The History of the Sufferings of the Church of Scotland from the restoration to the Revolution,* ed. Rev. Robert Burns (Glasgow: Blackie, Fullarton and Co., 1830), 4:396.

30. *The Works of Robert Louis Stevenson,* Vailima edition, vol. 24, (London: William Heinemann, 1923), 131.

31. Hewison, *The Covenanters,* 2:430.

32. SOME REMARKABLE PASSAGES OF THE LIFE AND DEATH OF MR. ALEXANDER PEDEN . . . *A third Edition with Amendments* . . . EDINBURGH / Collected and Published by Patrick Walker . . . MDCCXXVIII (portion of the title-page reproduced in *Six Saints of the Covenant,* ed. D. Hay Fleming, vol. 1 [London: Hodder and Stoughton, 1901]).

33. Alexander Smellie, *Men of the Covenant* (London: Andrew Melrose, 1908), 2:242.

34. Patrick Walker, in *Six Saints of the Covenant,* 1:107.

35. Hewison, *The Covenanters,* 2:501.

EPILOGUE

1. The Robert Louis Stevenson Club, "The Memory of Robert Louis Stevenson," Seventh Annual Report for Year Ending 30th September 1926. Widener Library, Harvard University. November 13, 1925.

2. "Mr. Stevenson's Art," *New York Daily Tribune,* October 13, 1889, 12

3. Review of *The Merry Men, New York Daily Tribune,* February 24, 1887, 6.

4. William Vaughan Moody and Robert Morss Lovett, *A History of English Literature* (New York: Charles Scribner's Sons, 1907), 383.

5. G. W. S., "Stevenson's Place in Literature," *New York Tribune,* December 30, 1894, 16.

6. "A Bra' Story," *New York Times,* August 1, 1886, 9.

7. Ibid.

8. "Recent Novels," *Nation,* May 19, 1887, 430; "Our Library Table," *Athenaeum,* March 5, 1887, 318.

9. "Rumoured Death of R. L. Stevenson: Sketch of His Career," *Glasgow Herald,* December 18, 1894.

10. Emile Legouis and Louis Cazamian, *A History of English Literature* (New York: Macmillan, 1931), 1308.

11. Harold Frederick, "A Literary Catastrophe," *New York Times,* March 15, 1896, 22.

12. G. W. S., "Stevenson's Place in Literature," *New York Tribune,* December 23, 1894, 16.

13. George Stronach, December [18?], 1894, newspaper cutting pasted in a volume of *The Merry Men and Other Tales and Fables* (London: Chatto and Windus, 1887). Huntington Library, RB 448891.

14. G. W. S., "Stevenson's Place in Literature," 16; "Death of Robert Louis Stevenson," *Chicago Daily Tribune,* December 18, 1894, 6.

15. "Robert Louis Stevenson," *Dial,* January 1, 1895, 3.

16. Editorial, *Scotsman,* December 18, 1894.

17. Editorial, *Glasgow Herald,* December 18, 1894.

18. Joseph Jacobs, "Mr. Robert Louis Stevenson," *Athenaeum,* December 22, 1894, 863.

19. G. W. S., "Stevenson's Place in Literature," 16; "Robert Louis Stevenson," *New York Times,* November 10, 1895, 31.

20. "Rumoured Death of R. L. Stevenson"; "Death of Mr. R. Louis Stevenson," *Daily Free Press* (Aberdeen), December 19, 1894; "Recent Novels," *Nation,* December 14, 1893, 452.

21. "Recent Fiction," *Dial,* October 16, 1893, 226.

INDEX

Page numbers in italics refer to illustrations